English-Swahili
Swahili-English

Word to Word™
Bilingual Dictionary

Compiled by:
C. Sesma, M.A.

Translated by:
Angelica Christin

Bilingual Dictionaries, Inc.

Swahili Word to Word™ Bilingual Dictionary
1st Edition © Copyright 2009

Published in the United States by:

Bilingual Dictionaries, Inc.
PO Box 1154
Murrieta, CA 92562
T: (951) 461-6893 • F: (951) 461-3092
www.BilingualDictionaries.com

ISBN13: 978-0-933146-55-6
ISBN: 0-933146-55-8

Preface

Bilingual Dictionaries, Inc. is committed to providing schools, libraries and educators with a great selection of bilingual materials for students. Along with bilingual dictionaries we also provide ESL materials, children's bilingual stories and children's bilingual picture dictionaries.

Sesma's Swahili Word to Word Bilingual Dictionary was created specifically with students in mind to be used for reference and testing. This dictionary contains approximately 16,000 entries targeting common words used in the English language.

List of Irregular Verbs

present - past - past participle

arise - arose - arisen
awake - awoke - awoken, awaked
be - was - been
bear - bore - borne
beat - beat - beaten
become - became - become
begin - began - begun
behold - beheld - beheld
bend - bent - bent
beseech - besought - besought
bet - bet - betted
bid - bade (bid) - bidden (bid)
bind - bound - bound
bite - bit - bitten
bleed - bled - bled
blow - blew - blown
break - broke - broken
breed - bred - bred
bring - brought - brought
build - built - built
burn - burnt - burnt *
burst - burst - burst
buy - bought - bought
cast - cast - cast
catch - caught - caught
choose - chose - chosen
cling - clung - clung

come - came - come
cost - cost - cost
creep - crept - crept
cut - cut - cut
deal - dealt - dealt
dig - dug - dug
do - did - done
draw - drew - drawn
dream - dreamt - dreamed
drink - drank - drunk
drive - drove - driven
dwell - dwelt - dwelt
eat - ate - eaten
fall - fell - fallen
feed - fed - fed
feel - felt - felt
fight - fought - fought
find - found - found
flee - fled - fled
fling - flung - flung
fly - flew - flown
forebear - forbore - forborne
forbid - forbade - forbidden
forecast - forecast - forecast
forget - forgot - forgotten
forgive - forgave - forgiven
forego - forewent - foregone
foresee - foresaw - foreseen
foretell - foretold - foretold

forget - forgot - forgotten	**light** - lit * - lit *
forsake - forsook - forsaken	**lose** - lost - lost
freeze - froze - frozen	**make** - made - made
get - got - gotten	**mean** - meant - meant
give - gave - given	**meet** - met - met
go - went - gone	**mistake** - mistook - mistaken
grind - ground - ground	**must** - had to - had to
grow - grew - grown	**pay** - paid - paid
hang - hung * - hung *	**plead** - pleaded - pled
have - had - had	**prove** - proved - proven
hear - heard - heard	**put** - put - put
hide - hid - hidden	**quit** - quit * - quit *
hit - hit - hit	**read** - read - read
hold - held - held	**rid** - rid - rid
hurt - hurt - hurt	**ride** - rode - ridden
hit - hit - hit	**ring** - rang - rung
hold - held - held	**rise** - rose - risen
keep - kept - kept	**run** - ran - run
kneel - knelt * - knelt *	**saw** - sawed - sawn
know - knew - known	**say** - said - said
lay - laid - laid	**see** - saw - seen
lead - led - led	**seek** - sought - sought
lean - leant * - leant *	**sell** - sold - sold
leap - lept * - lept *	**send** - sent - sent
learn - learnt * - learnt *	**set** - set - set
leave - left - left	**sew** - sewed - sewn
lend - lent - lent	**shake** - shook - shaken
let - let - let	**shear** - sheared - shorn
lie - lay - lain	**shed** - shed - shed

shine - shone - shone
shoot - shot - shot
show - showed - shown
shrink - shrank - shrunk
shut - shut - shut
sing - sang - sung
sink - sank - sunk
sit - sat - sat
slay - slew - slain
sleep - sleep - slept
slide - slid - slid
sling - slung - slung
smell - smelt * - smelt *
sow - sowed - sown *
speak - spoke - spoken
speed - sped * - sped *
spell - spelt * - spelt *
spend - spent - spent
spill - spilt * - spilt *
spin - spun - spun
spit - spat - spat
split - split - split
spread - spread - spread
spring - sprang - sprung
stand - stood - stood
steal - stole - stolen
stick - stuck - stuck
sting - stung - stung
stink - stank - stunk

stride - strode - stridden
strike - struck - struck (stricken)
strive - strove - striven
swear - swore - sworn
sweep - swept - swept
swell - swelled - swollen *
swim - swam - swum
take - took - taken
teach - taught - taught
tear - tore - torn
tell - told - told
think - thought - thought
throw - threw - thrown
thrust - thrust - thrust
tread - trod - trodden
wake - woke - woken
wear - wore - worn
weave - wove * - woven *
wed - wed * - wed *
weep - wept - wept
win - won - won
wind - wound - wound
wring - wrung - wrung
write - wrote - written

Those tenses with an * also have regular forms.

English-Swahili

Bilingual Dictionaries, Inc.

Abbreviations

a - article
n - noun
e - exclamation
pro - pronoun
adj - adjective
adv - adverb
v - verb
iv - irregular verb
pre - preposition
c - conjunction

A

abandon *v* telekeza

abandonment *n* ukiwa, ukatavu

abbot *n* mtawa

abbreviate *v* fupisha

abbreviation *n* kifupi

abdicate *v* jiuzulu

abdication *n* kujiuzulu

abdomen *n* tumbo

abduct *v* teka nyara

abduction *n* kutekwa nyara

aberration *n* ukengefu

abhor *v* chukia

abide by *v* tii

ability *n* uwezo

ablaze *adj* waka

able *adj* weza

abnormal *adj* sio kawaida

aboard *adv* chomboni

abolish *v* komesha

abort *v* acha

abortion *n* toa mimba

abound *v* jaa tele

about *pre* kuhusu

about *adv* kote kote

above *pre* juu

abreast *adv* sambamba

abridge *v* fupisha

abroad *adv* nje

abrogate *v* batilisha

abruptly *adv* ghafla

absence *n* ukosekanaji

absent *adj* kukosekana

absolute *adj* kabisa

absolution *n* msamaha

absolve *v* futia dhambi

absorb *v* nyonya, fyonza

absorbent *adj* -a kufyonza

abstain *v* jinyima

abstinence *n* kujinyima

abstract *adj* nadharia

absurd *adj* -a kiupuuzi

abundance *n* wingi

abundant *adj* -a wingi

abuse *v* nyanyasa

abuse *n* unyanyasaji

abysmal *adj* -siopimika

abyss *n* kina kirefu

academic *adj* kitaaluma

academy *n* chuo

accelerate *v* harakisha

accelerator *n* kichapuzi

accent *n* lafudhi

accept *v* kubali

acceptable *adj* -a kubalika

acceptance *n* kukubali

access *n* kuingilia

accessible *adj* kufikia

accident *n* ajali

accidental *adj* bahati mbaya

acclaim *v* shangilia

acclimatize *v* zoea mazingira

accommodate *v* patia nafasi

accompany *v* sindikiza

accomplice *n* msaidizi

accomplish *v* fanikiwa

accord *n* makubaliano

according to *pre* kufuatana na

accordion *n* kodiani

account *n* akaunti, taarifa

account for *v* eleza

accountable *adj* wajibika

accountant *n* mhasibu

accumulate *v* kusanya

accuracy *n* usahihi

accurate *adj* sahihi

accusation *n* tuhuma

accuse *v* tuhumu

accustom *v* zoea

ace *n* dume

ache *n* maumivu

achieve *v* fanikiwa

achievement *n* mafanikio

acid *n* tindikali

acidity *n* uchachu

acknowledge *v* tambua

acoustic *adj* akustika

acquaint *v* fahamiana

acquaintance *n* jamaa

acquire *v* pata

acquisition *n* pato

acquit *v* toa hatiani

acquittal *n* achia huru

acre *n* eka

across *pre* kukatisha

act *v* fanya

action *n* tendo

activate *v* anzisha

activation *n* uanzishaji

active *adj* hai

activity *n* shughuli

actor *n* mchezaji

actress *n* mchezaji

actual *adj* halisi

actually *adv* kwa kweli

acute *adj* kali

adamant *adj* -a kusisitiza

adapt *v* rekebisha

adaptable *adj* suluhia

adaptation *n* marekebisho

adapter *n* adapta

add *v* ongeza

addicted *adj* tawaliwa

addiction *n* kutawaliwa

addictive *adj* ya uraibu

addition *n* jumlisha

additional *adj* nyongeza

address *n* anwani

address *v* hutubia

addressee *n* mwandikiwa

adequate *adj* ya kutosha

adhere *v* shikilia

adhesive *adj* -a kunata

adjacent *adj* pembeni

adjective *n* kivumishi

adjoin *v* pakana

adjoining *adj* kupakana

adjourn *v* funga

adjust *v* rekebisha

adjustable *adj* -a rekebishika

adjustment *n* marekebisho

administer *v* toa, tawala

admirable *adj* -a kusifika

admiral *n* admeri

admiration *n* husudu

admire *v* husudu

admirer *n* ashiki

admissible *adj* kubalika

admission *n* kuingia, kukiri

admit *v* kubali

admittance *n* kuingia

admonish *v* onya

admonition *n* onyo

adolescence *n* ujana

adolescent *n* kijana

adopt *v* panga

adoption *n* kupanga

adoptive *adj* -a kupanga

adorable *adj* mahaba

adoration *n* kusujudu

adore *v* sujudu

adorn *v* pamba

adrift *adv* kwa kuelea

adulation *n* kusifu mno

adult *n* mtu mzima

adulterate *v* haribu

adultery *n* uzinzi

advance *v* songa mbele

advance *n* maendeleo

advantage *n* faida

Advent *n* Majilio

adventure *n* ujasiri

adverb *n* kielezi

adversary *n* adui

adverse *adj* kinyume

adversity *n* shida

advertise *v* tangaza

advertising *n* kutangaza

advice *n* ushauri

advisable *adj* -a busara

advise *v* kushauri

adviser *n* mshauri

advocate *v* tetea

aeroplane *n* ndege

aesthetic *adj* ujumi

afar *adv* kwa mbali

affable *adj* bashasha

affair *n* tukio

affect *v* athiri

affection *n* upendo

affectionate *adj* pendo

affiliate *v* ushirika

affiliation *n* shirikisho

affinity *n* uhusiano

affirm *v* thibitisha

affirmative *adj* -a kukubali

affix *v* bandika

afflict *v* dhuru

affliction *n* sikitiko

affluence *n* utajiri

affluent *adj* tajiri

afford *v* uwezo

affordable *adj* -enye kumudika

affront *v* tukana

affront *n* tusi

afloat *adv* kwa kuelea

afraid *adj* ogopa

afresh *adv* upya

after *pre* baada

afternoon *n* mchana

afterwards *adv* baadae

again *adv* tena

against *pre* dhidi

age *n* umri

agency *n* uwakala

agenda *n* ajenda

agent *n* wakala

agglomerate *v* kongomana

aggravate *v* kuza ubaya

aggravation *n* kukuza ubaya

aggregate *v* kusanya

aggression *n* shambulio

aggressive *adj* mgomvi

aggressor *n* mshari

aghast *adj* staajabu

agile *adj* nyumbufu

agitator *n* mchokozi

agnostic *n* -enye shaka

agonize *v* teseka

agonizing *adj* -a kuteseka

agony *n* maumivu

agree *v* kubali

agreeable *adj* -a kukubalika

agreement *n* makubaliano

agricultural *adj* ya kilimo

agriculture *n* kilimo

ahead *pre* mbele

aid *n* msaada

aid *v* saidia

aide *n* msaidizi

ailing *adj* ugua

ailment *n* ugonjwa

aim *v* lenga

aimless *adj* bila lengo

air *n* hewa

air *v* achia, kausha

aircraft *n* ndege

airfare *n* nauli

airfield *n* uwanja

airline *n* shirika la ndege

airtight *adj* -siopitisha hewa

aisle *n* njia kati ya viti

ajar *adj* wazi

akin *adj* kama

alarm *n* kamsa

alarm clock *n* saa ya kengele

alarming *adj* hofisha

alcoholic *adj* kileo

alcoholism *n* ulevi

alert *n* makini

alert *v* tahadharisha

algebra *n* aljebra

alien *n* mgeni

alight *adv* waka

align *v* linganisha

alignment *n* mfuatano

alike *adj* sawasawa

alive *adj* hai

all *adj* yote

allegation *n* lawama

allege *v* dai

allegedly *adv* inavyodaiwa

allegiance *n* utii

allegory *n* istiara

allergic *adj* mzio wa

allergy *n* mzio

alleviate *v* tuliza

alley *n* njia

alliance *n* ushirikiano

allied *adj* kuungana

alligator *n* mamba

allocate *v* gawia

allot *v* toa

allotment *n* mgawanyo

allow *v* ruhusu

allowance *n* posho, ruhusa

alloy *n* aloi

allure *n* haiba, vutia

alluring *adj* kuvutia

allusion *n* dokezo

ally *n* rafiky

ally *v* ungana

almanac *n* shajara

almighty *adj* -enye enzi

almond *n* lozi

almost *adv* nusura

alms *n* sadaka

alone *adj* pekee

along *pre* pamoja na

alongside *pre* ubavuni

aloof *adj* -enye unyanya

aloud *adv* kwa sauti

alphabet *n* alfabeti

already *adv* tayari

alright *adv* sawasawa

also *adv* pia

altar *n* madhabahuni

alter *v* badilisha

alteration *n* badiliko

altercation *n* mzozo

alternate *v* pokezana

alternate *adj* -a mpokezano

alternative *n* budi, badala

although *c* japokuwa

altitude *n* mwinuko

altogether *adj* pamoja

aluminum *n* aluminiamu

always *adv* daima

amass *v* kusanya

amaze *v* staajabisha

amazement *n* mastaajabu

ambassador *n* Balozi

ambiguous *adj* tatanisha

ambition *n* tamaa

ambivalent *adj* yumba

ambulance *n* gari la wagonjwa

ambush *v* vamia kwa kuvizia

amenable *adj* tiifu

amend *v* sahihisha

amendment *n* masahihisho

amenities *n* huduma

American *adj* Mmarekani

amiable *adj* mwema

amicable *adj* urafiki

amid *pre* katikati

ammonia *n* amonia

ammunition *n* risasi

amnesty *n* msamaha

among *pre* kati ya

amoral *adj* kutojali

amortize *v* lipa

amount *n* kiasi

amount to *v* fikia

amphibious *adj* -a maji

ample *adj* tele
amplifier *n* amplifaya
amplify *v* kuza sauti
amputate *v* kata
amputation *n* kukata kiungo
amuse *v* furahisha
amusement *n* kiburudisho
amusing *adj* burudani
analogy *n* analojia
analysis *n* uchambuzi
analyze *v* chambua
anarchist *n* mwasi
anarchy *n* tawala huria
anatomy *n* elimu mwili
ancestor *n* mhenga
ancestry *n* ukoo
anchor *n* nanga
anchovy *n* dagaa
ancient *adj* kongwe
and *c* na
anecdote *n* kisa,
anemia *n* safura
anemic *adj* -a na safura
anesthesia *n* nusu kaputi
anew *adv* upya
angel *n* malaika
angelic *adj* kimalaika
anger *v* kasirisha

anger *n* hasira
angle *n* pembe
Anglican *adj* Anglikana
angry *adj* kasirika
anguish *n* uchungu
animal *n* mnyama
animate *v* changamsha
animation *n* uhai
animosity *n* uadui
ankle *n* kiwiko cha mguu
annex *n* kiambatanisho
annexation *n* kuteka
annihilate *v* teketeza
annihilation *n* kuteketeza
anniversary *n* ukumbusho
annotate *v* fafanua
annotation *n* ufafanuzi
announce *v* tangaza
announcement *n* matangazo
announcer *n* mtangazaji
annoy *v* kera
annoying *adj* kukera
annual *adj* kila mwaka
annul *v* futa
annulment *n* mfuto
anoint *v* takasa, bariki
anonymity *n* kutokuwa na jina
anonymous *adj* bila jina

another *adj* ingine

answer *v* jibu

answer *n* jawabu

ant *n* siafu

antagonize *v* kasirisha

antecedent *n* kitangulizi

antecedents *n* historia

antelope *n* paa

antenna *n* udevu, arieli

anthem *n* wimbo wa taifa

antibiotic *n* kiuavijasumu

anticipate *v* tarajia

anticipation *n* matumaini

antidote *n* kiuasumu

antipathy *n* kutopenda

antiquated *adj* kuukuu

antiquity *n* zamani za kale

anvil *n* fuawe

anxiety *n* wasiwasi

anxious *adj* -a wasiwasi

any *adj* yoyote

anybody *pro* yeyote

anyhow *pro* kwa vyovyote

anyone *pro* yeyote

anything *pro* chochote

apart *adv* pembeni

apathy *n* utepetevu

ape *n* nyani

apex *n* kilele

apiece *adv* kila moja

apocalypse *n* mteketeo

apologize *v* omba msamaha

apology *n* msamaha

apostle *n* mtume

apostolic *adj* kiinjili

apostrophe *n* apostrofi

appall *v* shangaza

appalling *adj* ya kushangaza

apparel *n* vazi

apparent *adj* mbayana

apparently *adv* -a kuonekana

apparition *n* mzuka

appeal *n* rufaa, omba

appeal *v* kata rufaa

appealing *adj* kuomba

appear *v* tokea

appearance *n* kujitokeza

appease *v* ridhisha

appeasement *n* kuridhisha

appendicitis *n* kidole tumbo

appendix *n* kiambatanisho

appetite *n* hamu ya kula

applaud *v* shangilia

applause *n* makofi

apple *n* tofaa

appliance *n* kifaa

applicable *adj* husika

applicant *n* mwombaji

application *n* maombi

apply *v* omba

apply for *v* omba

appoint *v* teua

appointment *n* uteuzi, miadi

appraisal *n* tathmini

appraise *v* kadiria

appreciate *v* thamini

appreciation *n* shukurani

apprehend *v* kamata, hofia

apprehensive *adj* -a hofu

apprentice *n* mwanafunzi

approach *v* sogelea, karibia

approach *n* kukaribia

approachable *adj* ingilika

approbation *n* sifa

appropriate *adj* kufaa

approval *n* kibali

approve *v* kubali, idhinisha

approximate *adj* -a karibia

April *n* Aprili

apron *n* kimori, aproni

aptitude *n* uwezo

aquarium *n* tangi samaki

aquatic *adj* majini

aqueduct *n* mfereji daraja

Arabic *adj* Kiarabu

arable *adj* ya kulima

arbiter *n* msuluhishi

arbitrary *adj* holela

arbitrate *v* patanisha

arbitration *n* usuluhishi

arc *n* tao

arch *n* tao

archaeology *n* elimu kale

archaic *adj* zamani

archbishop *n* askofu mkuu

architect *n* msanifu majengo

ardent *adj* shauku

ardor *n* hamasa

arduous *adj* gumu, kuchonga

area *n* eneo

argue *v* bishana

argument *n* mabishano

arid *adj* kame

arise *iv* inuka, tokea

arithmetic *n* hesabu

ark *n* safina

arm *n* mkono

arm *v* mpa silaha

armaments *n* zana za vita

armed *adj* na silaha

armor *n* gamba la kujihami

armpit *n* kwapa**

army *n* jeshi
aromatic *adj* ya kunukia
around *pro* kuzunguka
arouse *v* amsha
arrange *v* panga
arrangement *n* mipangilio
array *n* maonyesho
arrest *v* kamata
arrest *n* kukamata
arrival *n* kuwasili
arrive *v* fika
arrogance *n* ufidhuli, jeuri
arrogant *adj* mfidhuli, mjeuri
arrow *n* mshale
arsenal *n* ghala la silaha
arsenic *n* aseniki, asenia
art *n* sanaa
artery *n* mshipa
arthritis *n* yabisi kavu
artichoke *n* rubaruti
article *n* makala
articulate *v* tamka
articulation *n* kutamka
artificial *adj* bandia
artillery *n* silaha za vita
artisan *n* fundi
artist *n* msanii
artistic *adj* -a kiusanii

artwork *n* usanii
as *c* wakati
as *adv* kama
ascend *v* panda
ascendancy *n* kupanda
ascertain *v* hakikisha
ascetic *adj* kujinyima
ash *n* majivu
ashamed *adj* kuona aibu
ashore *adv* pwani
ashtray *n* chombo cha jivu
aside *adv* pembeni
aside from *adv* mbali na
ask *v* uliza
asleep *adj* kulala
asparagus *n* asparaga
aspect *n* mwelekeo
asphalt *n* lami
asphyxiate *v* nyima pumzi
asphyxiation *n* kukosa pumzi
aspiration *n* mategemeo
aspire *v* tegemea, lenga
aspirin *n* aspirini
assail *v* shambulia
assailant *n* mshambulizi
assassin *n* muuaji
assassinate *v* ua
assassination *n* mauaji

assault *n* mapigo

assault *v* piga, shambulia

assemble *v* kusanya

assembly *n* mkusanyiko

assent *v* kubali, idhinisha

assert *v* sisitiza

assertion *n* msisitizo

assess *v* kadiria, tathmini

assessment *n* kadirio, tathmini

asset *n* mali

assets *n* rasilimali

assign *v* gawa, toa

assignment *n* uteuzi

assimilate *v* fyonza

assimilation *n* kufyonza

assist *v* saidia

assistance *n* usaidizi

associate *v* shirikisha

association *n* ushirikiano

assorted *adj* tofauti

assume *v* dhani, fikiri

assumption *n* dhana

assurance *n* ahadi, bima

assure *v* hakikishia

asterisk *n* alama ya nyota

asthma *n* pumu

asthmatic *adj* -a na pumu

astonish *v* shangaza

astonishing *adj* kushangaza

astound *v* staajabisha

astounding *adj* ya ajabu

astray *v* potea, potosha

astrologer *n* mnajimu

astrology *n* unajimu

astronaut *n* mwanaanga

astronomer *n* mamajusi

astronomic *adj* -a falaki, kubwa

astronomy *n* falaki

astute *adj* janja, mwerevu

asunder *adv* vipande

asylum *n* kimbilio, hifadhi

at *pre* kwa, kwenye

atheism *n* kukana Mungu

atheist *n* mkana Mungu

athlete *n* mwanariadha

atmosphere *n* angakewa

atmospheric *adj* -a hewa

atom *n* atomu, chembe

atomic *adj* -a nyuklia

atone *v* lipia

atonement *n* kutubu, toba

atrocious *adj* kikatili

atrocity *n* ukatili

attach *v* ambatanisha

attachment *n* wambiso

attack *n* shambulio

attack v shambulia

attacker n jambazi

attain v fikia

attainable adj kupatikana

attainment n kupatikana

attempt v jaribu

attempt n jaribio

attend v hudhuria

attendance n mahudhurio

attendant n mhudumu

attention n uangalifu

attentive adj mwangalifu

attenuate v punguza

attenuating adj -a kupunguza

attest v thibitisha

attic n dari

attitude n mkao, mtazamo

attorney n wakili

attract v vutia

attraction n mvutano, kivutio

attractive adj kuvutia

attribute v dhania

auction n mnada

auction v nadi

auctioneer n dalali

audacious adj jasiri, hodari

audacity n ushupavu

audible adj -a kusikika

audience n hadhira

audit v kagua

auditorium n ukumbi

augment v ongeza

August n Agosti

aunt n shangazi

auspicious adj -enye ahadi

austere adj kali

austerity n ugumu, ukali

authentic adj halisi

authenticate v dhihirisha

authenticity n uhalisi

author n mwandishi

authoritarian adj -a mabavu

authority n mamlaka

authorization n mamlaka

authorize v idhinisha

auto n gari

autograph n sahihi

automobile n gari

autonomous adj huru

autonomy n kujitawala

autumn n kipupwe

auxiliary adj msaidizi

avail v jipatia, nufaika

availability n upatikanaji

available adj patikana

avalanche n poromoko

avarice *n* uchoyo, ubadili
avaricious *adj* -a kiuchoyo
avenge *v* lipiza kisasi
avenue *n* barabara
average *n* wastani
averse *adj* kutopenda
aversion *n* kutopenda
avert *v* zuia, geuka
aviator *n* mwanaanga
avid *adj* shauku
avoid *v* epuka
avoidable *adj* epukika
avoidance *n* kuepuka
avowed *adj* dhahiri
await *v* ngojea
awake *iv* amka, amsha
awake *adj* tambua
awakening *n* kuamka
award *v* tuza
award *n* tuzo, zawadi
aware *adj* fahamu
awareness *n* ufahamu
away *adv* mbali
awe *n* heshima
awesome *adj* -a maajabu
awful *adj* mbaya
awkward *adj* ngumu
awning *n* mfuniko

ax *n* shoka
axiom *n* usemi
axis *n* mhimili
axle *n* ekseli

B

babble *v* ropoka
baby *n* mtoto
babysitter *n* yaya
bachelor *n* kapera
back *n* mgongo
back *adv* nyuma
back *v* rudi
back down *v* kubali, jitoa
back up *v* rudi nyuma
backbone *n* uti wa mgongo
backfire *v* lipukia, geukia
background *n* asili
backing *n* kuunga mkono
backlash *n* upinzani, mlegeo
backlog *n* kiporo
backpack *n* shanta
backup *n* kuunga mkono
backward *adj* nyuma, zezeta

B

backwards *adv* Kinyume

backyard *n* ua

bacon *n* nyama ya nguruwe

bacteria *n* bakteria

bad *adj* mbaya

badge *n* beji

badly *adv* vibaya

baffle *v* shangaza

bag *n* mfuko

baggage *n* mizigo

baggy *adj* -a kupwaya

bail *n* dhamana

bail out *v* dhamini, okoa

bailiff *n* dalali

bait *n* chambo

bake *v* oka

baker *n* mwoka

bakery *n* mikate inapo okwa

balance *v* sawazisha

balance *n* mizani

balcony *n* roshani

bald *adj* kipara

bale *n* robota

ball *n* mpira

balloon *n* puto

ballot *n* karatasi ya kura

ballroom *n* ukumbi wa dansi

balm *n* marhamu

balmy *adj* kuburudisha

bamboo *n* ulanzi

ban *n* kizuizi, marufuku

ban *v* zuia, kataza

banality *n* kawaida sana

banana *n* ndizi

band *n* bendi

bandage *n* bendeji

bandage *v* funga bendeji

bandit *n* jangili

bang *v* piga, bamiza

banish *v* fukuza

banishment *n* kizuizini

bank *n* benki

bankrupt *v* filisika

bankrupt *adj* kufilisika

bankruptcy *n* kufilisika

banner *n* bango

banquet *n* dhifa

baptism *n* ubatizo

baptize *v* batiza

bar *n* baa, mche

bar *v* zuia

barbarian *n* mshenzi

barbaric *adj* -a kiushenzi

barbarism *n* ushenzi

barber *n* kinyozi

bare *adj* tupu

barefoot *adj* peku peku

barely *adv* nadra

bargain *n* makubaliano

bargain *v* patana

bargaining *n* kupatana

barge *n* mashua

bark *v* bweka

bark *n* gome

barley *n* shayiri

barn *n* zizi

barometer *n* barometa

barrage *n* mvua ya risasi

barrel *n* pipa, gudulia

barren *adj* tasa, bure

barricade *n* boma

barrier *n* kizuizi

barring *pre* ila, isipokuwa

barter *v* mali kwa mali

base *n* kituo, besi

base *v* simama

baseless *adj* bila msingi

basement *n* handaki

bashful *adj* -enye aibu

basic *adj* kimsingi

basics *n* muhimu, msingi

basin *n* beseni

basis *n* msingi

bask *v* furahia

basket *n* kikapu

basketball *n* mpira wa kikapu

bastard *n* mwanaharamu

bat *n* popo

batch *n* idadi, bechi

bath *n* bafu

bathe *v* oga

bathroom *n* bafuni

bathtub *n* bafu

baton *n* kirungu

battalion *n* batalioni

batter *v* gonga, piga

battery *n* betri

battle *n* mapigano

battle *v* pigana

battleship *n* manowari

bay *n* ghuba,

bayonet *n* singe

bazaar *n* maduka ya soko

be *iv* kuwa

be born *v* kuzaliwa

beach *n* pwani

beacon *n* kimulimuli

beak *n* mdomo wa ndege

beam *n* mwonzi

bean *n* harage

bear *n* dubu

bear *iv* beba, stahimili

bearable adj kustahimili

beard n ndevu nyingi

bearded adj -enye ndevu

bearer n mbebaji

beast n mnyama

beat iv piga

beat n pigo, mdundo

beaten adj -liopigwa, -lioshindwa

beating n mapigo

beautiful adj mzuri

beautify v pendezesha

beauty n uzuri

beaver n panya buki

because c kwa sababu

because of pre kwa sababu ya

beckon v ita

become iv kuwa

bed n kitanda

bedding n mashuka

bedroom n chumba cha kulala

bedspread n shuka la juu

bee n nyuki

beef n nyama ya ng'ombe

beef up v weka sawa

beehive n mzinga wa nyuki

beer n bia

beet n kiazisukari

beetle n kombamwiko

before adv kabla, mbele ya

before pre kabla

beforehand adv awali

befriend v fanya urafiki

beg v omba

beggar n ombaomba

begin iv anza

beginner n mwanafunzi

beginning n mwanzo

beguile v laghai

behalf (on) adv (kwa) niaba

behave v taadabu

behavior n tabia

behead v chinja, kata kichwa

behind pre nyuma

behold iv ona, tazama

being n kiumbe

belated adj tuili

belch v cheua

belch n kucheua

belfry n mnara wa kengele

Belgian adj Mbelgiji

Belgium n Ubelgiji

belief n imani

believable adj kuaminika

believe v amini

believer n muumini

belittle v dhalilisha

bell *n* kengele

bell pepper *n* pilipili hoho

belligerent *adj* mgomvi

belly *n* tumbo

belly button *n* kitovu

belong *v* milikiwa na, wa

belongings *n* mali ya

beloved *adj* mpendwa

below *adv* chini

below *pre* chini ya

belt *n* mkanda

bench *n* benchi

bend *iv* pinda

bend down *v* inama

beneath *pre* chini ya

benediction *n* baraka

benefactor *n* mfadhili

beneficial *adj* kufaa

beneficiary *n* mrithi

benefit *n* manufaa

benefit *v* nufaika

benevolence *n* ukarimu

benevolent *adj* mkarimu

benign *adj* mpole, hafifu

bequeath *v* rithisha

bereaved *adj* kufiwa

bereavement *n* kilio

beret *n* bereti

berserk *adv* pagawa

berth *n* kitanda

beseech *iv* sihi, omba

beset *iv* shambuliwa

beside *pre* kando ya

besides *pre* isitoshe

besiege *iv* zingira

best *adj* nzuri kupita

bestial *adj* kinyama

bestiality *n* unyama

bestow *v* toa zawadi

bet *iv* pinga

bet *n* dau

betray *v* saliti

betrayal *n* usaliti

better *adj* bora

between *pre* kati ya

beverage *n* kinywaji

beware *v* jihadhari

bewilder *v* staajabisha

bewitch *v* loga

beyond *adv* pasipojulikana

bias *n* upendeleo

bible *n* biblia

biblical *adj* kibiblia

bibliography *n* bibliografia

bicycle *n* baiskeli

bid *n* zabuni

bid *iv* arifia, amuru

big *adj* kubwa

bike *n* baiskeli

bile *n* nyongo

bill *n* bili

billiards *n* biliadi

billion *n* bilioni

bin *n* pipa

bind *iv* funga

binding *adj* kufunga

binoculars *n* darubini

biography *n* wasifu

biological *adj* kibiolojia

biology *n* biolojia

bird *n* ndege

birth *n* kizazi

biscuit *n* biskuti

bishop *n* askofu

bison *n* nyati

bit *n* kipande

bite *iv* mega

bite *n* kumega, ng'ata

bitter *adj* chungu

bitterly *adv* kwa uchungu

bitterness *n* uchungu

bizarre *adj* sio ya kawaida

black *adj* nyeusi

blackboard *n* ubao

blackmail *n* mlungula

blackmail *v* lungula

blackness *n* weusi

blackout *n* giza, kuzimia

blacksmith *n* mhunzi

bladder *n* kibofu cha mkojo

blade *n* wembe, ubapa

blame *n* lawama

blame *v* laumu

blameless *adj* bila lawama

bland *adj* -siopendeza

blank *adj* wazi, nafasi tupu

blanket *n* blanketi

blaspheme *v* kufuru

blasphemy *n* kukufuru

blast *n* mlipuko

blaze *v* moto

bleach *v* buluu

bleach *n* dawa ya madoa

bleed *iv* toa damu

bleeding *n* toka damu

blemish *n* doa

blemish *v* tia doa

blend *n* mchanganyiko

blend *v* changanya

blender *n* mchanganyaji

bless *v* bariki

blessed *adj* -enye heri

bolster

blessing *n* baraka

blind *v* pofua

blind *adj* kipofu

blindly *adv* bila kuona

blindness *n* upofu

blink *v* pepesa

bliss *n* raha mustarehe

blister *n* malengelenge

blizzard *n* dhoruba ya theluji

bloated *adj* kuvimba gesi

block *n* pande kubwa

block *v* zuia

blockade *v* zingia, zingira

blockade *n* uzio, zingio

blockage *n* kizuizi

blood *n* damu

bloodthirsty *adj* mwuaji

bloody *adj* ilio na damu

bloom *v* nawiri, stawi

blossom *v* chanua

blot *n* doa

blot *v* tia doa

blouse *n* blauzi

blow *n* mpigo

blow *iv* puliza

blow out *iv* zima

blow up *iv* lipua

blowout *n* kubatilisha

bludgeon *v* piga na rungu

blue *adj* buluu

blueprint *n* plani

bluff *v* danganya

blunder *n* hitilafu

blunt *adj* butu, wazi

bluntness *n* uwazi

blur *v* tia ukungu

blurred *adj* fifia

blush *v* ona aibu, iva uso

blush *n* wekundu wa uso

boar *n* nguruwe pori

board *n* ubao

board *v* panda

boast *v* jivuna, jisifu

boat *n* boti

bodily *adj* kimwili

body *n* mwili

bog *n* kinamasi

bog down *v* zama, titia

boil *v* chemsha

boil down to *v* ishia, fupisha

boil over *v* furika

boiler *n* hodhi

boisterous *adj* machachari

bold *adj* thabiti, jasiri

boldness *n* ujasiri, ushupavu

bolster *v* saidia

B

bolt *n* komeo

bolt *v* bana komeo

bomb *n* bomu

bomb *v* lipua bomu

bombshell *n* fadhaa

bond *n* pingu, mapatano

bondage *n* utumwa

bone *n* mfupa

bone marrow *n* uboho wa mfupa

bonfire *n* moto wa kambi

bonus *n* turuhani

book *n* kitabu

bookcase *n* kabati la vitabu

bookkeeper *n* mhasibu

bookkeeping *n* uhasibu

booklet *n* kijarida, kijitabu

bookseller *n* muuza vitabu

bookstore *n* duka la vitabu

boom *n* boriti

boom *v* stawi, lia

boost *v* ongeza, saidia

boost *n* unga mkono

boot *n* buti, teke

booth *n* kibanda

booty *n* mali ya wizi

booze *n* pombe, kileo

border *n* mpaka

border on *v* pakana na

borderline *adj* mpaka

bore *v* toboa, chosha

bored *adj* choshwa

boredom *n* uchokezi

boring *adj* kuchosha

born *adj* -a kuzaliwa

borough *n* wilaya

borrow *v* azima

bosom *n* kifua

boss *n* bosi

boss around *v* tawala tawala

bossy *adj* mkorofi

botany *n* botania

botch *v* haribu

both *adj* wote wawili

bother *v* sumbua

bothersome *adj* sumbufu

bottle *n* chupa

bottleneck *n* kikwazo

bottom *n* chini, matako

bottomless *adj* tele

bough *n* tawi

boulder *n* jabali

boulevard *n* njia pana

bounce *v* dunda

bounce *n* mdundo, pigo

bound *adj* kufungwa

bound for *adj* elekea

boundary *n* mpaka

boundless *adj* bila mpaka

bounty *n* tuzo, zawadi

bourgeois *adj* kibwanyenye

bow *n* upinde

bow *v* inama

bow out *v* jitoa, ondoka

bowels *n* uchengele

bowl *n* bakuli

box *n* boksi, kasha

boxer *n* bondia

boxing *n* ndondi

boy *n* mvulana

boycott *v* susa, gomea

boyfriend *n* mpenzi wa kiume

boyhood *n* ujana, utoto

bra *n* sidiria

brace for *v* jitayarishe

bracelet *n* bangili

bracket *n* kiango, bano

brag *v* tamba

braid *n* butu, msuko

brain *n* ubongo

brainwash *v* tia kasumba

brake *n* kangaga

brake *v* breki

branch *n* tawi

branch office *n* ofisi ya tawi

branch out *v* panuka

brand *n* chapa, aina

brand-new *adj* mpya kabisa

brandy *n* brandi

brat *adj* kitwana

brave *adj* jasiri

bravely *adv* kijasiri

bravery *n* ujasiri

brawl *n* mzozo

breach *n* ufa, kulegalega

bread *n* mkate

breadth *n* upana

break *n* kukatika, ufa

break *iv* vunja

break away *v* kutoroka

break down *v* hali hafifu

break free *v* jiweke huru

break in *v* vunja ili kuingia

break off *v* ondoa, kata

break open *v* vunja kufungua

break out *v* zuka

break up *v* achana

breakable *adj* -a kuvunjika

breakdown *n* kuharibika

breakfast *n* kifungua kinywa

breakthrough *n* chomoza

breast *n* ziwa

breath *n* pumzi

breathe *v* pumua

breathing *n* kupumua

breathtaking *adj* -a kufurahisha

breed *iv* zaa, zalisha

breed *n* jamii, aina

breeze *n* upepo mwanana

brethren *n* ndugu

brevity *n* ufupi

brew *v* pika

bribe *v* honga

bribe *n* hongo

bribery *n* kuhonga

brick *n* tofali

bricklayer *n* mwashi

bridal *adj* -a kutambuza

bride *n* bibi harusi

bridegroom *n* bwana harusi

bridge *n* daraja

bridle *n* hatamu

brief *adj* fupi

brief *v* eleza

briefcase *n* mkoba

briefing *n* maelezo

briefly *adv* kwa kifupi

briefs *n* chupi

brigade *n* brigedi, kikosi

bright *adj* -enye kung'aa

brighten *v* ng'arisha

brightness *n* ung'aro

brilliant *adj* -a kung'aa

brim *n* mdomo, pomoni

bring *iv* leta

bring back *v* rudisha

bring down *v* shusha

bring up *v* pandisha

brink *n* ukingoni

brisk *adj* haraka, nyepesi

Britain *n* Uingereza

British *adj* Mwingereza

broad *adj* pana, nyanda

broadcast *v* tangaza

broadcast *n* tangazo

broadcaster *n* mtangazaji

broaden *v* panua

broadly *adv* kwa ujumla

brochure *n* kijarida

broil *v* banika

broiler *n* jiko la kubanikia

broke *adj* kuchacha

broken *adj* kuvunjika

bronchitis *n* mkamba

bronze *n* shaba nyekundu

broom *n* ufagio

broth *n* supu

brothel *n* danguro

brother *n* kaka, ndugu

brotherhood *n* undugu
brotherly *adj* kindugu
brow *n* paji la uso
brown *adj* rangi ya udongo
browse *v* tafuna
browser *n* kivinjari
bruise *n* jeraha
bruise *v* chubua, vilia
brush *n* brashi
brush *v* piga brashi
brush aside *v* kufukuza
brush up *v* kupiga msasa
brusque *adj* mkali
brutal *adj* kikatili
brutality *n* ukatili
brutalize *v* fanya ukatili
brute *adj* mkatili
bubble *n* povu
bubble gum *n* ubani
buck *n* dume
bucket *n* ndoo ya maji
buckle *n* bakoli
buckle up *v* funga
bud *n* chipukizi
buddy *n* rafiki
budge *v* sogea
budget *n* bajeti
buffalo *n* nyati

bug *n* kunguni, mdudu
bug *v* udhi, sumbua
build *iv* jenga
builder *n* mjenzi
building *n* jengo
buildup *n* ongezeko
bulb *n* kitunguu, balbu
bulge *n* vimba, tokeza
bulk *n* wingi, bonge
bulky *adj* kubwa
bull *n* dume, fahali
bulldoze *v* lazimisha
bullet *n* risasi
bully *adj* kuonea, katili
bulwark *n* kizuizi, ukingo
bum *n* matako
bump *n* nundu
bump into *v* kutana na
bumper *n* kubwa mno
bumpy *adj* -enye matuta
bunch *n* kititia, fungu
bundle *n* mzigo, furushi
bundle *v* fungasha
bunker *n* handaki, ghala
buoy *n* boya
burden *n* mzigo, udhia
burden *v* sumbua
burdensome *adj* -enye usumbufu

B
C

bureau *n* dawati, ofisi
bureaucracy *n* urasimu
bureaucrat *n* mrasimu
burglar *n* mwizi
burglarize *v* iba
burglary *n* wizi
burial *n* mazishi
burn *iv* choma, unguza
burn *n* jeraha la moto
burp *v* cheua
burp *n* cheuzi
burrow *n* tundu la mnyama
burst *iv* pasuka
burst into *v* vamia
bury *v* zika
bus *n* basi
bus *v* nenda kwa basi
bush *n* kichaka
business *n* biashara
businessman *n* mfanya biashara
bust *n* kifua
bustling *adj* kwa pilikapilika
busy *adj*
but *c* ila
butcher *n* bucha
butchery *n* bucha
butler *n* mhudumu mkuu
butt *n* kichungi

butter *n* siagi
butterfly *n* kipepeo
button *n* kifungo
buttonhole *n* tundu la kifungo
buy *iv* nunua
buy off *v* honga
buyer *n* mnunuzi
buzz *n* mvumo
buzz *v* vuma
buzzard *n* shakevale
buzzer *n* kengele
by *pre* kwa
bye *e* kwa heri
bypass *v* kwepa
by-product *n* chumo la ziada
bystander *n* mtazamaji

C

cab *n* teksi, kebu
cabbage *n* kabichi
cabin *n* kichumba
cabinet *n* kabati
cable *n* kebo
cafeteria *n* mgahawa

cage *n* kizimba

cake *n* keki

calamity *n* janga

calculate *v* kokotoa

calculation *n* mkokotoo

calculator *n* kikokotoo

calendar *n* kalenda

calf *n* ndama

caliber *n* ubora, ukubwa

calibrate *v* pima

call *n* wito

call *v* ita

call off *v* sitisha

call on *v* omba, tembelea

call out *v* ita

calling *n* wito

callous *adj* -enye sugu

calm *adj* tulivu

calm *n* mtulivu, kutulia

calm down *v* tulia

calorie *n* kalori

calumny *n* kashfa, uzushi

camel *n* ngamia

camera *n* kamera

camouflage *v* ficha

camouflage *n* maficho

camp *n* kambi

camp *v* piga kambi

campaign *v* fanya kampeni

campaign *n* kampeni

campfire *n* moto wa kambi

can *iv* hifadhi mkebeni

can *v* weza kufanya

can *n* kopo, mkebe

canal *n* mfereji

canary *n* chiriku

cancel *v* futa, sitisha

cancellation *n* kufuta, kusitisha

cancer *n* sarakani, kansa

cancerous *adj* -enye kansa

candid *adj* wazi

candle *n* mshumaa

candor *n* uwazi

candy *n* pipi, peremende

cane *n* henzirani, asa

canister *n* kopo, mkebe

canned *adj* kwenye kopo

cannibal *n* mla watu

cannon *n* mzinga

canoe *n* ngalawa

canonize *v* dumisha

cantaloupe *n* tikiti maji

canteen *n* kantini

canvas *n* turubai

canyon *n* korongo

cap *n* kofia

C

C

capability *n* uwezo

capable *adj* kuweza

capacity *n* uwezo

cape *n* rasi

capital *n* makao makuu

capital letter *n* herufi kubwa

capitalism *n* ubepari

capitulate *v* salimu amri

capsize *v* pinduka

capsule *n* kidonge

captain *n* kapteni

captivate *v* pendezwa mno

captive *n* kutekwa

captivity *n* kifungoni

capture *v* teka, kamata

capture *n* kuteka

car *n* gari

carat *n* karati

caravan *n* gari nyumba

carburetor *n* kabureta

carcass *n* mzoga

card *n* kadi

cardboard *n* kadibodi

cardiac *adj* -a moyo

cardiology *n* taaluma ya moyo

care *n* utunzaji, uangalizi

care *v* tunza, jali

care about *v* thamini, jali

care for *v* tunza, uguza

career *n* amali, kazi

carefree *adj* -siojali

careful *adj* uangalifu

careless *adj* uzembe

caretaker *n* mwangalizi

cargo *n* mzigo

caring *adj* kujali

carnal *adj* -a mwili

carol *n* wimbo wa kikristo

carpenter *n* seremala

carpentry *n* useremala

carpet *n* zulia, jamvi

carriage *n* gari

carrot *n* karoti

carry *v* beba

carry on *v* endelea

carry out *v* fanya

cart *n* mkokoteni, kigari

cart *v* beba

cartoon *n* katuni

cartridge *n* ganda, kidau

carve *v* chonga

case *n* sanduku

cash *n* fedha, pesa

cashier *n* keshia

casino *n* kasino

casket *n* kijaluba, kikasha

casserole *n* maziga

cassock *n* joho

cast *iv* tupa

castaway *n* alie mtengwa

caste *n* tabaka, hadhi

castle *n* ngome, husuni

casual *adj* sio rasmi

casualty *n* majeruhi

cat *n* paka

catalog *n* katalogi

catalog *v* orodhesha

cataract *n* mtoto wa jicho

catastrophe *n* janga

catch *iv* shika

catch up *v* wahi

catching *adj* kushika, kupata

catchword *n* wito, kidahizo

catechism *n* katekisimu

category *n* namna, jamii

cater to *v* hudumia

caterpillar *n* kiwavi

cathedral *n* kanisa kuu

catholic *adj* katoliki

Catholicism *n* Ukatoliki

cattle *n* ng'ombe

cauliflower *n* koliflawa

cause *n* sababu, chanzo

cause *v* sababisha, leta

caution *n* tahadhari

cautious *adj* kwa tahadhari

cave *n* pango

cave in *v* bomoka

cavern *n* pango, shimo

cavity *n* uwazi

cease *v* acha

ceaselessly *adv* bila kuacha

ceiling *n* dari

celebrate *v* sherehekea

celebration *n* sherehe

celebrity *n* mtu mashuhuri

celery *n* figili

celestial *adj* -a mbinguni

celibacy *n* ukapera

celibate *adj* kapera, mseja

cellphone *n* simu ya mkononi

cement *n* saruji, sementi

cemetery *n* makaburini

censorship *n* ukaguzi, udhibiti

censure *v* kanya, laumu

census *n* sensa

cent *n* senti

centenary *n* miaka mia

center *n* kati, kituo

center *v* weka katikati

centimeter *n* sentimeta

central *adj* -a katikati

C

century *n* karne

ceramic *n* kauri

cereal *n* nafaka

cerebral *adj* -a ubongo

ceremony *n* sherehe

certain *adj* uhakika, fulani

certainty *n* kwa uhakika

certificate *n* cheti, hati

certify *v* thibitisha

chagrin *n* majonzi

chain *n* mnyororo

chain *v* funga na mnyororo

chainsaw *n* msumeno

chair *n* kiti

chair *v* ongoza mkutano

chairman *n* mwenyekiti

chalet *n* kibanda

chalice *n* bilauri

chalk *n* chaki

chalkboard *n* ubao wa kuandika

challenge *v* pinga

challenge *n* changamoto

chamber *n* chumba

champ *n* bingwa

champion *n* bingwa

champion *v* tetea, pigania

chance *n* nafasi

chandelier *n* thurea

change *v* badilisha

change *n* mabadiliko

channel *n* mlangobahari

chant *n* uimbaji

chaos *n* vurugu, fujo

chaotic *adj* kwa vurugu

chapel *n* kanisa dogo

chaplain *n* mchungaji

chapter *n* sura, tawi

char *v* unguza

character *n* tabia

characteristic *adj* tabia

charade *n* utani

charbroil *adj* choma

charcoal *n* mkaa

charge *v* toza, amuru

charge *n* gharama

charisma *n* haiba

charismatic *adj* -enye haiba

charitable *adj* -enye hisani

charity *n* fadhila, sadaka

charm *v* vutia

charm *n* haiba

charming *adj* -enye haiba

chart *n* ramani, chati

charter *n* mkataba

charter *v* kodi

chase *n* msako**

C

chase v fukuza, kimbiza

chase away v fukuza

chasm n korongo

chaste adj safi

chastise v gombeza, adhibu

chastisement n adhabu

chastity n utawa, ubikira

chat v zungumza

chauffeur n dereva

cheap adj rahisi, duni

cheat v ibia, tapeli

cheater n tapeli

check n ukaguzi

check v kagua,kataza

check in v ukaguzi

check up n ukaguzi

checkbook n kitabu cha hundi

cheek n shavu

cheekbone n kituguta

cheeky adj fidhuli

cheer v shangilia

cheer up v changamka

cheerful adj mchangamfu

cheers n afya! kwaheri

cheese n jibini

chef n mpishi

chemical adj kemikali

chemist n mkemia

chemistry n kemia

cherish v tunza, thamini

chess n sataranji, chesi

chest n kifua, sanduku

chew v tafuna

chick n kifaranga, kigori

chicken n kuku

chicken out v ogopa

chicken pox n tetekuwanga

chide v gombeza

chief n mtemi, mkuu

chiefly adv hasa

child n mtoto

childhood n utotoni

childish adj -a kitoto

childless adj tasa, gumba

children n watoto

chill n baridi

chill v fanya baridi, poza

chill out v poa

chilly adj baridi, ubaridi

chimney n dohani, meko

chimpanzee n sokwe

chin n kidevu

chip n kipande, chenga

chisel n patasi

chocolate n chokoleti

choice n chaguo, uchaguzi

C

choir *n* kwaya
choke *v* paliwa
cholera *n* kipindupindu
cholesterol *n* kolesteroli
choose *iv* chagua
choosy *adj* chaguzi,
chop *v* kata kata
chop *n* kipande
chopper *n* mtema, mkataji
chore *n* kazi
chorus *n* mkarara, kiitikio
christen *v* batiza
christening *n* ubatizo
christian *adj* mkristo
Christianity *n* Ukristo
Christmas *n* Krisimasi
chronic *adj* sugu
chronicle *n* tarikhi
chronology *n* mpangilio
chubby *adj* kinene
chuckle *v* cheka chinichini
chunk *n* kipande
church *n* kanisa
chute *n* mwamvuli
cigar *n* biri
cigarette *n* sigareti
cinder *n* jivu
cinema *n* sinema

cinnamon *n* mdalasini
circle *n* mduara, duara
circle *v* zunguka
circuit *n* mzunguko
circular *adj* -a mviringo
circulate *v* zunguka
circulation *n* mzunguko
circumcise *v* tairi
circumcision *n* kutahiri
circumstance *n* mazingira
circus *n* sarakasi
cistern *n* tangi la maji
citizen *n* raia, mwananchi
citizenship *n* uraia
city *n* jiji
civic *adj* -a uraia
civil *adj* -a kiraia
civilization *n* ustaarabu
civilize *v* staarabisha
claim *v* dai
claim *n* madai
clam *n* chaza
clamor *v* makelele
clamp *n* kibanio, gango
clan *n* ukoo
clandestine *adj* -a siri
clap *v* piga makofi
clarification *n* ufafanuzi

clarify *v* fafanua

clarinet *n* zumari

clarity *n* uwazi

clash *v* gongana

clash *n* kugongana

class *n* darasa, aina

classic *adj* -liomaarufu

classroom *n* darasa

classy *adj* maridadi

clause *n* sharti, kishazi

claw *n* kucha

claw *v* parura

clean *adj* safi

clean *v* safisha

cleaner *n* msafishaji

cleanliness *n* usafi

cleanse *v* osha, safisha

cleanser *n* -a kusafisha

clear *adj* -a wazi

clear *v* ondoa, toa

clearance *n* kusafisha

clear-cut *adj* dhairi kabisa

clearly *adv* vizuri

clearness *n* kueleweka

cleft *n* ufa, mwanya

clemency *n* huruma

clench *v* kunja, kaza sana

clerical *adj* -a ukarani

clerk *n* karani

clever *adj* -enye akili

click *v* alika, bofya

client *n* mteja

clientele *n* wateja

cliff *n* jabali

climate *n* hali ya hewa

climatic *adj* -a hali ya hewa

climax *n* kilele, mshindo

climb *v* panda

climbing *n* kupanda

clinch *v* bana

cling *iv* ng'ang'ania

clinic *n* zahanati, kliniki

clip *v* kata, punguza

clipping *n* kukata

cloak *n* joho

clock *n* saa ya ukutani

clog *v* ziba, zibwa

cloister *n* makazi ya watawa

close *v* funga

close *adj* kufuga

close to *pre* karibu na

closed *adj* fungwa

closely *adv* kwa karibu

closet *n* kabati

closure *n* ufungaji

clot *n* donge la damu

cloth *n* nguo

clothe *v* vaa

clothes *n* mavazi

clothing *n* vazi

cloud *n* wingu

cloudless *adj* bila mawingu

cloudy *adj* na mawingu

clown *n* chale

club *n* klabu, rungu

club *v* piga rungu

clue *n* dalili, ishara

clumsiness *n* uzuzu

clumsy *adj* goigoi, wa hovyo

cluster *n* kundi, fungu

cluster *v* kusanyika

clutch *n* klachi, kunyakua

coach *v* kufundisha mtu

coach *n* daraja la pili

coaching *n* kufundisha

coagulate *v* ganda

coagulation *n* mgando

coal *n* mkaa

coalition *n* muungano

coarse *adj* -a matusi

coast *n* pwani, ufuko

coastal *adj* -a pwani

coastline *n* ukanda wa pwani

coat *n* koti

coax *v* bembeleza

cob *n* bunzi

cobweb *n* tandu ya buibui

cocaine *n* kokein, unga

cock *n* jogoo

cockpit *n* dungu

cockroach *n* mende

cocktail *n* kokteli

cocky *adj* kwa majivuno

cocoa *n* kakao

coconut *n* nazi

cod *n* chewa

coefficient *n* kizidishi

coerce *v* lazimisha

coercion *n* kulazimisha

coexist *v* ishi pamoja

coffee *n* kahawa

coffin *n* jeneza

cohabit *v* kaa kinyumba

coherent *adj* eleweka

cohesion *n* mshikamano

coin *n* sarafu

coincidence *n* ulinganifu

coincidental *adj* -a kutotarajia

cold *adj* -a baridi

coldness *n* ubaridi

colic *n* chango

collaborate *v* shirikiana

C

collaboration *n* ushirikiano
collaborator *n* mshiriki
collapse *v* anguka:zirai
collapse *n* kuanguka; kuzirai
collar *n* kola, ukosi
collarbone *n* mfupa wa bega
collateral *adj* -a nyongeza
collect *v* kusanya
collection *n* mkusanyiko
collector *n* mkusanya
college *n* chuo
collide *v* gongana
collision *n* mgongano
cologne *n* marashi
colon *n* nukta pacha
colonel *n* kanali
colonial *adj* kikoloni
colonization *n* ukoloni
colonize *v* anzisha ukoloni
colony *n* koloni
color *n* rangi
color *v* paka rangi
colossal *adj* kubwa sana
colt *n* mwanafarasi
column *n* nguzo; safu
coma *n* kuzimia
comb *n* chanuo; kitana
comb *v* chana

combat *n* mapigano
combat *v* pigana
combatant *n* mpiganaji
combination *n* mchanganyiko
combine *v* changanya
combustible *n* kuwaka
combustion *n* mwako
come *iv* njoo
come about *v* tokea
come across *v* kutana na
come apart *v* achia, chanika
come back *v* rudi
come down *v* shuka
come forward *v* njoo
come from *v* toka, tokea
come in *v* ingia
come out *v* tokezea
come over *v* njoo, karibia
come up *v* chipua, kuwa
comeback *n* kurudi ulingoni
comet *n* kimondo
comfort *n* faraja
comfortable *adj* -a faraja
comforter *n* chuchu
comical *adj* -a kuchekesha
coming *n* kuja
coming *adj* -a kuja
comma *n* mkato, koma

C

command *v* amrisha

commander *n* kamanda, amiri

commandment *n* amri

commemorate *v* adhimisha

commence *v* anza

commend *v* sifu, tukuza

commendation *n* sifa

comment *v* toa wazo

comment *n* wazo, oni

commerce *n* biashara

commercial *adj* -a biashara

commission *n* tume

commit *v* tenda, fanya

commitment *n* jukumu

committee *n* kamati

common *adj* -a kawaida

commotion *n* ghasia, vurugu

communicate *v* wasiliana

communion *n* komunyo

communism *n* ukomunisti

communist *adj* komunisti

community *n* jamii

commute *v* punguza

compact *adj* -liobanwa sana

companion *n* mwenzi

companionship *n* urafiki

company *n* kampuni

comparative *adj* linganishi

compare *v* linganisha

comparison *n* mlingano

compartment *n* chumba kidogo

compass *n* dira

compassion *n* huruma, upole

compassionate *adj* -enye huruma

compatibility *n* mchukuano

compatible *adj* -a mchukuano

compatriot *n* ndugu

compel *v* lazimisha

compelling *adj* -a kulazimisha

compensate *v* kufidia

compensation *n* fidia

compete *v* shindana,

competence *n* uwezo, ujuzi

competent *adj* -enye ujuzi

competition *n* mchuano

competitive *adj* -a mchuano

competitor *n* mshindani

compile *v* tayarisha

complain *v* lalamika

complaint *n* lalamiko

complement *n* kijazilizo

complete *adj* nzima

complete *v* maliza

completely *adv* kabisa

completion *n* kukamilika

complex *adj* ngumu

complexion *n* rangi ya asili

complexity *n* ugumu, utata

compliance *n* ridhaa

compliant *adj* -a ridhaa

complicate *v* tatanisha

complication *n* matatizo

complicity *n* ushiriki

compliment *n* sifa, pongezi

complimentary *adj* -a kusifu

comply *v* tekeleza

component *n* sehemu shiriki

compose *v* tunga

composed *adj* kwa kutulia

composer *n* mtunzi

composition *n* utunzi

compost *n* mbolea

composure *n* utulivu

compound *n* mchanganyiko

comprehend *v* elewa

comprehensive *adj* -a kueleweka

compress *v* shindilia

compression *n* mshindilio

comprise *v* tengenezwa na

compromise *n* muafaka

compromise *v* fanya muafaka

compulsion *n* shurutisho

compulsory *adj* -a lazima

compute *v* kisia

computer *n* kompyuta

comrade *n* ndugu, rafiki

con man *n* tapeli

conceal *v* ficha

concede *v* kubali

conceited *adj* kwa kujivuna

conceive *v* pata mimba

concentrate *v* nuika

concentration *n* mkusanyiko

concentric *adj* -a kati moja

concept *n* wazo, fikra

conception *n* utungaji

concern *v* husika

concern *n* shughuli

concerning *pre* kuhusu

concert *n* onyesho la muziki

concession *n* makubaliano

conciliate *v* suluhisha

conciliatory *adj* -a kupatanisha

conciousness *n* umakini

concise *adj* kwa kifupi

conclude *v* kamilisha

conclusion *n* hitimisho

concoct *v* buni, tunga

concoction *n* ubunifu

concrete *n* zege

concrete *adj* -a zege

concur *v* kubaliana**

C

C

concurrent *adj* -a mfuatano
condemn *v* hukumu, laumu
condemnation *n* hukumu, lawama
condensation *n* uoevukaji
condense *v* fupisha
condescend *v* dhalilika
condiment *n* kiungo
condition *n* sharti
conditional *adj* -a kutegemea
conditioner *n* dawa ya kuboresha
condo *n* nyumba
condolences *n* rambirambi
condone *v* puuzia
conducive *adj* -a kufaa kwa
conduct *n* mwenendo
conduct *v* ongoza, simamia
conductor *n* kondakta
cone *n* koni; pia
confer *v* tunza; shauriana
conference *n* mkutano
confess *v* kiri, tubu
confession *n* kukiri, kutubu
confessional *n* -a kukiri
confidant *n* msiri
confide *v* ambia siri
confidence *n* imani
confident *adj* kuamini
confidential *adj* -a siri

confine *v* fungia
confinement *n* kifungo
confirm *v* thibitisha
confirmation *n* uthibitisho
confiscate *v* nyang'anya
confiscation *n* unyang'anyi
conflict *n* ugomvi
conflict *v* pingana
conflicting *adj* -a kupingana
conform *v* fuata desturi
conformity *n* utiifu wa desturi
confound *v* shangaa sana
confront *v* kabiliana
confrontation *n* makabiliano
confuse *v* tatanisha, tatiza
confusing *adj* -a kutatiza
confusion *n* utata
congenial *adj* -a urafiki
congested *adj* -liosongamana
congestion *n* msongamano
congratulate *v* pongeza
congratulations *n* hongera
congregate *v* kusanyika
congregation *n* usharika
congress *n* bunge
conjecture *n* kubahatisha
conjugal *adj* -a unyumba
conjugate *v* nyambua kitenzi

conjunction *n* kiunganishi

conjure up *v* ita, kumbusha

connect *v* unganisha

connection *n* uhusiano

connote *v* maanisha

conquer *v* twa kwa nguvu

conqueror *n* mtekaji

conquest *n* utekaji

conscience *n* dhamiri, dhamira

conscious *adj* -enye fahamu

conscript *n* mwanajeshi

consecrate *v* tukiza

consecration *n* kutukuza

consecutive *adj* mfululizo

consensus *n* muafaka

consent *v* kubali

consent *n* makubaliano

consequence *n* tokeo

consequent *adj* kutokana

conservation *n* hifadhi

conservative *adj* ukale

conserve *v* hifadhi

conserve *n* jamu

consider *v* fikiria kuhusu

considerable *adj* kubwa

consideration *n* fikiria, kufikiri

consignment *n* mzigo

consist *v* tegemea, husu

consistency *n* msimamo

consistent *adj* -enye msimamo

consolation *n* faraja

console *v* fariji, liwaza

consolidate *v* zatiti, imarisha

consonant *n* konsonanti

conspiracy *n* njama

conspirator *n* mla njama

conspire *v* kula njama

constancy *n* uthabiti

constant *adj* uimara, uthabiti

constellation *n* kundi la nyota

consternation *n* fadhaa, hofu

constipate *v* funga choo

constipated *adj* funga choo

constipation *n* kufunga choo

constitute *v* unda

constitution *n* katiba

constrain *v* lazimisha

constraint *n* shurutisho

construct *v* jenga

construction *n* jengo

consul *n* balozi mdogo

consulate *n* kanseli

consult *v* tafuta ushauri,

consultation *n* ushauri

consume *v* kula, tumia

consumer *n* mtumiaji**

consumption *n* utumiaji, ulaji

contact *v* wasiliana na

contact *n* mawasiliano

contagious *adj* -a kuambukiza

contain *v* weka ndani

container *n* chombo

contaminate *v* najisi

contamination *n* kunajisi

contemplate *v* tafakari

contemporary *adj* -a kisasa

contempt *n* dharau

contend *v* pambana

contender *n* mgombea

content *adj* kwa kuridhika

content *v* ridhika,

contentious *adj* shari, -a ugomvi

contents *n* vilivyomo ndani

contest *n* mashindano

contestant *n* mshindani

context *n* muktadha

continent *n* bara

continental *adj* -a bara

contingency *n* uwezekano

contingent *adj* iwezayo kutokea

continuation *n* kuendelea

continue *v* endelea

continuity *n* kuendelea

continuous *adj* kwa kuendelea

contour *n* umbo; kontua

contraband *n* magendo,

contract *v* fanya mkataba

contract *n* mkataba

contradict *v* pinga, pingana

contradiction *n* tofauti, hitilafu

contrary *adj* kinyume

contrast *v* kwa kinyume

contrast *n* kinyume

contribute *v* changa

contribution *n* mchango

contributor *n* mfadhili

contrition *n* majuto

control *n* udhibiti

control *v* dhibiti

controversial *adj* kuleta utata

controversy *n* utata, mgogoro

convalescent *adj* kupata afueni

convene *v* itisha

convenience *n* -a kufaa

convenient *adj* -a kufaa

convention *n* desturi, mila

conventional *adj* -a kimila

converge *v* kutana

conversation *n* mazungumzo

converse *v* zungumza

conversely *adv* kwa kinyume

conversion *n* badiliko

C

convert *v* badilisha

convey *v* wasilisha

convict *v* mfungwa

conviction *n* kutiwa hatiani

convince *v* sadikisha

convincing *adj* kusadikisha

convoluted *adj* -lioviringika

convoy *n* msafara

convulse *v* tikisa sana

cook *v* pika

cook *n* mpishi

cookie *n* biskuti

cooking *n* kupika

cool *adj* -a baridi

cool *v* fanya baridi

cool down *v* poa

cooling *adj* -a kupooza

coolness *n* ubaridi; utulivu

cooperate *v* shirikiana

cooperation *n* ushirikiano

cooperative *adj* kushirikiana

coordinate *v* ratibu

coordination *n* uratibu

coordinator *n* mratibu

cop *n* askari, polisi

cope *v* weza, mudu

copper *n* shaba

copy *v* nakili

copy *n* nakala

copyright *n* hakimiliki

cord *n* kamba

cordial *adj* kunjufu

cordless *adj* bila waya

cordon *n* safu ya kizuizi

cordon off *v* zunguka

core *n* kiini

cork *n* kizibo

corn *n* nafaka, mahindi

corner *n* kona

cornerstone *n* jiwe la msingi

cornet *n* buruji

corollary *n* matokeo

coronary *adj* -a moyo

coronation *n* kutawazwa

corporal *adj* -a mwili

corporal *n* koplo

corporation *n* shirika

corpse *n* maiti

corpulent *adj* nene sana

corpuscle *n* chembe

correct *v* sahihisha

correct *adj* sahihi

correction *n* masahihisho

correlate *v* onyesha uwiano

correspond *v* andikiana na

correspondent *n* mwandishi

C

corresponding *adj* -a kulingana
corridor *n* ushoroba
corroborate *v* thibitisha
corrode *v* babua
corrupt *v* haribu, rubuni
corrupt *adj* mla rushwa
corruption *n* ufisadi
cosmetic *n* kipodozi
cosmic *adj* -a ulimwengu
cosmonaut *n* mwanaanga
cost *iv* gharimu
cost *n* gharama
costly *adj* -enye gharama
costume *n* vazi
cottage *n* nyumba
cotton *n* pamba
couch *n* kochi
cough *n* kukohoa
cough *v* kohoa
council *n* halmashauri
counsel *v* toa ushauri
counsel *n* ushauri, wakili
counselor *n* mshauri
count *v* hesabu
countenance *n* unga mkono
counter *n* kaunta
counter *v* pinga
counteract *v* kinza, zuia

counterfeit *v* ughushi
counterfeit *adj* bandia ghushi
counterpart *n* mwenzi
countess *n* mke wa lodi
countless *adj* bila hesabu
country *n* nchi
countryman *n* mwananchi
countryside *n* nje ya mji
county *n* mkoa, jimbo
couple *n* viwili, wawili
coupon *n* kuponi
courage *n* ujasiri, ushujaa
courageous *adj* shujaa
courier *n* mjumbe, tarishi
course *n* somo, kozi
court *n* mahakama
court *v* tongoza, chumbia
courtesy *n* adabu, heshima
courthouse *n* mahakama
courtship *n* posa, uchumba
courtyard *n* ua
cousin *n* binamu
covenant *n* agano
cover *n* mfuniko
cover *v* funika
cover up *v* ficha, ficha
coverage *n* maelezo
covert *adj* -a siri

coverup n kuficha

covet v tamani

cow n ng'ombe

coward n mwoga

cowardice n woga

cowardly adv -enye woga

cowboy n mchunga ng'ombe

crab n kaa

crack n ufa

crack v fanya ufa

cradle n kitanda cha mtoto

craft n kazi za mkono

craftsman n fundistadi

cram v jaza; bukua

cramp n kakamaa

cramped adj -liobanwa

crane n winchi; korongo

crank n hendeli

cranky adj -enye kisirani

crap n mavi

crash n mgongano

crash v gonga, vunjika

crass adj kubwa

crater n shimo

crave v tamani

craving n hamu kubwa

crawl v tambaa

crayon n penseli ya rangi

craziness n kichaa, wazimu

crazy adj wazimu, kichaa

creak n sauti ya mkwaruzo

cream n malai

creamy adj -a malai

crease n kunjo

crease v kunja kunja

create v umba

creation n uumbaji

creative adj mbunifu

creativity n ubunifu

creator n muumba

creature n kiumbe

credibility n uaminifu

credible adj wa kuaminika

credit n mkopo; heshima

creditor n mwia

creed n kanuni za imani

creek n ghuba; hori

creep v tamba

creepy adj -a kuogopesha

cremate v choma maiti

crest n kilele

crevice n ufa mdogo

crew n baharia

crib n hori

cricket n nyenje, senene

crime n uhalifu

C

criminal *adj* mhalifu

cripple *adj* kilema

cripple *v* lemaza

crisis *n* hali ya hatari

crisp *adj* kaukau

crispy *adj* -a kaukau

criss-cross *v* kingama

criterion *n* kigezo

critical *adj* -a kukosoa

criticism *n* ukosoaji

criticize *v* kosoa

critique *n* mapitio, kukosoa

crocodile *n* mamba

crony *n* mwandani

crook *n* jambazi; bakora

crooked *adj* -a kihuni

crop *n* zao

cross *n* msalaba

cross *adj* kwa hasira

cross *v* vuka; kasirisha

cross out *v* futa

crossing *n* kivuko

crossroads *n* njia panda

crosswalk *n* kivuko

crossword *n* fumbo la maneno

crouch *v* chuchumaa

crow *n* kunguru

crow *v* wika

crowbar *n* nondo

crowd *n* umati

crowd *v* songa, jaza

crowded *adj* -liojazana

crown *n* taji

crown *v* pamba

crowning *n* utawala; taji

crucial *adj* -a muhimu sana

crucifix *n* msalaba

crucifixion *n* sulubu

crucify *v* sulubu

crude *adj* sio adilifu

cruel *adj* katili

cruelty *n* ukatili

cruise *v* vinjari

crumb *n* chembechembe

crumble *v* meng'enya

crunchy *adj* -a kutafuna

crusade *n* vita vitakatifu

crusader *n* mpigania haki

crush *v* gandamiza

crushing *adj* mgandamizo

crust *n* gamba

crutch *n* gongo

cry *n* mlio

cry *v* lia

cry out *v* piga uyole

crying *n* kulia

crystal *n* fuwele

cub *n* mtoto wa (simba)

cube *n* mchemraba

cubic *adj* -a mchemraba

cubicle *n* kichumba

cucumber *n* tango

cuff *n* sijafu; pingu

cuisine *n* jiko

culminate *v* ishia, malizikia

culpability *n* hatia

culprit *n* mkosefu

cult *n* madhehebu

cultivate *v* lima

cultivation *n* kilimo

cultural *adj* -a utamaduni

culture *n* utamaduni

cumbersome *adj* -a udhia

cunning *adj* wa ujanja

cup *n* kikombe

cupboard *n* kabati

curable *adj* wa kupona

curator *n* mwangalizi

curb *v* zuia, dhibiti

curb *n* kizuio

curdle *v* ganda

cure *v* ponyesha

cure *n* dawa

curfew *n* ashiya

curiosity *n* udadisi

curious *adj* -a kushangaza

curl *v* fanya mawimbi

curl *n* wimbi, mkunjo

currency *n* pesa

current *adj* -a kisasa

currently *adv* kwa sasa

curse *v* laana, radhi

curtail *v* fupisha, zuia

curtain *n* pazia

curve *n* mchirizo

curve *v* pinda, kunja

cushion *n* mto

cushion *v* kinga, linga

cuss *v* tukana

custard *n* faluda

custodian *n* mwangalizi

custody *n* uangalizi; utunzaji

custom *n* mila, desturi

customary *adj* kwa mila

customer *n* mteja

custom-made *adj* -a kupima

customs *n* forodha

cut *n* mkato, ukataji

cut *iv* kata

cut back *v* punguza

cut down *v* angusha, kata

cut off *v* tenga

C
D

cut out *v* ondoa
cute *adj* nzuri, -a kuvutia
cutlery *n* vilia
cutter *n* mkataji; dau
cycle *n* baiskeli
cyclone *n* kimbunga
cylinder *n* silinda
cynic *adj* -enye bezo
cynicism *n* bezo
cypress *n* mvinje
cyst *n* uvimbe
czar *n* zari

D

dad *n* baba
dagger *n* jambia, sime
daily *adv* kila siku
dam *n* bwawa
damage *n* uharibifu, hasara
damage *v* haribu, athiri
damaging *adj* -a kuathiri
damn *v* laani
damnation *n* laana

damp *adj* -enye unyevu
dampen *v* lowesha
dance *n* dansi
dance *v* cheza
dancing *n* kucheza
dandruff *n* mba
danger *n* hatari
dangerous *adj* -a hatari
dangle *v* ning'iniza
dare *v* thubutu
dare *n* kuthubutu
daring *adj* -sioogopa
dark *adj* giza
darken *v* fanya giza
darkness *n* giza
darling *adj* mpenzi
darn *v* tilia
dart *n* kishale; datsi
dash *v* harakisha
dashing *adj* nadhifu
data *n* data
database *n* benki ya data
date *n* tarehe
date *v* weka tarehe
daughter *n* binti
daughter-in-law *n* mkamwana
daunt *v* ogopesha, tia hofu
daunting *adj* -a kutia hofu

D

dawn *n* alfajiri

day *n* siku

daydream *v* njozi za tamaa

daze *v* tia bumbuwazi

dazed *adj* kwa bumbuwazi

dazzling *adj* kung'ara

de luxe *adj* -a fahari

deacon *n* shemasi

dead *adj* -liokufa

dead end *n* njia isiyo toka

deaden *v* fifisha

deadline *n* muda wa mwisho

deadlock *adj* mvutano

deadly *adj* -a kuua

deaf *adj* kiziwi

deafen *v* fanya kiziwi

deafness *n* uziwi

deal *iv* fanya biashara

deal *n* makubaliano

dealer *n* muuzaji

dean *n* paroko

dear *adj* mpenzi

dearly *adv* kupenda mno

death *n* kifo

death toll *n* idadi ya wafu

death trap *n* mtego wa kifo

debase *v* dhalilisha

debatable *adj* -a mashaka

debate *v* jadiliana

debate *n* majadiliano

debit *n* makato

debrief *v* hoji

debris *n* kifusi

debt *n* deni

debtor *n* mdaiwa

debunk *v* fichua, umbua

debut *n* anza

decade *n* miaka kumi

decapitate *v* kata kichwa

decay *v* oza

decay *n* kuoza

deceased *adj* kufariki

deceit *n* ulaghai

deceitful *adj* -a kudanganya

deceive *v* laghai

December *n* Disemba

decency *n* ungwana

decent *adj* -enye heshima

deception *n* udanganyifu

deceptive *adj* -a udanganyifu

decide *v* amua

deciding *adj* -enye kuamua

decimal *adj* desimali

decimate *v* angamiza

decipher *v* fumbua, fasiri

decision *n* uamuzi**

decisive *adj* dhahiri

deck *n* sitaha

declaration *n* tamko

declare *v* tangaza

declension *n* mnyambuliko

decline *v* kataa

decline *n* mwinamo

decompose *v* oza, haribika

décor *n* nakshi, pambo

decorate *v* pamba

decorative *adj* -a kupamba

decorum *n* adabu

decrease *v* punguza

decrease *n* kupungua

decree *n* sheria, amri

decree *v* hukumu

decrepit *adj* dhaifu, kongwe

dedicate *v* tabaruku

dedication *n* wakfu;bidii

deduce *v* fasiri

deduct *v* punguza, toa

deduction *n* punguzo

deed *n* hati, tendo

deem *v* dhani

deep *adj* nyingi, nene

deepen *v* panua

deer *n* mbawala

deface *v* haribu sura

defame *v* chafua jina

defeat *v* shinda

defeat *n* kushindwa

defect *n* kasoro

defect *v* saliti, toroka

defection *n* kuasi, ukimbizi

defective *adj* -enye kasoro

defend *v* tetea

defendant *n* mshtakiwa

defender *n* mteteaji

defense *n* utetezi

defenseless *adj* bila kinga

defer *v* ahirisha

defiance *n* ukaidi, dharau

defiant *adj* -enye dharau

deficiency *n* upungufu

deficient *adj* pungufu

deficit *n* hasara

defile *v* chafua; najisi

define *v* eleza maana

definite *adj* kwa hakika

definition *n* maana

definitive *adj* -a kumalizia

deflate *v* toa upepo

deform *v* lemaza

deformity *n* kilema

defraud *v* laghai, danganya

defray *v* lipia

D

defrost v yeyusha barafu
deft adj mwerevu
defuse v tegua
defy v dharau, asi
degenerate v haribika tabia
degradation n uduni
degrade v kuvunjia heshima
degrading adj -a kuaibisha
degree n shahada; kiwango
dehydrate v kausha maji
deign v ridhia
deity n uungu
dejected adj -enye huzuni
delay v chelewesha
delay n kuchelewa
delegate v agiza, tuma
delegate n mjumbe
delegation n ujumbe
delete v futa
deliberate v fikiri, waza
deliberate adj kwa kudhamiria
delicacy n busara
delicate adj dhaifu; nyeti
delicious adj tamu
delight n kufurahisha
delight v furahisha
delightful adj wa kufurahisha
delinquency n uhalifu wa kitoto

delinquent adj kijana mhalifu
deliver v wasilisha
delivery n kuwasilisha
delude v danganya, ghilibu
deluge n mafuriko
delusion n madanganyo
demand v dai
demand n madai, matakwa
demanding adj -enye kuhitaji
demean v dhalilisha
demeaning adj -a kudhalilisha
demeanor n mwenendo
demented adj kichaa
demise n kifo
democracy n demokrasia
democratic adj -a kidemokrasia
demolish v bomoa
demolition n kubomoa
demon n shetani
demonstrate v onyesha
demonstrative adj kwa kuonyesha
demoralize v vunja moyo
demote v shusha cheo
den n pango
denial n ukanushaji
denigrate v adhiri, umbua
Denmak n Denmark
denominator n asili

denote v onyesha

denounce v shitaki

dense adj nene

density n unene; uzito

dent v gonga, bonyeza

dent n kibonyeo

dental adj -a meno

dentist n mganga wa meno

dentures n meno ya bandia

deny v kataa, kana

deodorant n odorono

depart v ondoka

department n idara

departure n kuondoka

depend v tegemea

dependable adj wa kutegemea

dependence n kutegemea

depict v sawiri, fafanua

deplete v maliza, punguza

deplore v sikitikia

deploy v eneza

deport v fukuza nchini

depose v pindua

deposit n amana, rubuni

deprave adj potoa

depravity n upotovu

depreciate v pungua thamani

depress v huzunisha

depressing adj -a kuhuzunisha

depression n unyong'onyevu

deprivation n kunyima

deprive v nyima

deprived adj -siojiweza

depth n kina

derail v acha njia ya reli

deranged adj kichaa

derelict adj mahame

deride v dharau, cheka

derivative adj kinyambuo

derive v tokana na

derogatory adj -a kudharau

descend v kushuka

descendant n mzawa

descent n mteremko

describe v eleza, fafanua

description n maelezo

descriptive adj -a maelezo

desecrate v kufuru

desegregate v komesha ubaguzi

desert n jangwa

desert v acha; telekeza

deserted adj -liotelekezwa

deserter n mhaini

deserve v stahili

deserving adj anaye stahili

design n mchoro, usanifu

designate v onyesha

desirable adj -a kutakiwa

desire n matakwa

desire v taka, tamani

desist v jizuia, acha

desk n dawati

desolate adj -lioachwa

desolation n ukiwa, upweke

despair n kukata tamaa

despicable adj hafifu

despise v chukia

despite c licha ya

despondent adj -enye majonzi

despot n mdhalimu

despotic adj kwa kidhalimu

dessert n kitindamlo

destination n mwelekeo

destiny n Mungu; bahati

destitute adj fukara

destroy v angamiza

destroyer n mwangamizi

destruction n uangamizi

destructive adj -a kuangamiza

detach v bandua, kata

detail n habari

detail v orodhesha

detain v weka kizuizini

detect v ng'amua, gundua

detective n mpelelezi

detention n gereza, kizuizi

deter v zuia

deteriorate v dhoofika

deterioration n uchakavu

determination n kusudio

determine v amua

deterrence n kizuizi

detest v chukia

detestable adj -a kuchukiza

detonate v lipua

detonation n mlipuko

detonator n kilipulio

detour n kipengee

detriment n madhara

detrimental adj -enye madhara

devaluation n kushuka thamani

devalue v shusha thamani

devastate v teketeza, haribu

devastating adj -a kuteketeza

devastation n maangamizi

develop v jenga; pata; kua

development n maendeleo

deviation n ukengefu

device n chombo, kitu

devil n shetani

devious adj ujanja; utapeli

devise v tunga

D

devoid *adj* kosefu

devote *v* jitoa mhanga

devotion *n* utawa

devour *v* bugia

devout *adj* kwa dhati

dew *n* umande

diabetes *n* kisukari

diabolical *adj* -a kishetani

diagnose *v* tambua ugonjwa

diagonal *adj* -a mshazari

diagram *n* kielezo

dial *v* piga simu

dial tone *n* mlio wa simu

dialect *n* lahaja

dialogue *n* maongezi

diameter *n* kipenyo

diamond *n* almasi

diaper *n* nepi

diarrhea *n* kuharisha

dice *n* dadu

dictate *v* amuru

dictatorial *adj* -a kiimla

dictionary *n* kamusi

die *v* kufa, fariki

die out *v* ishia, fifia

diet *n* chakula, mlo

differ *v* tofautiana

difference *n* tofauti

different *adj* tofauti

difficult *adj* ngumu

difficulty *n* ugumu

diffuse *v* sambaza

dig *iv* lima

digest *v* meng'enya

digestion *n* umeng'enyaji

digit *n* kidole; tarakimu

dignify *v* tukuza, kweza

dignity *n* hadhi

digress *v* badili mada

dilapidated *adj* -liochakaa

dilemma *n* mashaka

diligence *n* juhudi ya kazi

dilute *v* punguza nguvu

dim *adj* hafifu

dim *v* fifisha

dimension *n* kipimo

diminish *v* punguza

dine *v* kula mlo wa jioni

diner *n* mgahawa

dining room *n* chumba cha kulia

dinner *n* mlo wa jioni

diocese *n* dayosisi

diphthong *n* irabu unganifu

diploma *n* stashahada

diplomacy *n* diplomasia

diplomatic *adj* -a kidiplomasia

dire *adj* mbaya sana

direct *adj* -lionyooka

direct *v* elekeza

direction *n* uelekeo

director *n* mkurugenzi

directory *n* kitabu cha simu

dirt *n* udongo, uchafu

dirty *adj* chafu

disability *n* kilema

disabled *adj* mlemavu

disadvantage *n* madhara

disagree *v* pingana, kataa

disagreeable *adj* -siopendeza

disagreement *n* upinzani

disappear *v* toweka, potea

disappearance *n* kutoweka

disappoint *v* katisha tamaa

disappointing *adj* -a kuvunja moyo

disappointment *n* masikitiko

disapproval *n* kutoridhika

disapprove *v* chukia

disarm *v* tuliza

disaster *n* balaa

disastrous *adj* -a balaa

disband *v* tawanya

disbelief *n* kutoamini

disburse *v* lipa

discard *v* tupa

discern *v* tambua, vumbua

discharge *v* ruhusu, toa

discharge *n* mfyatuko

disciple *n* mfuasi

discipline *n* nidhamu

disclaim *v* kanusha, kataa

disclose *v* fichua, gundua

discomfort *n* karaha

disconnect *v* kata, achanisha

discontent *adj* -sioridhika

discontinue *v* simamisha

discord *n* kutopatana

discordant *adj* -a kutopatana

discount *n* punguzo

discount *v* punguza bei

discourage *v* katisha tamaa

discourtesy *n* dharau

discover *v* gundua, vumbua

discovery *n* uvumbuzi

discredit *v* kutoamini

discreet *adj* mwangalifu

discrepancy *n* hitilafu, tofauti

discretion *n* busara

discriminate *v* bagua

discrimination *n* ubaguzi

discuss *v* jadili

discussion *n* majadiliano

disdain *n* dharau

disease *n* ugonjwa
disembark *v* shuka
disentangle *v* kunjua
disfigure *v* haribu sura
disgrace *n* aibu
disgrace *v* aibisha
disgraceful *adj* -a aibu
disgruntled *adj* -sioridhika
disguise *v* kujigeuza
disguise *n* kujigeuza
disgust *n* kichefuchefu
disgusting *adj* -enye kuchefua
dish *n* sahani, chombo
dishearten *v* vunja moyo
dishonest *adj* mdanganyifu
dishonesty *n* kwa udanganyifu
dishonor *n* aibu
dishonorable *adj* kwa kutia aibu
dishwasher *n* mwosha vyombo
disillusion *n* zindua
disinfect *v* ua vijidudu
disintegrate *v* momonyoka
disintegration *n* mmomonyoko
disk *n* sahani, kisahani
dislike *v* chukia
dislike *n* chuki
dislocate *v* tengua
dislodge *v* sogeza

disloyal *adj* -enye kuasi
disloyalty *n* uasi
dismal *adj* mbaya sana
dismantle *v* bomoa
dismay *n* hofu
dismay *v* tia hofu
dismiss *v* fukuza
dismissal *n* kufukuzwa
dismount *v* shuka, teremka
disobedience *n* ukaidi
disobedient *adj* kwa ukaidi
disobey *v* kaidi
disorder *n* vurugu
disorganized *adj* bila mpangilio
disown *v* kana, kataa
disparity *n* hitilafu, tofauti
dispatch *v* tuma
dispel *v* tawanya
dispensation *n* kutoa dawa
dispense *v* gawa, toa
dispersal *n* usambazaji
disperse *v* sambaza
displace *v* hamisha
display *n* maonyesho
display *v* onyesha
displease *v* kasirisha
displeasing *adj* -a kukasirisha
displeasure *n* maudhi

disposal *n* kutupa, uondoaji
dispose *v* tupa; panga
disprove *v* kanusha
dispute *n* ubishani
dispute *v* bisha
disqualify *v* zuia
disregard *v* dharau, puuzia
disrepair *n* haribika
disrespect *n* kosa heshima
disrupt *v* vuruga
disruption *n* vurugu
dissatisfied *adj* kutoridhika
disseminate *v* sambaza
dissent *v* pinga
dissident *adj* mpinzani
dissimilar *adj* -siofanana
dissipate *v* tawanya
dissolute *adj* -a kihasharati
dissolution *n* kuvunjika
dissolve *v* yeyuka, vunjika
dissonant *adj* -enye hitilafu
dissuade *v* shauri vingine
distance *n* umbali
distant *adj* -a mbali
distaste *n* chuki
distasteful *adj* -enye kuchukiza
distill *v* pika
distinct *adj* wazi, dhahiri

distinction *n* kutofautisha
distinctive *adj* -a kutofautisha
distinguish *v* tofautisha
distort *v* badilika
distract *v* vuta kwingine
distraction *n* kuvuta mawazo
distraught *adj* -enye kufadhaishwa
distress *n* mateso, majonzi
distressing *adj* tia wasiwasi
distribute *v* gawa,
distribution *n* mgao
district *n* wilaya
distrust *n* kutoamini
distrust *v* tilia shaka
distrustful *adj* kwa mashaka
disturb *v* sumbua
disturbance *n* usumbufu
disturbing *adj* -a kusumbua
disunity *n* kutopatana
disuse *n* acha kutumika
ditch *n* kidimbwi, mtaro
dive *v* piga mbizi
diver *n* mpiga mbizi
diverse *adj* tofauti
diversify *v* panua
diversion *n* mchepuo
diversity *n* anuwai
divert *v* chepusha

D

D

divide *v* gawanya

dividend *n* gawio

divine *adj* -a Mungu

diving *n* kupiga mbizi

divinity *n* Mungu, utakatifu

division *n* mgawanyo

divorce *n* talaka

divorce *v* taliki

divorcee *n* mtalaka

divulge *v* toboa, toa wazi

dizziness *n* kizunguzungu

do *iv* fanya

docile *adj* kwa upole

docility *n* upole

dock *n* gudi

dock *v* guda

doctor *n* daktari, mganga

doctrine *n* msingi, kanuni

document *n* makala, waraka

documentation *n* nyaraka

dodge *v* kwepa

dog *n* mbwa

dogmatic *adj* -a imani

dole out *v* toa, gawa

doll *n* mwanasesere

dollar *n* dola

dolphin *n* pomboo, panji

dome *n* kuba

domestic *adj* -a nyumbani

domesticate *v* fuga

dominate *v* tawala

domination *n* utawala

dominion *n* utawala, miliki

donate *v* toa msaada

donation *n* msaada

donkey *n* punda

donor *n* mfadhili, mtoaji

doom *n* maangamizi

door *n* mlango

doorway *n* mlangoni

dope *n* mkorogo

dormitory *n* bweni

dosage *n* kipimo

dossier *n* jalada

dot *n* nukta

double *adj* -a kufanana

double *v* mara mbili

double-cross *v* saliti

doubt *n* mashaka

doubt *v* shuku

doubtful *adl* -a mashaka

dough *n* kinyunga, donge

dove *n* njiwa

down *adv* chini

down payment *n* malipo ya amana

downcast *adj* -enye huzuni

downfall *n* anguko

downhill *adv* mteremko

downpour *n* mvua kubwa

downsize *v* punguza

downstairs *adv* kuelekea chini

down-to-earth *adj* -a mambo halisi

downtown *n* mjini

downturn *n* kushuka

dowry *n* mahari

doze *n* usingizi

doze *v* sinzia

dozen *n* dazeni

draft *n* mswadajaribio

draft *v* andika jaribio

draftsman *n* mchoraji ramani

drag *v* burura

drain *v* fyonza, toa maji

drainage *n* kupita kwa maji

dramatic *adj* -a tamthilia

dramatize *v* igiza tamthilia

drape *n* pazia

drastic *adj* kali, -enye athari

draw *n* mvuto; sare

draw *iv* chora

drawback *n* kizuizi

drawer *n* mrasimu

drawing *n* mchoro

dread *v* hofia

D

dreaded *adj* anaye hofiwa

dreadful *adj* mbaya sana

dream *iv* ota

dream *n* ndoto

dress *n* vazi

dress *v* vaa

dressing *n* kuvaa

dried *adj* kauka

drift *v* elea

drift apart *v* kwenda mrama

drill *v* toboa

drill *n* kekee

drink *iv* kunywa

drink *n* kinywaji

drinkable *adj* -a kunyweka

drinker *n* mnywaji

drip *v* tiririka

drip *n* tone

drive *n* ujia; bidii

drive *iv* endesha

drive at *v* elekea, lenga

drive away *v* ondoka

driver *n* dereva

drizzle *v* nyunya

drizzle *n* manyunyu

drop *n* tone; punguzo

drop *v* angusha

drop in *v* tembelea

drop off v shusha
drop out v acha, jitenga
drought n ukame
drown v zama
drowsy adj kwa usingizi
drug n dawa
drug v levya na dawa
drugstore n duka la dawa
drum n ngoma
drunk adj kulewa
drunkenness n ulevi
dry v kausha
dry adj kavu
dryclean v fua bila maji
dual adj mbili
dubious adj -a mashaka
duck n bata
duck v kwepa, inama
duct n kifereji
due adj -enye kustahili
duel n pambano
dues n haki
dull adj butu
duly adv ipasavyo
dumb adj bubu
dummy n mjinga, mwigo
dummy adj -a bandia
dump v tupa

dump n jalala
dung n kinyesi, samadi
dupe v danganya
duplicate v nakala, kifani
duplication n kunakili
durable adj -a kudumu
duration n muda, kipindi
during pre wakati
dusk n magharibi
dust n vumbi
dusty adj -enye vumbi
Dutch adj Mdachi
duty n jukumu
dwarf n mbilikimo
dwell iv ishi
dwelling n makazi
dwindle v fifia
dye v tia rangi
dye n rangi
dying adj kufariki
dynamic adj -a elimumwendo
dynamite n baruti
dynasty n ufalme

E

each *adj* kila moja

each other *adj* wao kwa wao

eager *adj* -enye hamu

eagerness *n* shauku

eagle *n* tai

ear *n* sikio

earache *n* kuumwa sikio

early *adv* mapema

earmark *v* tia alama,

earn *v* pata

earnestly *adv* kwa bidii

earnings *n* mapato

earring *n* hereni

earth *n* dunia

earwax *n* nta ya sikio

ease *v* rahisisha

ease *n* urahisi

easily *adv* kwa urahisi

east *n* mashariki

Easter *n* Pasaka

eastern *adj* -a mashariki

easterner *n* wa mashariki

easy *adj* rahisi

eat *iv* kula

eat away *v* lika

eavesdrop *v* sikiliza kwa siri

ebb *v* kupwa, fifia

eccentric *adj* wa pekee

echo *n* mwangwi

eclipse *n* kupatwa

ecology *n* ekolojia

economical *adj* wekevu

economize *v* weka akiba

economy *n* uwekevu

ecstasy *n* upeo wa furaha

ecstatic *adj* -enye kujaa furaha

edge *n* ukingo

edible *adj* -enye kuliwa

edifice *n* jengo kubwa

edit *v* hariri

edition *n* toleo, chapisha

educate *v* elimisha

educational *adj* -a kuelimisha

eerie *adj* -a kutia hofu

effect *n* tokea; mali

effective *adj* -enye kufaa

effectiveness *n* kufaa

efficiency *n* utendaji bora

efficient *adj* madhubuti

effigy *n* sanamu

effort *n* juhudi, bidii

effusive *adj* -enye hisia kali

egg *n* yai

egg white *n* ute wa yai

egoism *n* ubinafsi

egoist *n* mbinafsi

eight *adj* nane

eighteen *adj* kumi na nane

eighth *adj* wa nane

eighty *adj* themanini

either *adj* yoyote

either *adv* au, ama

eject *v* toa

elapse *v* pita

elastic *adj* nyumbufu

elated *adj* kwa furaha

elbow *n* kiko

elder *n* mkubwa

elderly *adj* mzee

elect *v* chagua

election *n* uchaguzi

electric *adj* -a umeme

electrician *n* fundi umeme

electricity *n* umeme

electrify *v* weka umeme

electrocute *v* ua kwa umeme

elegance *n* madaha

elegant *adj* -enye madaha

element *n* kitu

elementary *adj* -a msingi

elephant *n* tembo

elevate *v* inua

elevation *n* mwinuko

elevator *n* lifti

eleven *adj* kumi na moja

eleventh *adj* -a kumi na moja

eligible *adj* -enye kufaa

eliminate *v* ondosha, futa

eloquence *n* ufasaha, umbuji

else *adv* tena, zaidi

elsewhere *adv* penginepo

elude *v* epuka

elusive *adj* -a kuepuka

emaciated *adj* -enye kudhoofika

emanate *v* toa

emancipate *v* komboa

embalm *v* tia maiti dawa

embark *v* panda; anza

embarrass *v* aibisha

embassy *n* ubalozi

embellish *v* pamba, remba

embezzle *v* imba

embitter *v* chukiza

emblem *n* nembo, ishara

embody *v* fanya tashihisi

emboss *v* tuna

embrace *v* kumbatia

embrace *n* kukumbatia

embroider *v* tarizi

E

embroidery *n* taraza	**enclosure** *n* boma
embroil *v* chochea ugomvi	**encompass** *v* kwa pamoja
embryo *n* kiinitete	**encounter** *v* kutana
emerald *n* zumaradi	**encounter** *n* kukutana
emerge *v* ibuka	**encourage** *v* tia moyo
emergency *n* dharura	**encroach** *v* ingilia mali ya
emigrant *n* mhamaji	**encyclopedia** *n* kamusi elezo
emigrate *v* hama, hajiri	**end** *n* mwisho
emission *n* mtawanyo	**end** *v* maliza
emit *v* toa	**end up** *v* ishia
emotion *n* hisia	**endanger** *v* hatarisha
emotional *adj* -enye hisia	**endeavor** *v* jaribu
emperor *n* mfalme mkuu	**endeavor** *n* jitihada, juhud
emphasis *n* msisitizo	**ending** *n* mwisho
emphasize *v* sisitiza	**endless** *adj* bila mwisho
empire *n* ufalme	**endorse** *v* idhinisha
employ *v* ajiri	**endorsement** *n* kuidhinisha
employee *n* mwajiriwa	**endure** *v* stahimili, vumilia
employer *n* mwajiri	**enemy** *n* adui
employment *n* ajira	**energetic** *adj* -enye nguvu
empress *n* mke wa mfalme	**energy** *n* nguvu, bidii
emptiness *n* utupu	**enforce** *v* tekeleza
empty *adj* tupu	**engage** *v* ajiri;anzisha
empty *v* ondoa	**engaged** *adj* poswa
enable *v* wezesha	**engagement** *n* ajira; chumbiwa
enchant *v* pendezwa	**engine** *n* injini
encircle *v* zunguka	**engineer** *n* mhandisi
enclose *v* fungia, zungushia	**England** *n* Uingereza

English adj Mwingereza
engrave v andika
engraving n kuandika
engulf v mezwa
enhance v ongeza
enjoy v furahia, faidi
enjoyable adj -a kufurahisha
enjoyment n raha, starehe
enlarge v kuza, ongeza
enlargement n ukuzaji
enlighten v -enye kujulishwa
enlist v jiunga
enormous adj kubwa mno
enough adv -a kutosha
enrage v gadhabisha
enrich v tajirisha
enroll v orodhesha
enrollment n uandikishaji
ensure v hakikisha
entail v ingiza
entangle v tatiza
enter v ingia
enterprise n shughuli
entertain v chekesha
entertaining adj kuburudisha
entertainment n burudani
enthrall v vutia sana
enthralling adj -a kuvutia

enthuse v onyesha shauku
enthusiasm n shauku
entice v shawishi
enticement n kishawishi
enticing adj -a kushawishi
entire adj yote
entirely adv kabisa
entrance n kiingilio, mlango
entreat v sihi
entree n kifungua mlo
entrepreneur n mjasirimali
entrust v amini, kabidhi
entry n mwingilio, kuingia
envelop v funga, funika
envelope n bahasha
envious adj -enye wivu
environment n mazingira
envisage v wazia
envoy n mjumbe
envy n wivu
envy v onea wivu
epilepsy n kifafa
episode n tukio
epistle n waraka
epitomize v kuwa mfano wa
equal adj sawa
equality n usawa
equate v sawadhisha

equation *n* mgawo

equator *n* ikweta

equilibrium *n* mlingano, usawa

equip *v* andaa

equipment *n* vifaa

equivalent *adj* sawa na

era *n* kipindi

eradicate *v* komesha

erase *v* futa

eraser *n* kifuto

erect *v* simamisha

erect *adj* wima

err *v* kosea

errand *n* ujumbe, utume

erroneous *adj* -a makosa

error *n* kosa

erupt *v* lipuka, fumuka

eruption *n* mlipuko

escalate *v* ongezeka

escalator *n* ngazi za umeme

escapade *n* utundu

escape *v* toroka

escort *n* msindikizaji

esophagus *n* umio

especially *adv* haswa

espionage *n* upelelezi

essay *n* juhudi; insha

essence *n* arki; chimbuko

essential *adj* -a muhimu

establish *v* anzisha

estate *n* shamba kubwa

esteem *v* heshimu sana

estimate *v* kadiria

estimation *n* kadirio

estranged *adj* walio tengana

estuary *n* hori

eternity *n* milele

ethical *adj* -a uadilifu

ethics *n* uadilifu

etiquette *n* adabu

euphoria *n* furaha kubwa

Europe *n* Ulaya

European *adj* Mzungu

evacuate *v* hama

evade *v* epuka

evaluate *v* wakifia

evaporate *v* vukiza

evasion *n* ukwepaji

evasive *adj* -a kukwepa

eve *n* mkesha

even *adj* sawasawa

even if *c* hata kama

even more *c* zaidi

evening *n* jioni

event *n* tukio, jambo

eventuality *n* tukio la dharura**

eventually *adv* mwishoni
everlasting *adj* -a milele
every *adj* kila
everybody *pro* kila mmoja
everyday *adj* kila siku
everyone *pro* kila mtu
everything *pro* vyote
evict *v* fukuza
evidence *n* uthibitisho
evil *n* uovu
evil *adj* -enye uovu
evoke *v* amsha
evolution *n* mabadiliko
evolve *v* endelea kukua
exact *adj* dhahiri
exaggerate *v* zidisha, kuza
exalt *v* tukuza
examination *n* mtihani
examine *v* chunguza, pima
example *n* mfano
exasperate *v* chosha, udhi
excavate *v* chimba
exceed *v* zidisha, pita
exceedingly *adv* kupita kiasi
excel *v* fanya vizuri kuliko
excellent *adj* bora sana
except *pre* kasoro
exception *n* jambo la pekee

exceptional *adj* -sio ya kawaida
excerpt *n* dondoo
excess *n* ziada
excessive *adj* -a ziada
exchange *v* badilisha
excite *v* sisimua
excitement *n* mfadhaiko
exciting *adj* -a kusisimua
exclaim *v* tamka ghafla
exclude *v* tenga
excruciating *adj* -a kutesa sana
excursion *n* matembezi
excuse *v* samehe
excuse *n* kisingizio
execute *v* tekeleza; ua
executive *n* mkurugenzi
exemplary *adj* -a mfano
exemplify *v* onyesha mfano
exempt *adj* samehe
exemption *n* ruhusu
exercise *n* zoezi
exercise *v* fanya mazoezi
exert *v* tumia
exertion *n* jitihada
exhaust *v* chosha
exhausting *adj* -a kuchosha
exhaustion *n* uchovu
exhibit *v* onyesha

exhibition n maonyesho

exhort v sihi sana

exile v fukuzia uhamishoni

exile n kuishi uhamishoni

exist v kuwepo

existence n uhai, kuishi

exit n kutoka

exodus n utokaji, uhamaji

exonerate v toa hatiani

exorbitant adj kubwa sana

exorcist n kaimu

exotic adj -a kigeni

expand v panua

expansion n upanuzi

expect v tegemea

expectancy n tazamio, tarajio

expectation n tegemeo

expediency n manufaa

expedient adj -enye manufaa

expedition n haraka, hima

expel v fukuza

expenditure n matumizi

expense n gharama

expensive adj -enye gharama

experience n mazoea

experiment n jaribio

expert adj mjuzi

expiate v fidia

expiation n kufidia

expiration n kufika mwisho

expire v fika mwisho]

explain v eleza

explicit adj -a wazi

explode v lipuka, fumuka

exploit v tumia, tumikisha

exploit n vitendo; ushujaa

exploitation n utumiaji

explore v chunguza

explorer n mchunguzi

explosion n mlipuko

explosive adj -enye kulipuka

export v safirisha

expose v fichua

exposed adj kilicho fichuliwa

express adj eleza

expression n usemi, neno

expressly adv kwa dhati

expropriate v nyang'anya

expulsion n kufukuzwa

exquisite adj bora sana

extend v ongeza, panua

extension n upanuzi

extent n kiasi, ukubwa

extenuating adj -a kupunguza

exterior adj nje

exterminate v angamiza

external *adj* -a nje
extinct *adj* --liokufa
extinguish *v* zima
extort *v* toza kwa lazima
extortion *n* kutoza kwa nguvu
extra *adv* zaidi
extract *v* chimba
extraneous *adj* -siomuhimu
extravagance *n* ubadhirifu
extravagant *adj* mbadhirifu
extreme *adj* mno
extremist *adj* mkereketwa
extremities *n* vikomo
extricate *v* nasua
extroverted *adj* mcheshi
exude *v* toa
exult *v* sifia
eye *n* jicho
eyebrow *n* nyusi
eye-catching *adj* -a kuvutia
eyeglasses *n* miwani
eyelash *n* kope
eyelid *n* kope
eyesight *n* uwezo wa kuona
eyewitness *n* shahidi

F

fable *n* hadithi
fabric *n* kitambaa
fabricate *v* tunga
fabulous *adj* nzuri sana
face *n* uso
face up to *v* kubali
facet *n* upande
facilitate *v* rahisisha
facing *pre* -enye kutazama
fact *n* ukweli
factor *n* kitu
factory *n* kiwanda
factual *adj* -a ukweli
faculty *n* uwezo; kitivo
fad *n* haja
fade *v* fifia
faded *adj* -liofifia
fail *v* shindwa
failure *n* kushindwa
faint *v* zimia
faint *n* kuzimia
faint *adj* hafifu
fair *n* soko; maonyesho
fair *adj* nzuri; haki
fairness *n* weupe; haki

fairy *n* kishetani; basha

faith *n* imani

faithful *adj* mwaminifu

fake *v* igiza

fake *adj* bandia

fall *n* mwanguko

fall *iv* anguka

fall back *v* rudi nyuma

fall behind *v* chelewa

fall down *v* anguka

fall through *v* shindikana

fallacy *n* uwongo

fallout *n* athari

falsehood *n* uwongo

falsify *v* ghushi

falter *v* jikwaa; babaika

fame *n* umaarufu

familiar *adj* mzoefu

family *n* familia

famine *n* njaa

famous *adj* mashuhuri

fan *n* mshabiki; feni

fanatic *adj* mlokole

fancy *adj* wazo, tamanio

fang *n* jino chonge

fantastic *adj* -a ajabu

fantasy *n* njozi

far *adv* mbali

F

faraway *adj* mbali sana

farce *n* utani

fare *n* nauli

farewell *n* kwa heri

farm *n* shamba

farmer *n* mkulima

farming *n* ukulima

farther *adv* mbali zaidi

fascinate *v* vutia sana

fashion *n* mtindo

fashionable *adj* -a kisasa

fast *adj* haraka

fasten *v* funga

fat *n* mafuta

fat *adj* nene

fatal *adj* -a kuua

fate *n* majaliwa, riziki

fateful *adj* -a majaliwa

father *n* baba

fatherhood *n* ubaba

father-in-law *n* baba mkwe

fatherly *adj* -a kibaba

fathom out *v* elewa

fatigue *n* uchovu

fatten *v* nenepesha

fatty *adj* -a mafuta

faucet *n* bomba

fault *n* kosa

faulty *adj* -enye hitilafu
favor *n* upendeleo
favorable *adj* -a upendeleo
favorite *adj* kipenzi
fear *n* uoga
fearful *adj* -a uoga
feasible *adj* iwezekanayo
feast *n* tafrija
feat *n* kitendo
feather *n* nyoya
feature *n* sura; makala
February *n* Februari
fed up *adj* kifu, choka
federal *adj* -a shirikisho
fee *n* karo
feeble *adj* nyonge
feed *iv* lisha
feedback *n* maoni rejea
feel *iv* hisi
feeling *n* hisia
feelings *n* hisia, maoni
feet *n* miguu
feign *v* jifanya
fellow *n* mwenza
fellowship *n* ujamaa
felon *n* mhalifu
felony *n* uhalifu
female *n* mwanamke

feminine *adj* -a kike
fence *n* ugo
fencing *n* zungusho
fend *v* tunza
fend off *v* kinga
fender *n* ngao, dafrau
ferment *v* chacha
ferment *n* uchachu
ferocious *adj* kali
ferocity *n* ukali
ferry *n* kivuko
fertile *adj* -enye rutuba
fertility *n* rutuba; uzazi
fertilize *v* rutubisha
fervent *adj* -a shauku
fester *v* tunga usaha
festive *adj* -a sherehe
festivity *n* sherehe
fetid *adj* -a kunuka
fetus *n* kilenge
feud *n* uadui
fever *n* homa
feverish *adj* homa
few *adj* chache
fewer *adj* chache zaidi
fiancé *n* mchumba
fiber *n* nyuzi
fickle *adj* kigeugeu

fiction *n* kubuniwa

fictitious *adj* -a kubuniwa

fiddle *n* fidla; uwongo

fidelity *n* uaminifu

field *n* mgunda

fierce *adj* kali

fiery *adj* moto

fifteen *adj* kumi na tano

fifth *adj* -a tano

fifty *adj* hamsini

fifty-fifty *adv* nusu kwa nusu

fig *n* tini

fight *iv* gombana

fight *n* ugomvi

fighter *n* mgomvi

figure *n* umbo; mchoro

figure out *v* tambua, elewa

file *v* piga tupa

file *n* jalada; tupa

fill *v* jaza

filling *n* kijazio

film *n* filamu

filter *n* chujio

filter *v* chuja

filth *n* uchafu

filthy *adj* chafu

fin *n* pezi

final *adj* -a mwisho

finalize *v* malizia

finance *v* lipia

financial *adj* -a fedha

find *iv* tafuta

find out *v* gundua

fine *n* faini

fine *v* toza faini

fine *adv* vizuri

fine *adj* -enye kupendeza

fine print *n* herufi ndogo

finger *n* kidole

fingernail *n* kucha

fingerprint *n* alama ya kidole

fingertip *n* ncha ya kidole

finish *v* maliza

Finland *n* Ufini

Finnish *adj* -a Kifini

fire *v* washa

fire *n* moto

firearm *n* silaha

firecracker *n* fataki

fireman *n* mzimamoto

fireplace *n* pa kuotea moto

firewood *n* kuni

fireworks *n* fataki

firm *adj* imara

firm *n* kampuni

firmness *n* uimara**

first *adj* kwanza

fish *n* samaki

fisherman *n* mvuvi

fishy *adj* -a samaki

fist *n* ngumi

fit *n* kushikwa

fit *v* enea

fitness *n* ukakamavu

fitting *adj* -a kufaa

five *adj* tano

fix *v* tengeneza

flag *n* bendera

flame *n* ulimi wa moto

flammable *adj* -a kuungua

flank *n* ubavu, upande

flare *n* mwanga

flare-up *v* mlipuko

flash *n* nuru

flashlight *n* kurunzi, tochi

flashy *adj* maridadi

flat *n* ghorofa

flat *adj* tambarare

flatten *v* laza, nyoosha

flatter *v* sifia

flattery *n* sifa

flaunt *v* onyesha

flavor *n* ladha

flaw *n* dosari

flawless *adj* bila dosari

flea *n* kiroboto

flee *iv* kimbia, toroka

fleet *n* kundi

fleeting *adj* -a kupita

flesh *n* mwili

flex *v* kunja

flexible *adj* -a kunjika

flicker *v* meta meta

flier *n* mrukaji

flight *n* safari ya ndege

flimsy *adj* nyembamba

flip *v* rusha, geuza

flirt *v* bemba

float *v* elea

flock *n* kundi

flog *v* piga

flood *v* furika

flooding *n* kufurika

floodlight *n* taa kubwa

floor *n* sakafu

flop *n* kuporomoka

floss *n* uzi

flour *n* unga

flourish *v* chanua

flow *v* tiririka

flow *n* mtiririko

flower *n* ua**

F

flu _n_ mafua

fluctuate _v_ panda na shuka

fluently _adv_ bila shida

fluid _n_ umaji

flunk _v_ feli

flush _v_ vuta maji; iva uso

flute _n_ filimbi

flutter _v_ papatika

fly _iv_ ruka

fly _n_ nzi

foam _n_ povu

focus _n_ kiini

focus on _v_ lenga

foe _n_ adui

fog _n_ ukungu

foggy _adj_ -enye ukungu

foil _v_ kwamisha

fold _v_ kunja

folder _n_ jalada

folks _n_ watu

folksy _adj_ -a kiurafiki

follow _v_ fuata

follower _n_ mfuasi

folly _n_ wazimu

fond _adj_ penda

fondle _v_ papasa

fondness _n_ mapenzi

food _n_ chakula

foodstuff _n_ vyakula

fool _v_ danganya

fool _adj_ mpumbavu

foolproof _adj_ mathubuti

foot _n_ mguu

football _n_ mpira wa miguu

footnote _n_ tanbihi

footprint _n_ alama ya mguu

footstep _n_ hatua

footwear _n_ viatu

for _pre_ ya

forbid _iv_ kataza

force _n_ nguvu

force _v_ lazimisha

force _adj_ -a lazima

forecast _iv_ tabiri

forefront _n_ mstari wa mbele

foreground _n_ mandharimbele

forehead _n_ paji

foreign _adj_ -a kigeni

foreigner _n_ mgeni

foreman _n_ msimamizi

foremost _adj_ -a kwanza

foresee _iv_ bashiri

foreshadow _v_ onyesha dalili

foresight _n_ kuona mbele

forest _n_ msitu

foretaste _n_ hisia mapema

foretell _v_ tabiri

forever _adv_ milele

forewarn _v_ tahadharisha

foreword _n_ utangulizi

forfeit _v_ poteza

forge _v_ fua vyuma; ghushi

forgery _n_ kughushi

forget _v_ sahau

forgivable _adj_ -a kusameheka

forgive _v_ samehe

forgiveness _n_ msamaha

fork _n_ uma

form _n_ umbo; muundo

formal _adj_ -a rasmi

formality _n_ utaratibu

formalize _v_ fanya rasmi

formally _adv_ kwa rasmi

format _n_ muundo

formation _n_ kuumbika

former _adj_ -a awali

formerly _adv_ zamani

formidable _adj_ -enye kutisha

formula _n_ njia, fomula

forsake _iv_ telekeza

fort _n_ ngome

forthcoming _adj_ ijayo

forthright _adj_ -a uaminifu

fortify _v_ zatiti

fortitude _n_ ujasiri

fortress _n_ ngome

fortunate _adj_ -enye bahati

fortune _n_ mali

forty _adj_ arobaini

forward _adv_ mbele

fossil _n_ kisukuku

foster _v_ lea

foul _adj_ -a kunuka

foundation _n_ msingi

founder _n_ mwanzilishi

foundry _n_ kalibu

fountain _n_ chemchem

four _adj_ nne

fourteen _adj_ kumi na nne

fourth _adj_ -a nne

fox _n_ mbweha

foxy _adj_ mjanja

fraction _n_ sehemu

fracture _n_ ufa, mpasuko

fragile _adj_ nyepesi

fragment _n_ kipande

fragrance _n_ manukato

fragrant _adj_ -a kunukia

frail _adj_ nyonge

frailty _n_ unyonge

frame _n_ fremu

frame _v_ weka fremu

framework *n* muundo
France *n* Ufaransa
franchise *n* uwakala; kura
frank *adj* kweli
frankly *adv* kwa ukweli
frankness *n* ukweli
frantic *adj* fadhaika
fraternal *adj* -a kindugu
fraternity *n* undugu
fraud *n* udanganyifu
fraudulent *adj* -a udanganyifu
freckle *n* kidoa cha ngozi
freckled *adj* -enye vidoa
free *v* achia huru
free *adj* huru
freedom *n* uhuru
freeway *n* barabara kuu
freeze *iv* ganda
freezer *n* friza
freezing *adj* -a kuganda
freight *n* mzigo
French *adj* -a Kifaransa
frenetic *adj* fadhaika
frenzied *adj* -a mfadhaiko
frenzy *n* mfadhaiko
frequency *n* mrudio
frequent *adj* mara kwa mara
frequent *v* zoea

fresh *adj* mbichi, mpya
freshen *v* safisha
freshness *n* usafi, upya
friar *n* mtawa
friction *n* mgongano
Friday *n* ljumaa
fried *adj* -a kukaanga
friend *n* rafiki
friendship *n* urafiki
fries *n* chipsi
frigate *n* manowari
fright *n* uoga
frighten *v* ogopesha
frightening *adj* -a kuogopesha
frigid *adj* wa baridi
fringe *n* pindo
frivolous *adj* -a upuuzi
frog *n* chura
from *pre* kutoka
front *n* mbele
front *adj* tangulia
frontage *n* upande wa mbele
frontier *n* mpaka
frost *n* sakitu, barafu
frostbite *n* kuganda ngozi
frostbitten *adj* -enye kuganda ngozi
frosty *adj* -enye sakitu
frown *v* kunja uso

F

frozen *adj* -lioganda
frugality *n* kubana matumizi
fruit *n* tunda
fruity *adj* -a matunda
frustrate *v* vunja moyo
frustration *n* kukata tamaa
fry *v* kaanga
frying pan *n* kikaangio
fuel *n* kuni, mafuta
fuel *v* chochea
fugitive *n* mkimbizi
fulfill *v* timiza
fulfillment *n* utimizaji
full *adj* jaa
fully *adv* kabisa
fumes *n* mioshi
fumigate *v* fukiza
fun *n* burudani
function *n* kazi
fund *n* hazina, mfuko
fund *v* gharimia, lipia
fundamental *adj* -a msingi
funds *n* pesa
funeral *n* kilio
fungus *n* uyoga
funny *adj* -a kuchekesha
furious *adj* -enye kukasirika
furiously *adv* kwa kukasirika

furnace *n* joko
furnish *v* toa, patia
furnishings *n* mapambo
furniture *n* fanicha
furor *n* msisimko
furrow *n* mtaro
furry *adj* -enye manyoya
further *adv* mbali zaidi
furthermore *adv* isitoshe
fury *n* hasira
fuse *n* fyuzi, fataki
fusion *n* myeyungano
fuss *n* pilikapilika
futile *adj* -sio na maana
future *n* maisha ya mbele

G

gadget *n* kifaa
gag *n* dhihaka; utani
gag *v* goka
gage *v* pima
gain *v* pata
gain *n* pato
gal *n* msichana

galaxy *n* kundi la nyota

gale *n* kimbunga

gallant *adj* -enye ujasiri

gallery *n* nyumba ya sanaa

gallon *n* galoni

gallows *n* majili

galvanize *v* gutusha, shtua

gamble *v* cheza kamari

game *n* mchezo

gang *n* kundi

gangrene *n* uozo wa mwili

gangster *n* jambazi

gap *n* upenyo

garage *n* gereji

garbage *n* pipa

garden *n* bustani

gardener *n* mtunza bustani

gargle *v* sukutua

garland *n* shada

garlic *n* kitunguu swaumu

garment *n* nguo

garnish *v* pamba, remba

garnish *n* kupamba

garrison *n* askari; ngome

garrulous *adj* maneno mengi

garter *n* mkanda wa soksi

gas *n* gesi

gash *n* jeraha

gasoline *n* petroli

gasp *v* tweta

gastric *adj* -a tumbo

gate *n* lango

gather *v* kusanya

gathering *n* mkusanyiko

gauge *v* pima

gauze *n* shashi

gaze *v* tazama

gear *n* gia; vifaa

geese *n* bata bukini

gem *n* kito

gender *n* jinsia; ngeli

gene *n* kinasaba

general *n* jumla

generalize *v* jumlisha

generate *v* zalisha

generation *n* uzalishaji

generator *n* jenerata

generic *adj* -a ainasafu

generosity *n* ukarimu

genetic *adj* -a vinasaba

genius *n* kipaji

genocide *n* mauaji

genteel *adj* -a kiungwana

gentle *adj* -a upole

gentleman *n* mwanaume

gentleness *n* upole**

G

genuflect _v_ piga magoti
genuine _adj_ halisi
geography _n_ jiografia
geology _n_ jiologia
geometry _n_ jiometri
germ _n_ kijidudu, kiini
German _adj_ Mjerumani
Germany _n_ Ujerumani
germinate _v_ mea, chipua
gerund _n_ kitezi
gestation _n_ ujauzito
gesticulate _v_ ashiria
gesture _n_ ishara
get _iv_ pata; chukua
get along _v_ patana, weza
get away _v_ ondoka
get back _v_ rudi
get by _v_ faa, kubalika
get down _v_ shuka
get down to _v_ anza
get in _v_ ingia
get off _v_ toka, teremka
get out _v_ ondoka, toka
get over _v_ njoo
get together _v_ kusanyika
get up _v_ inuka
geyser _n_ chemchem
ghastly _adj_ mbaya sana

ghost _n_ mzimu
giant _n_ jitu, pandikizi
gift _n_ zawadi
gifted _adj_ kipaji
gigantic _adj_ zinga
giggle _v_ chekelea
gimmick _n_ mbinu
ginger _n_ tangawizi
gingerly _adv_ kwa uangalifu
giraffe _n_ twiga
girl _n_ msichana
girlfriend _n_ rafiki wa kike
give _iv_ toa, patia
give away _v_ gawa
give back _v_ rudisha
give in _v_ kubali
give out _v_ achia, toa
give up _v_ kata tamaa
glacier _n_ mto wa barafu
glad _adj_ furahi
glamorous _adj_ wa haiba
glance _v_ angalia
glance _n_ kutupa jicho
gland _n_ tezi
glare _n_ mng'ao
glass _n_ kioo
glasses _n_ miwani
glassware _n_ vyombo vya kioo

gleam *n* mng'ao

gleam *v* ng'aa

glide *v* teleza

glimmer *n* dalili

glimpse *n* kupitisha macho

glimpse *v* pitisha macho

glitter *v* meta meta

globe *n* dunia, mviringo

globule *n* tone

gloom *n* utusitusi

gloomy *adj* -enye huzuni

glorify *v* tukuza

glorious *adj* -a kupendeza

glory *n* utukufu

gloss *n* mng'ao

glossary *n* faharasa

glossy *adj* -a kung'aa

glove *n* glavu

glow *v* mwanga

glucose *n* glukozi

glue *n* gundi

glue *v* gundisha

glut *n* furiko

glutton *n* mlafi

gnaw *v* guguna

go *iv* nenda

go ahead *v* endelea

go away *v* ondoka, toka

go back *v* rudi

go down *v* shuka

go in *v* ingia

go on *v* endelea

go out *v* toka nje

go over *v* rudia, pitia

go through *v* pita

go under *v* zama, titia

go up *v* panda

goad *v* chokoza

goal *n* bao, goli

goalkeeper *n* golikipa

goat *n* mbuzi

gobble *v* bugia, meza

God *n* Mungu

goddess *n* mungu wa kike

godless *adj* kikafiri

goggles *n* miwani ya jua

gold *n* dhahabu

golden *adj* -a dhahabu

good *adj* nzuri

good-looking *adj* mzuri

goodness *n* wema

goods *n* mali, vitu

goodwill *n* nia nzuri

goof *v* kosea

goof *n* mpumbavu

goose *n* bata bukini

G

gorge *n* korongo

gorilla *n* sokwe

gospel *n* injili

gossip *v* teta

gossip *n* umbea

gout *n* jongo

govern *v* ongoza

government *n* serikali

governor *n* gavana

gown *n* gauni

grab *v* nyakua

grace *n* madaha, neema

graceful *adj* -enye madaha

gracious *adj* -enye huruma

grade *n* daraja

gradual *adj* taratibu

graduate *v* hitimu, maliza

graduation *n* mahafali

graft *v* pandikiza

graft *n* chipukizi, hongo

grain *n* mbegu

gram *n* gramu

grammar *n* sarufi

grand *adj* kubwa

grandchild *n* mjukuu

granddad *n* babu

grandfather *n* babu

grandmother *n* bibi

grandparents *n* babu na bibi

grandson *n* mjukuu wa kiume

grandstand *n* jukwaa

granny *n* bibi

grant *v* toa

grant *n* idhini; msaada

grape *n* zabibu

grapefruit *n* balungi

grapevine *n* mzabibu

graphic *adj* -a grafu

grasp *n* kukamata

grasp *v* kamata

grass *n* majani

grassroots *adj* jamii shinani

grateful *adj* -a kushukuru

gratify *v* ridhika

gratifying *adj* -a kuridhisha

gratitude *n* shukurani

gratuity *n* posho

grave *adj* -a hatari, muhimu

grave *n* kaburi

gravel *n* kokoto

gravely *adv* -enye kokoto

graveyard *n* makaburini

gravitate *v* vutiwa

gravity *n* uzito

gravy *n* mchuzi

gray *adj* kijivu

grayish adj -a kijivu kijivu

graze v kwaruza; chunga

graze n mkwaruzo

grease v weka grisi

grease n grisi

greasy adj -a kuteleza

great adj kubwa

greatness n umaarufu

Greece n Ugiriki

greed n ulafi

greedy adj mlafi

Greek adj Mgiriki

green adj kijani

greet v salimia, amkia

greetings n salamu

gregarious adj chamgamfu

grenade n kombora

greyhound n mbwa

grief n majonzi

grievance n malalamiko

grieve v sikitikia, lilia

grill v banika

grill n oka; hoji

grim adj mkali

grimace n kukunja uso

grime n masizi

grind iv saga

grip v shika

grip n mkamato

gripe n maumivu

grisly adj -a kutisha

groan v guna

groan n maguno

groceries n mahitaji

groin n nena

groom n bwana harusi

groove n makwa; mfuo

gross adj jumla; chafu

grossly adv kw uchafu

grotesque adj -a kutisha

grotto n pango

grouch v nuna

grouchy adj -a kununa

ground n ardhi

ground floor n tabaka ya chini

groundless adj bila msingi

groundwork n kazi ya msingi

group n kundi

grow iv ota, kuwa

grow up v kuwa

growl v vuma, guna

grown-up n mtu mzima

growth n ukuaji

grudge n kinyongo

grudgingly adv kwa kinyongo

gruelling adj -a kuumiza

G

gruesome adj -a kutisha
grumble v lalamika
grumpy adj -enye kisirani
guarantee v hakikishia
guarantee n hakikisho
guarantor n mdhamini
guard n mlinzi
guardian n mtunzaji
guerrilla n gaidi,
guess v otea, kisia
guess n kisio
guest n mgeni
guidance n mwongozo
guide v ongoza, elekeza
guide n kiongozi
guidelines n maelekezo
guild n ushirika
guile n ujanja
guillotine n majili
guilt n hatia
guilty adj -enye hatia
guise n kujifanya
guitar n gita
gulf n ghuba
gull n shakwa
gullible adj danganyika
gulp v meza
gulp n kugugumia

gulp down v meza kwa pupa
gum n ufizi, gundi
gun n bunduki
gun down v ua
gunfire n mlio wa bunduki
gunman n mpiga bunduki
gunpowder n baruti
gust n kimbunga
gusto n kufurahia
gusty adj -a kimbunga
gut n utumbo
guts n ujasiri
gutter n mfumbi
guy n jamaa
guzzle v kunywa kwa pupa
gym n ukumbi wa michezo

H

habit n vazi
habitable adj -a kufaa kuishi
habitual adj -a kawaida
hack v katakata
haggle v bishana bei
hail n mvua mawe

hail *v* ita

hair *n* nywele

haircut *n* kukata nywele

hairdo *n* mtindo wa nywele

hairdresser *n* msusi

half *n* nusu

half *adj* nusu

hall *n* ukumbi

hallway *n* ususu

halt *v* simama

halve *v* gawanya nusu

ham *n* kiga; kiweo

hamlet *n* kijiji

hammer *n* nyundo

hammock *n* bembea

hand *n* mkono

hand down *v* rithi, shusha

hand in *v* wasilisha

hand out *v* gawa

hand over *v* kabidhi

handbag *n* pochi

handcuff *v* funga pingu

handcuffs *n* pingu

handful *n* mkono tele

handgun *n* bastola

handicap *n* kilema

handkerchief *n* kitambaa

handle *v* shika

handle *n* mpini

handout *n* msaada

handrail *n* uzio wa ngazi

handshake *n* kutoa mkono

handsome *adj* mzuri

handy *adj* -a kufaa

hang *iv* tundika, ning'iniza

hang on *v* subiri

hang up *v* tundika

hanger *n* rafu

hangup *n* tamaa kubwa

happen *v* tokea

happening *n* kutokea

happiness *n* furaha

happy *adj* furahi

harass *v* nyanyasa

harassment *n* unyanyasaji

harbor *n* bandari

hard *adj* ngumu

harden *v* fanya ngumu

hardly *adv* kwa nadra

hardness *n* ugumu

hardship *n* shida

hardware *n* vifaa vya ujenzi

hardwood *n* ubao mgumu

hardy *adj* hodari

hare *n* sungura

harm *v* umiza

H

H

harm _n_ hatari
harmful _adj_ -a hatari
harmonize _v_ onanisha
harmony _n_ uelewano
harp _n_ utari
harpoon _n_ chusa
harrowing _adj_ -enye kusikitisha
harsh _adj_ kali
harshly _adv_ kwa ukali
harshness _n_ ukali
harvest _n_ zao
harvest _v_ vuna
hashish _n_ bangi
hassle _v_ sumbua
hassle _n_ usumbufu
haste _n_ haraka
hasten _v_ harakisha
hastily _adv_ kwa haraka
hasty _adj_ upesi
hat _n_ kofia
hatchet _n_ kishoka
hate _v_ chukia
hatred _n_ chuki
haughty _adj_ -enye kiburi
haul _v_ beba, vuta
haunt _v_ wangia
have _iv_ kuwa na
have to _v_ bidika

haven _n_ bandari
havoc _n_ uharibifu
hawk _n_ mwewe
hay _n_ nyasi
haystack _n_ lundo la nyasi
hazard _n_ hatari
hazardous _adj_ -a hatari
haze _n_ ukungu
hazy _adj_ un-enyezi
he _pro_ yeye
head _n_ kichwa
head for _v_ weza
heading _n_ kichwa
head-on _adv_ uso kwa uso
headquarters _n_ makao makuu
headway _n_ maendeleo
heal _v_ pona
healer _n_ mganga
health _n_ afya
healthy _adj_ wa afya
heap _n_ lundo
heap _v_ lundikwa
hear _iv_ sikia
hearing _n_ kusikia
hearsay _n_ tetesi
hearse _n_ gari la jeneza
heart _n_ moyo
heartbeat _n_ pigo la moyo

heartburn *n* kiungulia

hearten *v* tia moyo

heartfelt *adj* -a dhati

hearth *n* pa kuotea moto

heartless *adj* katili

hearty *adj* bashasha

heat *v* pasha moto

heat *n* joto

heathen *n* mpagani

heating *n* usambazaji joto

heatwave *n* wimbi la joto

heaven *n* mbingu

heavenly *adj* -a mbingu

heaviness *n* uzito

heavy *adj* nzito

heckle *v* chambua

hectic *adj* heka heka

heed *v* tii

heel *n* kisigino

height *n* urefu

heighten *v* zidisha

heinous *adj* -a kuchukiza

heir *n* mrithi

heiress *n* mrithi wa kike

heist *n* wizi kwa silaha

helicopter *n* helikopta

hell *n* jahanamu

hello *e* habari

helm *n* usukani

helmet *n* helmeti

help *v* saidia

help *n* msaada

helper *n* msaidizi

helpful *adj* saidia

helpless *adj* -siomudu

hem *n* pindo

hemisphere *n* kizio

hemorrhage *n* kuvuja damu

hen *n* kuku

hence *adv* hivyo

henchman *n* kibaraka

her *adj* yeye

herald *v* tangaza

herald *n* mtabiri

herb *n* mmea

here *adv* hapa

hereby *adv* hivi sasa

hereditary *adj* -a kurithi

heresy *n* uasi

heretic *adj* mwasi

heritage *n* urithi

hermetic *adj* -sio ingiza hewa

hermit *n* mtawa

hernia *n* ngiri

hero *n* shujaa

heroic *adj* -a kishujaa

H

heroin *n* unga
heroism *n* ushujaa
hers *pro* yake
herself *pro* yeye mwenyewe
hesitant *adj* -a kusita
hesitate *v* sita
hesitation *n* kusita
heyday *n* wakati wa neema
hiccup *n* kwikwi
hidden *adj* -liofichwa
hide *iv* ficha
hideaway *n* maficho
hideous *adj* ya kutisha
high *adj* juu
highlight *n* kubainisha
highly *adv* sana
Highness *n* Mtukufu
highway *n* barabara kuu
hijack *v* teka
hijack *n* kuteka
hijacker *n* mtekaji
hike *v* tembea
hike *n* kutembea
hilarious *adj* -a kuchekesha
hill *n* kilima
hillside *n* kilimani
hilltop *n* kilele cha kilima
hilly *adj* -enye vilima

hilt *n* mpini
hinder *v* zuia
hindrance *n* kizuizi
hindsight *n* ufahamu
hinge *v* tegemea
hinge *n* bawaba
hint *n* dokezo
hint *v* dokeza
hip *n* kiuno
hire *v* ajiri
his *adj* yake
his *pro* yake
Hispanic *adj* asili ya Kispanish
hiss *v* zomea
historian *n* mwanahistoria
history *n* historia
hit *n* pigo
hit *iv* piga
hit back *v* rudishia kupiga
hitch *n* kikwazo
hitch up *v* unganisha
hitchhike *n* kuomba lifti
hitherto *adv* hadi sasa
hive *n* mzinga
hoard *v* kusanya
hoarse *adj* -enye madende
hoax *n* mzaha
hobby *n* upendeleo

hog _n_ nguruwe pori

hoist _v_ pandisha

hoist _n_ kupandisha

hold _iv_ shika

hold back _v_ zuia

hold on to _v_ shikilia

hold out _v_ shikilia

hold up _v_ kawiza

holdup _n_ ushikiliaji wa nguvu

hole _n_ tundu

holiday _n_ likizo

holiness _n_ utakatifu

Holland _n_ Uholanzi

hollow _adj_ -enye tundu

holy _adj_ takatifu

homage _n_ heshima

home _n_ nyumba

homeland _n_ nchi ya asili

homeless _adj_ bila pa kuishi

homely _adj_ -a kawaida

hometown _n_ makazi ya mjini

homicide _n_ mauaji

homily _n_ mahubiri

honest _adj_ -a kweli

honesty _n_ ukweli

honey _n_ asali

honeymoon _n_ fungate

honk _v_ piga honi

honor _n_ heshima

hood _n_ kifuniko

hoodlum _n_ kibaka

hoof _n_ kwato

hook _n_ ndoana

hooligan _n_ mhuni

hop _v_ ruka

hope _n_ tumaini

hopefully _adv_ kwa matumaini

horizon _n_ upeo wa macho

horizontal _adj_ -a ulalo

horn _n_ pembe

horrendous _adj_ mbaya sana

horrible _adj_ -a kutisha

horrify _v_ tisha

horror _n_ kitisho

horse _n_ farasi

hose _n_ mpira

hospital _n_ hospitali

hospitality _n_ ukarimu

hospitalize _v_ laza hospitali

host _n_ mwenyeji

hostage _n_ mateka

hostess _n_ mhudumu

hostile _adj_ -a adui

hostility _n_ uadui

hot _adj_ moto, joto

hotel _n_ hoteli

H

hound *n* mbwa

hour *n* saa

hourly *adv* kila saa

house *n* nyumba

household *n* kaya

housekeeper *n* mtunza nyumba

housework *n* kazi za ndani

hover *v* zunguka zunguka

how *adv* vipi

however *c* hata hivyo

howl *v* vuma

howl *n* mlio mkali

hub *n* kitovu

huddle *v* songamana

hug *v* kumbatia

hug *n* kukumbatia

huge *adj* kubwa sana

hull *n* kiunzi

hum *v* imba

human *adj* -a binadamu

human being *n* binadamu

humanities *n* sanaa

humankind *n* binadamu

humble *adj* -sio taka makuu

humbly *adv* kwa kunyenyekea

humid *adj* -enye unyevu

humidity *n* unyevu

humiliate *v* aibisha

humility *n* unyenyekevu

humor *n* vichekesho

humorous *adj* -a kuchekesha

hump *n* kibiongo

hunch *n* hisia

hunchback *n* -enye kibiongo

hunched *adj* -enye kupinda

hundred *adj* mia

hundredth *adj* -a mia

hunger *n* njaa

hungry *adj* -a na njaa

hunt *v* winda

hunter *n* mwindaji

hunting *n* kuwinda

hurdle *n* kikwazo

hurl *v* tupa

hurricane *n* kimbunga

hurriedly *adv* kwa haraka

hurry *v* harakisha

hurry up *v* harakisha

hurt *iv* umiza

hurt *adj* -a kuumiza

hurtful *adj* -a kuumiza

husband *n* mume

hush *n* ukimya

hush up *v* nyamaza

husky *adj* -a kukwaruza

hustle *n* kulaghai**

hut *n* kibanda
hydraulic *adj* haidroliki
hydrogen *n* haidrojeni
hyena *n* fisi
hygiene *n* usafi
hymn *n* wimbo
hyphen *n* kistariungio
hypnosis *n* kiinimacho
hypnotize *v* pumbaza akili
hypocrisy *n* unafiki
hypocrite *adj* mnafiki
hypothesis *n* nadharia
hysteria *n* mpagao
hysterical *adj* kupagawa

I

I *pro* mimi
ice *n* barafu
ice cream *n* malai
ice cube *n* tonge la barafu
ice skate *v* kuteleza barafu
iceberg *n* siwa barafu
icebox *n* jokofu
ice-cold *adj* baridi sana

icy *adj* -enye barafu
idea *n* wazo, dhana
ideal *adj* kipeo
identical *adj* sawa sawa
identify *v* tambua
identity *n* utambulisho
ideology *n* itikadi
idiom *n* nahau
idiot *n* mjinga
idiotic *adj* -a kijinga
idle *adj* isiotumika
idol *n* sanamu ya miungu
idolatry *n* kuabudu sanamu
if *c* kama
ignite *v* washa
ignorance *n* ujinga
ignorant *adj* mjinga
ignore *v* puuza, dharau
ill *adj* mgonjwa
illegal *adj* haramu, sio halili
illegible *adj* haisomeki
illegitimate *adj* sio halali
illicit *adj* haramu
illness *n* ugonjwa
illogical *adj* -sio na mantiki
illuminate *v* angaza, washa
illusion *n* uongo
illustrate *v* fafanua, chora

H
I

illustration 96

illustration *n* kielezo, mchoro
illustrious *adj* mashuhuri
image *n* picha
imagination *n* fikra, uwazo
imagine *v* fikiri, dhani
imbalance *n* kutolingana
imitate *v* iga, fuata
imitation *n* kuiga; bandia
immaculate *adj* safi kabisa
immature *adj* changa
immaturity *n* uchanga
immediately *adv* haraka
immense *adj* kubwa sana
immensity *n* ukubwa
immerse *v* tumbukiza
immersion *n* kutumbukiza
immigrant *n* mhamiaji
immigrate *v* hamia
immigration *n* uhamiaji
imminent *adj* karibia
immobile *adj* bila kujigusa
immoral *adj* ovu, fasiki
immorality *n* uovu, ufasiki
immortal *adj* -siokufa
immortality *n* kuishi milele
immune *adj* -siodhurika
immunity *n* kinga
immunize *v* kinga, chanja

immutable *adj* -siobadilika
impact *n* dharuba, athari
impact *v* athiri
impair *v* haribu
impartial *adj* adilifu
impatience *n* kosa subira
impatient *adj* bila subira
impeccable *adj* maasumu
impediment *n* kizuizi
impending *adj* kukaribia
imperfection *n* dosari
imperial *adj* -a kifalme
imperialism *n* ubeberu
impertinence *n* ufidhuli
impertinent *adj* fidhuli
impetuous *adj* -a harara
implacable *adj* -sio na huruma
implant *v* pandikiza
implement *v* tekeleza
implicate *v* husisha
implication *n* udhanifu
implore *v* sihi
imply *v* husisha
impolite *adj* -enye dharau
import *v* ingiza, leta
importance *n* umuhimu
importation *n* uingizaji
impose *v* lazimisha

imposing *adj* -a kushangaza
imposition *n* utozaji; udhia
impossibility *n* kutowezekana
impossible *adj* haiwezekani
impotent *adj* hanithi
impound *v* kamata, fungia
impoverished *adj* kufanywa fukara
impractical *adj* haitekelezeki
imprecise *adj* -enye makosa
impress *v* athiri, vutia
impressive *adj* -a kuvutia
imprison *v* funga, weka jela
impromptu *adv* -a papo hapo
improper *adj* -siosahihi
improve *v* boresha
improvement *n* maendeleo
improvise *v* tunga papo hapo
impulse *n* mchocheo
impulsive *adj* -a usukumizi
impure *adj* -enye najisi
in *pre* katika, kwenye
in depth *adv* kwa undani
inability *n* kutoweza
inaccessible *adj* -siofikiwa
inaccurate *adj* -sio sahihi
inadequate *adj* -siofaa
inadmissible *adj* -siokubalika
inappropriate *adj* -sio ya heshima

inasmuch as *c* kwa kiasi cha
inaugurate *v* simika
inauguration *n* kusimika
incalculable *adj* -siohesabika
incapable *adj* -sio na uwezo
incapacitate *v* kuzuia, lemaza
incarcerate *v* funga jela
incense *n* ubani
incentive *n* motisha
inception *n* auwali
incessant *adj* -a mfululizo
inch *n* inchi
incident *n* tukio
incidentally *adv* hivi
incision *n* upasuaji
incite *v* shawishi
incitement *n* kushawishi
inclination *n* mwelekeo
incline *v* mwinamo
include *v* weka pamoja na
inclusive *adv* pamoja na
income *n* mapato
incoming *adj* -a kuingia
incompatible *adj* -siopatana
incompetence *n* kutomudu
incompetent *adj* -siojimudu
incomplete *adj* -siokamilika
inconsistent *adj* -sioendana

inconvenient *adj* -enye khero
incorporate *v* shirikisha
incorrect *adj* -sio sahihi
increase *v* ongeza
increase *n* nyongeza
increasing *adj* -a kuongezeka
incredible *adj* -a ajabu
increment *n* ongezeko
incriminate *v* -a kutia hatiani
incur *v* ingia, pata
incurable *adj* -sio tibika
indecency *n* utovu wa adabu
indecision *n* kusita
indecisive *adj* anae sita
indeed *adv* kwa kweli
indefinite *adj* -sio na mwisho
indemnify *v* fidia
indemnity *n* fidia
independence *n* uhuru
independent *adj* huru
index *n* kielezo; faharisi
indicate *v* onyesha
indication *n* mwelekeo
indict *v* shitaki
indifference *n* kutojali
indifferent *adj* -siojali
indigent *adj* fukara, maskini
indigestion *n* kuvimbiwa

indirect *adj* -sio dhairi
indiscreet *adj* -sio na hadhari
indispensable *adj* -a lazima
indisposed *adj* kutojisika vizuri
indisputable *adj* -a uhakika
indivisible *adj* -siogawanyika
indoctrinate *v* chocheleza
indoor *adv* ndani
induce *v* shawishi
indulge *v* endekeza
indulgent *adj* upole; anasa
industry *n* kiwanda, utenzi
ineffective *adj* -siofaa
inefficient *adj* -sioweza
inept *adj* -sioelekevu
inevitable *adj* -siozuilika
inexpensive *adj* -sioghali
inexperienced *adj* -sio na uzoefu
inexplicable *adj* -sioelezeka
infallible *adj* -enye uhakika
infancy *n* utotoni
infant *n* mtoto mchanga
infect *v* ambukiza
infection *n* ambukzizo
infectious *adj* -a kuambukiza
infer *v* dokeza; hitimisha
inferior *adj* -a hadhi -a chini
infertile *adj* tasa, gumba

infested *adj* tapakaa, jaa
infidelity *n* uzinzi
infiltrate *v* penyeza
infiltration *n* kupenya
infinite *adj* -sio pimika
infirmary *n* zahanati
inflammation *n* uvimbe
inflate *v* puliza
inflation *n* mfumuko
inflexible *adj* -sio pinda
inflict *v* umiza
influence *n* shawishi
influential *adj* -enye uwezo
influenza *n* homa ya mafua
influx *n* uingiaji
inform *v* taarifu
informal *adj* -sio rasmi
informant *n* mtoa habari
information *n* habari
informer *n* mchongezi
infraction *n* kosa
infrequent *adj* -a mara chache
infuriate *v* kasirisha
infusion *n* kiziduo
ingenuity *n* maarifa, werevu
ingest *v* meza, vuta ndani
ingot *n* mkuo
ingrained *adj* -liotopea

ingratiate *v* jipendekeza
ingredient *n* kiambato
inhabit *v* ishi
inhabitant *n* mkazi
inhale *v* vuta
inherit *v* rithi
inheritance *n* urithi
inhibit *v* ishi
inhuman *adj* -a kin-ama
initial *adj* -a mwanzo
initially *adv* awali
initials *n* saini ndogo
initiate *v* anzisha
initiative *n* hatua, uamuzi
inject *v* dunga
injection *n* sindano
injure *v* umiza
injurious *adj* -enye kudhuru
injury *n* kidonda
injustice *n* uonevu, dhuluma
ink *n* wino
inkling *n* fununu
inland *adv* ndani ya nchi
inland *adj* bara
in-laws *n* wakwe
inmate *n* mfungwa
inn *n* hoteli
innate *adj* -a asili

inner *adj* -a ndani
innocent *adj* bila hatia
innovation *n* kufanya mageuzi
innuendo *n* kijembe, fumbo
innumerable *adj* -sio hesabika
input *n* pembejeo; ingizo
inquest *n* uchunguzi
inquire *v* uliza
inquiry *n* swali, uchunguzi
inquisition *n* udadisi
insane *adj* kichaa
insanity *n* wazimu
insatiable *adj* -sio tosheka
inscription *n* andiko, mchoro
insect *n* mdudu
insensitive *adj* -siohisi
inseparable *adj* -siotengana
insert *v* ingiza
insertion *n* ingizo
inside *adj* -a ndani
inside *pre* ndani ya
insignificant *adj* -sio na maana
insincere *adj* -a kinafiki
insincerity *n* unafiki
insinuate *v* singizia
insinuation *n* uchochezi
insipid *adj* dufu
insist *v* sisitiza

insistence *n* msisitizo
insolent *adj* -a kifidhuli
insoluble *adj* -sioyayuka
inspect *v* kagua
inspection *n* ukaguzi
inspector *n* mkaguzi
inspiration *n* wazo bunifu
inspire *v* tia moyo
instability *n* ugeugeu
install *v* weka, simika
installation *n* ufungaji
installment *n* mkupuo
instance *n* mfano
instant *n* muda mfupi
instantly *adv* papo hapo
instead *adv* badala
instigate *v* anzisha
instil *v* fundisha
instinct *n* silika
institute *v* chukua hatua
institution *n* taasisi
instruct *v* elekeza, fundisha
instructor *n* mwalimu
insufficient *adj* -siotosha
insulate *v* hami
insulation *n* kihami, uhami
insult *v* tukana, kashifu
insult *n* tusi, kashfa

insurance *n* bima
insure *v* katia bima
insurgency *n* uhasi, ghasia
insurrection *n* uhasi, ghasia
intact *adj* kamili
intake *n* uchukuaji
integrate *v* changanyika
integration *n* uchanganyikaji
integrity *n* uadilifu, uaminifu
intelligent *adj* -enye akili
intend *v* dhamiria
intense *adj* kali, -a nguvu
intensify *v* zidisha nguvu
intensity *n* nguvu
intensive *adj* shadidi
intention *n* nia
intercede *v* ombea, tetea
intercept *v* zuia njiani
intercession *n* utetezi
interchange *v* badilisha
interchange *n* kubadilisha
interest *n* upendeleo
interested *adj* kuvutiwa
interesting *adj* -a kuvutia
interfere *v* ingilia
interference *n* kuingilia
interior *adj* ndani
interlude *n* mapumziko

intermediary *n* msuluhishi
intern *v* mkufunzi
interpret *v* fafanua, tafsiri
interpretation *n* ufafanuzi
interpreter *n* mkalimani
interrogate *v* hoji
interrupt *v* katiza
interruption *n* ukatizaji
intersect *v* gawa kati
intertwine *v* sokota
interval *n* mapumziko
intervene *v* ingilia kati
intervention *n* kuingilia kati
interview *n* usaili
intestine *n* utumbo
intimacy *n* undani
intimate *adj* -a karibu
intimidate *v* tisha
intolerable *adj* -sio stahimilika
intoxicated *adj* lewa
intravenous *adj* ndani ya mshipa
intrepid *adj* shupavu
intricate *adj* -a kutatanisha
intrigue *n* njama
intriguing *adj* -a kushangaza
intrinsic *adj* -a asili
introduce *v* tambulisha
introduction *n* utangulizi

introvert *adj* pweke
intrude *v* ingilia
intruder *n* jambazi, mvamizi
intrusion *n* uingiliaji
intuition *n* hisia
inundate *v* furika
invade *v* vamia
invader *n* mvamizi
invalid *n* batili
invalidate *v* batilisha
invaluable *adj* -enye thamani
invasion *n* uvamizi
invent *v* buni, vumbua
invention *n* uvumbuzi
inventory *n* orodha
invest *v* wekeza
investigate *v* chunguza
investigation *n* uchunguzi
investment *n* uwekezaji
investor *n* mwekezaji
invisible *adj* -sioonekana
invitation *n* mwaliko
invite *v* karibisha
invoice *n* hati ya madai
invoke *v* omba kwa
involve *v* shirikisha
involved *v* shiriki, husika
involvement *n* kuhusika

inward *adj* -a ndani
inwards *adv* kwa ndani
iodine *n* iodini
irate *adj* -enye kuudhika
Ireland *n* Eire
Irish *adj* irishi
iron *n* chuma, feri
iron *v* piga pasi
ironic *adj* -a dhihaka
irony *n* dhihaka, kejeli
irrational *adj* -a kuto tumia akili
irrefutable *adj* -siopingika
irregular *adj* -sio ya msimu
irrelevant *adj* -sio husu
irresistible *adj* -sio stahimilika
irrespective *adj* bila kujali
irrevocable *adj* -sio tenguka
irrigate *v* mwagilia
irrigation *n* umwagiliaji
irritate *v* kera, udhi
irritating *adj* -a kukera
Islamic *adj* -a Kiislamu
island *n* kisiwa
isle *n* kisiwa
isolate *v* tenga
isolation *n* kutengwa
issue *n* suala
Italian *adj* Mwitaliano

italics *adj* italiki
Italy *n* Italia
itch *v* washa, washwa
itchiness *n* kuwashwa
item *n* kitu; dondoo
itemize *v* orodhesha
itinerary *n* utaratibu, njia
ivory *n* pembe ya ndovu

J

jackal *n* bweha
jacket *n* jaketi, koti
jail *n* gereza, jela
jail *v* funga jela
jam *n* jemu
janitor *n* mwangalizi
January *n* Januari
Japan *n* Ujapani
Japanese *adj* Mjapani
jar *n* chombo cha kiyoo
jasmine *n* myasmini
jaw *n* taya
jealous *adj* kwa wivu
jealousy *n* wivu

jeans *n* jinzi
jeopardize *v* hatarisha
jerk *v* tingisha
jerk *n* mshtuko
jersey *n* sweta
Jew *n* Myahudi
jewel *n* kito
jeweler *n* sonara
jewelry store *n* duka la sonara
Jewish *adj* -a Kiyahudi
job *n* kazi
jobless *adj* bila kaz
join *v* unga
joint *n* -a pamoja
jointly *adv* kwa pamoja
joke *n* utani, kichekesho
joke *v* tania
jokingly *adv* kwa kutania
jolly *adj* -a furaha
jolt *v* tikisa, shtua
jolt *n* mtikisiko
journal *n* gazeti; jarida
journey *n* safari
jovial *adj* bashasha
joy *n* furaha
joyful *adj* -a shangwe
joyfully *adv* kwa furaha
jubilant *adj* -a shangwe

I
J

Judaism *n* dini ya Kiyahudi
judge *n* jaji
judgment *n* hukumu
jug *n* balasi, jagi
juice *n* maji ya matunda
juicy *adj* -enye rojorojo
July *n* Julai
jump *v* ruka
jump *n* mruko, urukaji
junction *n* njia panda
June *n* Juni
jungle *n* pori, msitu
junior *adj* mdogo
junk *n* takataka
just *adj* -a haki
justice *n* haki
justify *v* halalisha
justly *adv* kwa haki
juvenile *n* mtoto
juvenile *adj* -a watoto

K

karate *n* karate
keep *iv* weka
keep on *v* endelea
keep up *v* endeleza
keg *n* kipipa
kettle *n* birika
key *n* ufunguo
keyboard *n* kinanda, kibodi
kick *v* piga teke
kickback *n* rushwa
kid *n* mtoto
kidnap *v* teka nyara
kidnapper *n* mteka nyara
kidnapping *n* kuteka nyara
kidney *n* figo
kidney bean *n* harage jekundu
kill *v* ua
killer *n* muuaji
killing *n* mauaji
kilogram *n* kilogramu
kilometer *n* kilometa
kilowatt *n* kilowati
kind *adj* aina
kindle *v* washa
kindly *adv* kwa ukarimu

kindness *n* ukarimu
king *n* mfalme
kingdom *n* ufalme
kinship *n* undugu
kiosk *n* kibanda, genge
kiss *v* busu
kiss *n* busu
kitchen *n* jikoni
kite *n* mwewe, tiara
kitten *n* Kitoto cha paka
knee *n* goti
kneecap *n* kifuniko cha goti
kneel *iv* piga magoti
knife *n* kisu
knight *n* shujaa
knit *v* fuma
knob *n* nundu, kirungu
knock *n* pigo, bamizo
knock *v* gonga
knot *n* fundo
know *iv* jua
know-how *n* ujuzi
knowingly *adv* kwa kujua
knowledge *n* ujuzi, elimu

L

lab *n* maabara
label *n* lebo
labor *n* kazi
laborer *n* kibarua
labyrinth *n* mzingile
lace *n* kimia
lack *v* kosa
lack *n* ukosefu, utovu
lad *n* kijana
ladder *n* ngazi
laden *adj* jaza
lady *n* bibi, binti
lagoon *n* wangwa
lake *n* ziwa
lamb *n* kondoo
lament *v* omboleza; jutia
lament *n* ombolezo
lamp *n* taa
lamppost *n* mlingoti wa taa
lampshade *n* chengeu
land *n* ardhi
land *v* tua
landing *n* kutua
landlocked *adj* -sio na bahari
landscape *n* sura ya nchi

K
L

lane *n* ujia
language *n* lugha
languish *v* dhoofika
lantern *n* kandili
lap *n* paja
lapse *n* kupita, kupotoka
lapse *v* pita, potea
larceny *n* wizi
large *adj* kubwa
larynx *n* zoloto
laser *n* leza
lash *n* kope
lash *v* chapa, piga
lash out *v* lipuka
last *v* dumu
last *adj* mwisho
last name *n* jina la ukoo
last night *adv* jana usiku
lasting *adj* -a kudumu
lastly *adv* mwisho
latch *n* kitasa
late *adv* kwa kuchelewa
lately *adv* hivi karibuni
later *adv* baadaye
later *adj* -a baadaye
lateral *adj* -a kando
latest *adj* -a sasa
lather *n* povu

latitude *n* latitudo
latter *adj* -a mwisho
laugh *v* cheka
laugh *n* kicheko
laughable *adj* -a kuchekesha
laughter *n* kicheko
launch *n* kushua chombo
launch *v* shua, zindua
laundry *n* udobi
lavatory *n* choo, msala
law *n* sheria
law-abiding *adj* mfuata sheria
lawful *adj* -a halali
lawmaker *n* mtunga sheria
lawn *n* uwanja wa nyasi
lawsuit *n* madai
lawyer *n* wakili
lax *adj* kizembe
laxative *adj* haluli
lay *n* namna
lay *iv* laza, weka
lay off *v* achisha kazi
layer *n* tabaka
layman *n* mtu wa kawaida
layout *n* ramani, mchoro
laziness *n* uvivu
lazy *adj* mvivu
lead *iv* ongoza

lead *n* uongozi;risasi

leaded *adj* -enye risasi

leader *n* kiongozi

leadership *n* uongozi

leading *adj* -a kuongoza

leaf *n* jani

leaflet *n* jani dogo

league *n* umoja, ligi

leak *v* vuja

leak *n* kuvuja

leakage *n* uvujaji

lean *adj* nyembamba

lean *iv* egemea

lean on *v* himiza

leaning *n* upendeleo

leap *iv* ruka

leap *n* mruko

leap year *n* mwaka mrefu

learn *iv* funza

learned *adj* -a usomi

learner *n* mwanafunzi

learning *n* kujifunza

lease *v* kodi

leash *n* kamba

least *adj* -a uchache

leather *n* ngozi

leave *iv* acha; ondoka

leave out *v* ondoa

lecture *n* mhadhara

ledger *n* leja

leftovers *n* mabaki, masalio

leg *n* mguu

legacy *n* urithi

legal *adj* -a halali

legality *n* uhalali

legalize *v* halalisha

legend *n* hekaya

legible *adj* -a kusomeka

legion *n* kikosi

legislate *v* tunga sheria

legislation *n* sheria

legitimate *adj* wa halali

leisure *n* starehe

lemon *n* limau

lemonade *n* maji ya limau

lend *iv* azima

length *n* urefu

lengthen *v* refusha

lengthy *adj* -a kirefu

leniency *n* huruma, upole

lenient *adj* -enye huruma

lense *n* mboni

Lent *n* Kwaresma

lentil *n* dengu

leopard *n* chui

leper *n* mkoma**

L

leprosy *n* ukoma

less *adj* kidogo

lessee *n* mpangaji

lessen *v* punguza

lesser *adj* ndogo zaidi

lesson *n* somo

lessor *n* mpangishaji

let *iv* panga, ruhusu

let down *v* angusha

let go *v* achia

let in *v* ingiza

let out *v* achia, fungulia

lethal *adj* -a kuua

letter *n* barua

level *v* sawazisha

level *n* kiwango

lever *n* wenzo

leverage *n* nguvu ya wenzo

levy *v* toza

lewd *adj* zinifu

liability *n* dhima

liable *adj* wajibika

liaison *n* uhusiano

liar *adj* mwongo

liberate *v* achia huru

liberation *n* uachiaji huru

liberty *n* uhuru

librarian *n* mkutubi

library *n* maktaba

lice *n* chawa

licence *n* leseni

license *v* toa leseni

lick *v* lamba

lid *n* kifuniko, mfuniko

lie *iv* lala

lie *v* sema uongo

lie *n* uongo

lieu *n* badala

lieutenant *n* luteni

life *n* maisha

lifeless *adj* -sio hai

lifestyle *n* namna ya kuishi

lifetime *adj* maisha yote

lift *v* inua

lift off *v* ruka, paa

lift-off *n* kupaa

ligament *n* kano

light *iv* washa, angaza

light *adj* nyepesi

light *n* mwanga

lighter *n* kiberiti, kiwashio

lighthouse *n* mnara wa taa

lighting *n* taa, mwanga

lightly *adv* kidogo

lightning *n* mwako wa radi

lightweight *n* nyepesi

likable *adj* -a kupendwa

like *pre* kama

like *v* penda

likelihood *n* uwezekano

likely *adv* wezekana

likeness *n* kufanana

likewise *adv* kadhalika

liking *n* mapenzi

limb *n* kiungo

lime *n* ndimu

limestone *n* gange

limit *n* kikomo

limit *v* zuia

limitation *n* udhaifu

limp *v* chechemea

limp *n* kuchechemea

linchpin *n* egemeo

line *n* mstari

linen *n* kitani, mashuka

linger *v* sita

lingering *adj* -a muda mrefu

lining *n* bitana

link *v* unganisha

link *n* kiungo

lion *n* simba

lioness *n* simba jike

lip *n* mdomo

liquid *n* kiowevu

liquidate *v* filisika

liquidation *n* kufilisi

liquor *n* pombe

list *v* orodhesha

list *n* orodha

listen *v* sikiliza

listener *n* msikilizaji

litany *n* litania

liter *n* lita

literal *adj* halisi, hasa

literally *adv* kihalisi

literature *n* fasihi

litigation *n* madai

litre *n* lita

litter *n* machela

little *adj* kidogo

little bit *n* kipande kidogo

liturgy *n* liturujia

live *adj* hai

live *v* ishi

live off *v* ishi kwa

live up *v* fikia matarajio

livelihood *n* riziki

liver *n* ini

livid *adj* -a kukasirika

living room *n* sebuleni

lizard *n* mjusi

load *v* jaza

L

load *n* mzigo
loaded *adj* -a kujazwa
loaf *n* boflo
loan *v* kopesha, azima
loan *n* mkopo
loathe *v* chukia
loathing *n* chuki
lobby *n* ukumbi, sebule
lobby *v* shawishi wabunge
lobster *n* koche
local *adj* -a kienyeji
locate *v* tambua; tafuta
located *adj* iko, inapatikana
location *n* mahali
lock *v* funga
lock *n* kufuli, kitasa
lock up *v* fungia, funga
locksmith *n* mfua makufuli
locust *n* nzige
lodge *v* ishi
lofty *adj* ndefu sana
log *n* gogo
log *v* kata mti
log in *v* fungua
log off *v* funga, jiondoe
logic *n* mantiki
logical *adj* -enye mantiki
loin *n* vizazi

loiter *v* randa
loneliness *n* upweke
lonely *adv* mpweke
lonesome *adj* -enye upweke
long *adj* ndefu
long for *v* tamani
longing *n* tamaa, shauki
longitude *n* longitudo
long-standing *adj* -a muda mrefu
long-term *adj* -a muda mrefu
look *n* mtazamo
look *v* tazama
look after *v* chunga
look at *v* tazama
look down *v* dharau
look for *v* tafuta
look forward *v* subiri kwa hamu
look into *v* chunguza
look out *v* kinga, tahadhari
look over *v* pitia, angalia
look through *v* pekua, tafua
looking glass *n* kioo
looks *n* sura, umbile
loom *n* mtande, mtanda
loom *v* jongea
loophole *n* mwanya
loose *v* legea
loose *adj* -a kulegea

loosen v legeza
loot v iba
loot n mali ya wizi
lord n bwana, mfalme
lordship n utawala juu ya
lose iv shindwa
loser n mshindwa
loss n kupoteza
lot adv nyingi
lotion n losheni
lots adj wingi
lottery n bahati nasibu
loud adj -a sauti -a juu
loudly adv kwa sauti
loudspeaker n kipaza sauti
lounge n sebule
louse n chawa
lousy adj -a ovyo
lovable adj anaependeka
love v penda
love n upendo
lovely adj nzuri
lover n mpenzi
loving adj -a upendo
low adj chini
lower adj chini zaidi
lowkey adj chini chini
lowly adj duni

loyal adj mwaminifu
loyalty n uaminifu
lubricate v lainisha
lubrication n ulainishaji
lucid adj timamu
luck n bahati
lucky adj -a na bahati
lucrative adj -enye faida
ludicrous adj -a kipuuzi
luggage n mzigo, sanduku
lukewarm adj vugu vugu
lull n utulivu
lumber n mbao, mti
luminous adj -enye mwanga
lump n bonge
lunacy n kichaa
lunatic adj -enye kichaa
lunch n mlo wa mchana
lung n pafu
lure v vutia
lurid adj -a kutisha
lurk v jificha, jibanza
lush adj -enye kustawi
lust v tamani
lust n ashiki
lustful adj -enye ashiki
luxurious adj -a kifahari
luxury n fahari, anasa

L

lyrics *n* maneno, shairi

M

machine *n* mashine
mad *adj* kichaa
madam *n* mama
madden *v* kasirisha
madly *adv* kwa kichaa
madman *n* kichaa
madness *n* wazimu
magazine *n* jarida
magic *n* uchawi
magician *n* mchawi
magistrate *n* hakimu
magnet *n* sumaku
magnetic *adj* -enye sumaku
magnetism *n* usumaku
magnificent *adj* -a fahari
magnify *v* kuza
magnitude *n* ukubwa
maid *n* binti
maiden *n* mwanamwali
mail *v* posti
mail *n* barua

mailbox *n* sanduku la posta
mailman *n* msambaza barua
maim *v* lemaza
main *adj* haswa
mainland *n* bara
mainly *adv* haswa
maintain *v* endeleza
maintenance *n* utuzaji
majestic *adj* -a kifalme
majesty *n* ufalme
major *n* meja, somo kuu
major *adj* kuu
major in *v* somea
majority *n* wingi
make *n* aina
make *iv* tengeneza
make up *v* tunga
make up for *v* fidia
maker *n* mtengenezaji
makeup *n* kipodozi
malaria *n* homa, malaria
male *n* mume
malevolent *adj* ovu
malfunction *n* kasoro, dosari
malice *n* ubaya
malign *v* fanyia shari
malignancy *n* uovu
malignant *adj* mbaya, ovu

mall *n* eneo la maduka
malnutrition *n* utapiamlo
mammal *n* mamalia
man *n* mwanaume
manage *v* weza
manageable *adj* -enye kuwezekana
management *n* utawala
manager *n* mkurugenzi
mandate *n* uwezo
mandatory *adj* -a lazima
maneuver *n* endesha
manger *n* hori
mangle *v* guruto
manhandle *v* burura
manhunt *n* msako wa mtu
maniac *adj* mwehu
manifest *v* onekana
manipulate *v* chezea
mankind *n* binadamu
manliness *n* udume
manly *adj* -a kidume
manner *n* namna
mannerism *n* tabia
manners *n* tabia
manpower *n* nguvu kazi
mansion *n* jumba kubwa
manslaughter *n* mauaji
manual *adj* -a mkono

manufacture *v* tengeneza
manure *n* mbolea
manuscript *n* mwandiko
many *adj* wengi
map *n* ramani
marble *n* marumaru
march *v* piga gwaride
march *n* gwaride
March *n* Machi
mare *n* farasi jike
margin *n* pambizo
marginal *adj* -a pambizoni
marine *adj* -a bahari
marital *adj* -a ndoa
mark *n* alama
mark *v* weka alama
mark down *v* punguza bei
market *n* soko
marksman *n* mlengaji hodari
marriage *n* ndoa
married *adj* oa/olewa
marrow *n* uboho
marry *v* ona
Mars *n* Mars
marshal *n* jemadari
martyr *n* shujaa
marvel *n* maajabu, shani
marvelous *adj* nzuri

M

masculine *adj* -a kiume
mash *v* ponda
mask *n* barakoa
mason *n* mwashi
masquerade *v* kujifanya
mass *n* misa, chungu
massage *n* kuchua
massage *v* chua
masseur *n* mchuaji
masseuse *n* mchuaji wa kike
massive *adj* kubwa sana
mast *n* mlingoti
master *n* bwana, mkuu
master *v* mudu
masterpiece *n* kazi bora
mastery *n* udhibiti
mat *n* mkeka
match *n* kiberiti, pambano
match *v* linganisha
mate *n* mwenza
material *n* kifaa
maternal *adj* -a mama
maternity *n* uzazi
math *n* hesabu
matriculate *v* andikisha
matrimony *n* ndoa
matter *n* suala
mattress *n* godoro

mature *adj* komaa
maturity *n* ukomavu
maul *v* rarua
maxim *n* maadili ya hekima
maximum *adj* kiasi cha juu
May *n* Mei
may *iv* weza
may-be *adv* labda
mayhem *n* fujo, vurugu
mayor *n* meya
maze *n* mzingile
meager *adj* nyembamba
meal *n* mlo
mean *iv* maanisha
mean *adj* choyo
meaning *n* maanisha
meaningful *adj* -a maana
meaningless *adj* -sio na maana
meanness *n* ubaya, uchoyo
means *n* inamaanisha
meantime *adv* wakati huo
meanwhile *adv* wakati huo
measles *n* surua
measure *v* pima
measurement *n* vipimo
meat *n* nyama
meatball *n* kababu
mechanic *n* mekanika

M

mechanism *n* mtambo

mechanize *v* tumia mashine

medal *n* nishani

medallion *n* nishani kubwa

meddle *v* ingilia, dakiza

mediate *v* suluhisha

mediator *n* msuluhishi

medication *n* tiba, dawa

medicinal *adj* -a dawa

medicine *n* dawa

mediocre *adj* -a kadiri

mediocrity *n* ukadiri

meditate *v* ziua, taamali

meditation *n* kuziua

medium *adj* -a njia

meekness *n* unyenyekevu

meet *iv* kutana

meeting *n* mkutano

melancholy *n* uzuni

mellow *adj* laini

mellow *v* tulia, poa

melodic *adj* -a sauti nzuri

melon *n* tikiti maji

melt *v* yayusha

member *n* mwanachama

membership *n* uwanachama

membrane *n* utambi

memento *n* kumbusho

memo *n* taarifa

memoirs *n* habari za maisha

memorable *adj* -sio sahaulika

memorize *v* kariri

memory *n* kumbukumbu

men *n* wanaume

menace *n* tishio

mend *v* tengeneza

menopause *n* kukoma hedhi

menstruation *n* hedhi

mental *adj* -a ubongo

mentality *n* akili, fikira

mentally *adv* kwa kichwa

mention *v* taja

mention *n* kutaja

menu *n* orodha ya vyakula

merchandise *n* mali

merchant *n* mfanya biashara

merciful *adj* -enye huruma

merciless *adj* -sio na huruma

mercury *n* zebaki

mercy *n* huruma

merely *adv* tu

merge *v* ungana, kutana

merger *n* muungano

merit *n* sifa, faida

merit *v* stahili

mermaid *n* nguva

M

merry *adj* -a furaha
mesh *n* wavu wa wire
mesmerize *v* pumbaza akili
mess *n* vurugu; bwalo
mess around *v* fanya masihara
mess up *v* bulunda
message *n* ujumbe
messenger *n* mjumbe
Messiah *n* Masiya
messy *adj* chafu
metal *n* chuma
metallic *adj* -a chuma
metaphor *n* sitiari
meteor *n* kimondo
meter *n* mita
method *n* njia
metric *adj* -a mita
metropolis *n* mji mkubwa
Mexican *adj* Mtu wa Mexico
mice *n* panya
microbe *n* kijidudu
microphone *n* kipaza sauti
microscope *n* hadubini
midair *n* -a angani
midday *n* mchana
middle *n* katikati
middleman *n* wakala
midget *n* mbilikimo

midnight *n* usiku wa manane
midwife *n* mkunga
mighty *adj* -enye nguvu
migraine *n* kipandauso
migrant *n* mhamiaji
migrate *v* hamia
mild *adj* -siokali
mildew *n* kuvu
mile *n* maili
mileage *n* umbali kwa maili
milestone *n* mango
militant *adj* mkereketwa
milk *n* maziwa
milky *adj* -a maziwa
mill *n* kinu
millennium *n* milenia
milligram *n* miligramu
millimeter *n* milimeta
million *n* milioni
millionaire *adj* milionea
mime *v* sanaa bubu
mince *v* saga
mincemeat *n* kima
mind *v* chunga
mind *n* akili
mindful *adj* -a tahadhari
mindless *adj* bila akili
mine *n* mgodi

M

mine v chimba

mine pro yangu

miner n mchimba mgodi

mineral n madini

mingle v changanyika

miniature n udogo

minimize v punguza

minimum n kiasi cha chini

miniskirt n mini

minister n waziri; mchungaji

minister v tumikia, hudumia

ministry n wizara

minor adj ndogo

minority n wachache

mint n mnanaa

mint v unda

minus adj toa

minute n dakika

miracle n muujiza

miraculous adj -a muujiza

mirage n mazingazi

mirror n kioo

misbehave v fanya utundu

miscalculate v kosea mahesabu

miscarriage n kuharibu mimba

miscarry v haribu mimba

mischief n utukutu, utundu

mischievous adj mtukutu, mtundu

misconduct n tabia mbaya

misconstrue v elewa vibaya

misdemeanor n kosa dogo

miser n bahili

miserable adj kukosa raha

misery n umaskini

misfit adj kaa vibaya

misfortune n bahati mbaya

misgivings n wasi, mashuku

misinterpret v elewa visivyo

misjudge v fikiri vibaya

mislead v ongoza vibaya

mismanage v endesha vibaya

misplace v poteza

misprint n mategu

miss v kosa; chelewa

miss n kukosa

missile n kombora

missing adj -sioonekana

mission n ujumbe, lengo

missionary n mmisionari

mist n ukungu

mistake iv kosea

mistake n kosa

mistaken adj -a makosa

mister n bwana

mistreat v tesa

mistreatment n mateso

M

mistress *n* kimada

mistrust *n* kutoamini

mistrust *v* tilia shaka

misty *adj* -enye ukungu

misunderstand *v* elewa vibaya

misuse *n* kutumia vibaya

mitigate *v* punguza, tuliza

mix *v* changanya

mixer *n* mchanganyaji

mixture *n* mchanganyiko

mix-up *n* utata

moan *v* pika kite

moan *n* kite

mob *v* songasonga

mob *n* kundi la ghasia

mobile *adj* -a kwenda

mobilize *v* hamasisha

mock *v* dhihakia, tania

mockery *n* dhihaki, utani

mode *n* namna, jinsi

model *n* aina

moderate *adj* punguza, tuliza

moderation *n* kiasi, wastani

modern *adj* -a kisasa

modest *adj* -siojivuna

modesty *n* staha

modify *v* badilisha

module *n* kipimo

moisten *v* lowesha

moisture *n* mvuke

molar *n* gego

mold *v* finyanga, subu

mold *n* kalibu; kuvu

moldy *adj* -enye kuvu

mole *n* fuko

molecule *n* molekuli

molest *v* baka, nyanyasa

mom *n* mama

moment *n* muda, kipindi

momentarily *adv* kipindi kifupi

momentous *adj* -a maana sana

monarch *n* mfalme

monarchy *n* ufalme

monastic *adj* -a utawa

Monday *n* Jumatatu

money *n* fedha, pesa

money order *n* hawala

monitor *v* fuatilia, simamia

monk *n* mtawa

monkey *n* kima, tumbili

monopoly *n* ukirithimba

monotonous *adj* -a kukinaisha

monotony *n* ukinaifu

monster *n* jitu, dubwana

monstrous *adj* -a kikatili

month *n* mwezi

monthly *adv* kwa mwezi

monumental *adj* -a ukumbusho

mood *n* hali

moody *adj* hali ya usununu

moon *n* mwezi

moor *v* tia nanga

mop *v* piga deki

moral *adj* adilifu, nyofu

moral *n* fundisho

morality *n* uadilifu

more *adj* zaidi

moreover *adv* zaidi ya hapo

morning *n* asubuhi

moron *adj* tahira

morphine *n* afyuni

morsel *n* kipande

mortal *adj* -enye kufa

mortality *n* kifo

mortar *n* kinu; chokaa

mortgage *n* rehani

mortification *n* udhalilishaji

mortify *v* dhalilisha

mosaic *n* mozaiki

mosque *n* msikiti

mosquito *n* mbu

moss *n* kuvumwani

most *adj* wengi wao

mostly *adv* kwa zaidi

motel *n* hoteli

moth *n* nondo

mother *n* mama

motherhood *n* umama

mother-in-law *n* mama mkwe

motion *n* mwendo

motionless *adj* simama

motivate *v* tia hamasa

motive *n* nia

motor *n* mota, injini

motorcycle *n* pikipiki

motto *n* wito

mouldy *adj* -enye kuvu

mount *n* mlima; kiunzi

mount *v* panda; weka

mountain *n* mlima

mountainous *adj* -enye milima

mourn *v* omboleza

mourning *n* maombolezo

mouse *n* panya

mouth *n* mdomo

move *n* kuhama, hatua

move *v* sogea, hama

move back *v* rudi nyuma

move forward *v* sogea mbele

move out *v* hama

move up *v* sogea mbele

movement *n* mwendo

M

movie *n* sinema
mow *v* fyeka
much *adv* sana
mucus *n* kamasi
mud *n* tope
muddle *n* vurugu
muddy *adj* -enye tope
muffle *v* fifisha
muffler *n* mafla
mug *v* pora
mugging *n* uporaji
mule *n* nyumbu
multiple *adj* nyingi
multiplication *n* kuzidisha
multiply *v* zidisha
multitude *n* idadi kubwa
mumble *v* nong'ona
mummy *n* mama
munch *v* tafuna
munitions *n* zana za vita
murder *n* mauaji
murderer *n* muuaji
murky *adj* -enye shaka
murmur *v* nong'ona
murmur *n* mnong'ono
muscle *n* msuli
mushroom *n* uyoga
music *n* musiki

M

musician *n* mwanamusiki
Muslim *adj* Mwislamu
must *iv* lazima
mustache *n* masharubu
mustard *n* haradali
muster *v* kusanya
mutate *v* badilika
mute *adj* bubu
mutilate *v* lemaza
mutiny *n* uashi
mutually *adv* kwa wote wawili
muzzle *v* zuia kusema
muzzle *n* pua na mdomo
my *adj* yangu
myself *pro* mimi
mysterious *adj* -a mwujiza
mystery *n* mwujiza
mystic *adj* -a mwujiza
mystify *v* tatanisha
myth *n* kisasili

N

nag *v* kefya, sumbua

nagging *adj* -a kukef-a

nail *n* kucha

naive *adj* wa asili

naked *adj* uchi

name *n* jina

namely *adv* haswa, yaani

nanny *n* yaya

nap *n* kusinzia

narrate *v* hadithia, eleza

narrow *adj* nyembamba

narrowly *adv* kwa kidogo

nasty *adj* mbaya

nation *n* taifa

national *adj* raia

nationality *n* uraia

nationalize *v* taifisha

native *adj* mzaliwa

natural *adj* -a asili

naturally *adv* kwa asili

nature *n* asili, mazingira

naughty *adj* mtundu

nausea *n* kichefuchefu

navel *n* kitovu

navigate *v* abiri

navigation *n* kuabiri

navy *n* uanamaji

navy blue *adj* baharia

near *pre* karibu na

nearby *adj* -a karibu

nearly *adv* karibia

nearsighted *adj* kutoona mbali

neat *adj* safi

neatly *adv* kwa usafi

necessary *adj* muhimu

necessitate *v* lazimu

necessity *n* ulazima

neck *n* shingo

necklace *n* mkufu

necktie *n* tai

need *v* hitaji

need *n* mahitaji, kuhitaji

needle *n* sindano

needless *adj* -sio hitajika

needy *adj* maskini

negative *adj* hasi

neglect *v* shindwa kujali

neglect *n* kutojali

negligence *n* uzembe

negligent *adj* mzembe

negotiate *v* jadiliana

negotiation *n* majadiliano

neighbor *n* jirani

N

neighborhood *n* ujirani

neither *adj* hakuna, wala

neither *adv* hata

nephew *n* mpwa

nerve *n* mshipa

nervous *adj* -a hofu

nest *n* kiota

net *n* wavu

Netherlands *n* Uholanzi

network *n* mtandao

neutralize *v* tangua, zimua

never *adv* kamwe

nevertheless *adv* hata hivyo

new *adj* mpya

newborn *n* mtoto mchanga

newcomer *n* mgeni

newly *adv* mpya

newlywed *adj* maharusi

news *n* habari

newsletter *n* jarida la habari

newspaper *n* gazeti

next *adj* alafu

next door *adj* -a jirani

nibble *v* mega kidogo

nice *adj* nzuri

nicely *adv* kwa uzuri

nickel *n* nikeli

nickname *n* jina la utani

nicotine *n* nikotini

niece *n* mpwa

night *n* usiku

nightmare *n* jinamizi

nine *adj* tisa

nineteen *adj* kumi na tisa

ninety *adj* tisini

ninth *adj* -a tisa

nip *n* mfinyo

nip *v* kata, finya

nipple *n* chuchu

nitrogen *n* nitrojeni

no one *pro* si mtu

nobility *n* uungwana

noble *adj* -a kiungwana

nobleman *adj* lodi

nobody *pro* sio mtu

nocturnal *adj* -a usiku

noise *n* kelele

noisily *adv* kwa kelele

noisy *adj* wa kelele

nominate *v* pendekeza

none *pre* hakuna, hata

nonetheless *c* hata hivyo

nonsense *n* upuuzi

nonstop *adv* bila kuacha

noon *n* adhuhuri

noose *n* kitanzi

N

nor *c* wala

norm *n* desturi, kanuni

normal *adj* kawaida

normalize *v* rudi kawaida

normally *adv* kwa kawaida

north *n* kaskazini

northern *adj* -a kaskazini

northerner *adj* wa kaskazini

Norway *n* Norway

Norwegian *adj* Mnorway

nose *n* pua

nostril *n* tundu la pua

nosy *adj* mdadisi

not *adv* sio mtu

notable *adj* -a kutambulika

notably *adv* hasa, hususan

notary *n* wakili

note *n* maelezo; noti

note *v* zingatia

notebook *n* daftari

nothing *n* bila

notice *v* ona, tazama

notice *n* taarifa

noticeable *adj* -a kuonekana

notification *n* taarifa

notify *v* toa taarifa

notion *n* wazo

notorious *adj* -a sifa mbaya

noun *n* nomino

nourish *v* lisha

nourishment *n* lishe

novel *n* riwaya

novelty *n* shani, upya

November *n* Novemba

novice *n* mwanafunzi

now *adv* sasa

nowadays *adv* siku hizi

nowhere *adv* si popote

noxious *adj* -a kudhuru

nozzle *n* nozeli

nuance *n* tofauti

nuclear *adj* -a nyuklia

nude *adj* uchi, utupu

nudism *n* kukaa uchi

nudist *n* mkaa uchi

nudity *n* uchi

nuisance *n* usumbufu

null *adj* batili

nullify *v* batilisha

numb *adj* -enye ganzi

number *n* tarakimu

numbness *n* Kurumbiza Ulaya

numerous *adj* kufa ganzi

nun *n* mtawa, sista

nurse *n* muuguzi, nesi

nurse *v* uguza

N

nursery n chekechea
nurture v lea, kuza
nut n tapo; nati
nutrition n lishe
nutritious adj -enye lishe
nut-shell n ganda; kokwa

O

oar n kasia
oasis n oasisi
oath n kiapo
oatmeal n oti
obedience n utiifu
obedient adj mtiifu
obese adj tipwatipwa
obey v tii
object v pinga
object n kitu
objection n upinzani
objective n lengo
obligate v lazimisha
obligatory adj -a lazima
oblige v lazimisha
obliged adj -a shukrani

obliterate v futa kabisa
oblivion n kusahauliwa
oblivious adj -sioelewa
oblong adj mstatili
obnoxious adj wa kuudhi
obscene adj chafu
obscenity n uchafu
obscure adj giza
obscurity n utusitusi
observation n uangalizi
observe v tazama
obsess v shikwa
obstacle n kizuizi
obstinacy n ukaidi, ubishi
obstinate adj mbishi
obstruct v zuia
obstruction n kizuizi
obtain v pata
obvious adj dhahiri, -liowazi
obviously adv ni dhahiri
occasion n nafasi, fursa
occult adj -a mizungu
occupant n mpangaji
occupation n kazi; ukaaji
occupy v ishi katika
occur v tokea
ocean n bahari
October n Octoba

octopus *n* pweza
ocurrence *n* tokeo
odd *adj* witiri
oddity *n* upekee, shani
odds *n* uwezekano
odious *adj* -a kuchukiza
odometer *n* -a maili
odor *n* harufu
odyssey *n* safari ndefu
of *pre* ya
off *adv* kutoka
offend *v* tusi
offense *n* kosa
offensive *adj* -a kuchukiza
offer *v* ahidi, toa
offer *n* zabuni
offering *n* sadaka
office *n* ofisi
officer *n* afisa
official *adj* -a serikali
officiate *v* simamia
offset *v* fidia
offspring *n* mtoto
off-the-record *adj* -sio rasmi
often *adv* mara kwa mara
oil *n* mafuta
ointment *n* malhamu
okay *adv* sawa

old *adj* mzee
old age *n* uzee
old-fashioned *adj* -a kizamani
olive *n* zaituni
omelette *n* kimanda
omen *n* ishara, dalili
ominous *adj* -a dalili mbaya
omission *n* kuacha
omit *v* acha, shindwa
on *pre* kwenye
once *adv* mara moja
once *c* mara
one *adj* moja
oneself *pre* binafsi
ongoing *adj* -a kuendelea
onion *n* kitunguu
onlooker *n* mtazamaji
only *adv* tu
onset *n* mwanzo
onslaught *n* shambulio
onwards *adv* na kuendelea
open *v* fungua
open *adj* wazi
open up *v* fungua
opening *n* nafasi
openness *n* uwazi
opera *n* opera
operate *v* endesha

O

operation *n* operesheni

opinion *n* oni, wazo

opinionated *adj* mkaidi

opium *n* afyuni

opponent *n* mpinzani

opportune *adj* -a kufaa

opportunity *n* nafasi, fursa

oppose *v* pinga

opposite *adj* -a mkabala

opposite *adv* kwa mkabala

opposite *n* mkabala

opposition *n* upinzani

oppress *v* gandamiza

oppression *n* ugandamizaji

opt for *v* chagua

optical *adj* -a macho

optician *n* fundi miwani

option *n* uchaguzi

optional *adj* -sio ya lazima

opulence *n* utajiri

or *c* au

oracle *n* uaguzi

orally *adv* kwa maneno

orange *n* chungwa

orbit *n* mzunguko

ordain *v* amuru

ordeal *n* msukosuko

order *n* amri, maagizo

ordinarily *adv* kwa kawaida

ordinary *adj* -a kawaida

ordination *n* kutawazwa

ore *n* madini

organ *n* kinanda

organism *n* kiumbe, mfumo

organist *n* mpiga kinanda

organization *n* taasisi

organize *v* panga

orient *n* mashariki

oriental *adj* -a mashariki

orientation *n* mwelekeo

oriented *adj* -lioelekea

origin *n* chimbuko, asili

original *adj* mwanzo

originally *adv* kwa asili

originate *v* tokea

ornament *n* pambo

ornamental *adj* -a kupamba

orphan *n* yatima

ostentatious *adj* wa kujivuna

ostrich *n* mbuni

other *adj* mwingine

otherwise *adv* vinginevyo

otter *n* fisi maji

ought to *iv* bidi

ounce *n* wakia

our *adj* yetu

ours *pro* zetu

ourselves *pro* sisi wenyewe

oust *v* pindua, toa

out *adv* nje

outbreak *n* kuzuka

outburst *n* mlipuko

outcast *adj* -liotengwa

outcome *n* matokeo

outcry *n* kilio

outdated *adj* -a zamani

outdo *v* zidi

outdoor *adv* wa nje

outdoors *adv* kwa nje

outer *adj* -a nje

outfit *n* vazi, patia vifaa

outgoing *adj* -changamfu

outgrow *v* acha

outing *n* ziara; matembezi

outlast *v* dumu kuliko

outlaw *v* kataza

outlet *n* mlango

outline *n* muhtasari

outline *v* eleza kwa kifupi

outlive *v* ishi kuliko

outlook *n* mtazamo

outmoded *adj* -a kizamani

outnumber *v* zidi wingi

outpouring *n* mbubujiko

output *n* uzalishaji

outrage *n* kitendo kiovu

outrageous *adj* -a kikatili

outright *adj* moja kwa moja

outrun *v* zidi mbio

outset *n* mwanzo

outshine *v* zidi umaridadi

outside *adv* nje

outsider *n* mtu wa nje

outskirts *n* kiunga

outstanding *adj* nzuri sana

outstretched *adj* -a kunyooshwa

outward *adj* mwelekeo

outweigh *v* zidi uzito

oval *adj* duara dufu

ovary *n* kifumba mbegu

ovation *n* makofi

oven *n* joko, tanuri

over *pre* juu

overall *adv* kwa ujumla

overboard *adv* kuzidisha

overcast *adj* ya mawingu

overcoat *n* koti kubwa

overcome *v* shinda

overdo *v* zidisha

overdone *adj* -a kuzidishwa

overdue *adj* -a kuchelewa

overflow *v* furika

O

overlap v pishana
overlook v kosa kuona
overpower v zidi nguvu
overrate v kisia kupita kiasi
override v puuza
overrule v batilisha
overrun v vamia
oversee v simamia
overshadow v zidi kwa haiba
oversight n kupitiwa
overstate v zidisha chumvi
overstep v vuka mpaka
overtake v pita, kuta
overthrow v pindua
overthrow n kupindua
overtime adv kazi ya ziada
overturn v pinduka; pindua
overview n muhtasari
overweight adj mnene
overwhelm v zidi nguvu
owe v daiwa
owl n bundi
own v miliki
own adj yangu
owner n mmilikaji
ownership n umilikaji
ox n fahali
oxen n ng'ombe maksai

oxygen n oksijeni
oyster n chaza

P

pace v tembea
pace n hatua
pacify v tuliza
pack v fungasha
package n kifurushi
pact n makubaliano
pad v jazia vitu laini
padding n vitu laini
paddle v piga makasia
padlock n kufuli
pagan adj mpagani
page n ukurasa
pail n ndoo
pain n maumivu
painful adj -a maumivu
painless adj bila maumivu
paint v piga rangi
paint n rangi
paintbrush n brashi ya rangi
painter n mpiga rangi

painting *n* kupiga rangi

pair *n* pea, jozi

pajamas *n* nguo za kulalia

pal *n* rafiki

palace *n* kasri

palate *n* kaakaa

pale *adj* -liokwajuka

paleness *n* kupauka

palm *n* kiganja

palpable *adj* -a kugusika

paltry *adj* -sio muhimu

pamper *v* bembeleza

pamphlet *n* kijarida

pan *n* sufuria

pancreas *n* kongosho

pander *v* endekeza

pang *n* maumivu

panic *n* hofu

panorama *n* mandhari yote

panther *n* chui mweusi

pantry *n* kabati ya chakula

pants *n* suruali; chupi

papacy *n* ofisi ya papa

paper *n* karatasi

paperwork *n* kazi ya ukarani

parable *n* hadithi ya kidini

parachute *n* parachuti

parade *n* gwaride

paradise *n* peponi

paragraph *n* aya

parakeet *n* kasuku

parallel *n* sambamba

paralysis *n* kupooza

paralyze *v* pooza

parameters *n* vipengele

paramount *adj* -a muhimu zaidi

parasite *n* kimelea

parcel *n* kifurushi

parcel post *n* posta ya mizigo

pardon *v* samehe

pardon *n* kusamehe

parenthesis *n* vifungo

parents *n* wazazi

parish *n* parokia

parishioner *n* paroko

parity *n* kiwango rasmi

park *v* egesha

park *n* mbuga, bustani

parking *n* maegesho

parliament *n* bunge

parochial *adj* -a parokia

parrot *n* kasuku

parsley *n* kotmiri

part *v* tenganisha

part *n* sehemu

partial *adj* -a sehemu

P

partially *adv* kwa kiasi

participate *v* shiriki

participation *n* kushiriki

particle *n* chembe

particular *adj* hasa

particularly *adv* maalumu hasa

parting *n* mgawanyiko

partisan *n* mfuasi

partition *n* mgawanyo

partly *adv* kwa sehemu

partner *n* mwenzi

partnership *n* ushirikiano

partridge *n* kwale

party *n* sherehe; chama

pass *n* kufaulu

pass *v* faulu, pita

pass around *v* pitisha

pass away *v* fariki

pass out *v* zimia

passage *n* njia, kupita

passenger *n* abiria

passer-by *n* mpita njia

passion *n* shauku, uchu

passive *adj* -a kutoonyesha hisia

passport *n* pasipoti

password *n* nywila

past *adj* -liopita

paste *v* gandisha

paste *n* gundi

pastime *n* burudani

pastor *n* mchungaji

pastry *n* kitobosha

pasture *n* malishoni

pat *n* kibonge

patch *v* weka kiraka

patch *n* kipande

patent *n* hakimiliki

patent *adj* -a wazi

paternity *n* ubaba

path *n* njia, ujia

pathetic *adj* -a kusikitisha

patience *n* subira

patient *adj* -enye subira

patio *n* baraza

patriot *n* mzalendo

patriotic *adj* -a kizalendo

patrol *n* doria

patron *n* mteja; mlezi

patronage *n* ulezi

patronize *v* dhalilisha

pattern *n* kielelezo

pawn *v* weka rehani

pawnbroker *n* mweka rehani

pay *n* mshahara

pay *iv* lipa

pay back *v* lipizia

pay off v lipa

payable adj -a kulipwa

paycheck n mshahara

payee n mlipwa

payment n malipo

pea n njegere

peace n amani

peaceful adj -a amani

peach n pichi

peacock n tausi

peak n kilele

peanut n karanga

pear n pera

pearl n lulu

peasant n mkulima

pebble n kokoto

peck v donoa

peck n kudonoa

peculiar adj -a ajabu

pedagogy n uelimishaji

pedal n pedeli

pedantic adj elimu ya vitabu

peel v menya

peel n maganda

peep v chungulia

peer n mwenzi, hirimu

pelican n mwari

pellet n marisawa

pen n kalamu ya wino

penalize v adhibu

penalty n adhabu

penance n toba

penchant n kupenda kitu

pencil n kalamu

pendant n kidani

pending adj -enye kusubiri

pendulum n penduli

penetrate v penya; ingilia

penicillin n penisilini

peninsula n rasi

penitent n mtu anayetubu

penniless adj bila senti

penny n senti, sarafu

pension n kiinua mgongo

pentagon n pembe tano

pent-up adj --liowekwa

people n watu

pepper n pili pili

per pre kwa

perceive v ona, gundua

percent adv kwa asilimia

percentage n asilimia

perception n mtazamo

perennial adj -a kudumu

perfect adj -sio na kasoro

perfection n ukamilifu

P

perforate *v* toboa

perforation *n* tundu

perform *v* cheza, tenda

performance *n* utendaji

perfume *n* manukato

perhaps *adv* labda

peril *n* hatari

perilous *adj* -a hatari

perimeter *n* mzingo

period *n* wakati, kipindi

perish *v* angamia

perishable *adj* -a kuharibika

permanent *adj* -a kudumu

permeate *v* penya katika

permission *n* idhini

permit *v* ruhusu

pernicious *adj* -a kudhuru

perpetrate *v* penya

persecute *v* sulubu

persevere *v* ng'ang'ania

persist *v* endelea

persistence *n* kung'ang'ania

persistent *adj* -a kuendelea

person *n* mtu

personal *adj* -a binafsi

personality *n* tabia, haiba

personify *v* kuwa mfano

personnel *n* wafanyakazi

perspective *n* mtazamo

perspiration *n* jasho

perspire *v* toka jasho

persuade *v* shawishi

persuasion *n* kushawishi

persuasive *adj* -a kushawishi

pertain *v* husu

pertinent *adj* -enye uhusiano

perturb *v* tia wasiwasi

perverse *adj* kaidi

pervert *v* potosha

pervert *adj* anaye potosha

pest *n* mdudu mharibifu

pester *v* sumbua

petal *n* petali

petite *adj* ndogo

petition *n* ombi

petrified *adj* -lioganda

petroleum *n* petroli

pettiness *n* uduni

petty *adj* duni

pew *n* benchi

phantom *n* shetani

pharmacist *n* mkemia

pharmacy *n* duka la dawa

phase *n* hatua

pheasant *n* kwale

phenomenon *n* tukio

philosopher *n* mwana falsafa

philosophy *n* falsafa

phobia *n* hofu

phone *n* simu

phone *v* piga simu

phoney *adj* bandia

phosphorus *n* fosforasi

photo *n* picha

photocopy *n* nakala kivuli

photograph *v* piga picha

photographer *n* mpiga picha

photography *n* upigaji picha

phrase *n* hukumu

physically *adj* kimwili

physician *n* daktari

physics *n* fizikia

pianist *n* mpiga piano

piano *n* piano

pick *v* okota

pick up *v* okota

pickup *n* pikapu

picture *n* picha

picture *v* fikiria, sawiri

picturesque *adj* -a kupendeza

pie *n* pai

piece *n* kipande

piecemeal *adv* kidogo kidogo

pier *n* gati

pierce *v* toboa

piercing *n* kutoboa

piety *n* ucha Mungu

pig *n* nguruwe

pigeon *n* njiwa

pile *v* rundika

pile *n* lundo

pile up *v* rundika

pilfer *v* iba kidogo

pilgrim *n* haji, hujaji

pilgrimage *n* hija

pill *n* kidonge

pillage *v* pora

pillar *n* nguzo, mhimili

pillow *n* mto

pillowcase *n* foronya

pilot *n* rubani

pimple *n* chunusi

pin *n* pini

pincers *n* koleo

pinch *v* finya

pinch *n* mfinyo

pine *n* msindano

pineapple *n* nanasi

pink *adj* waridi

pinpoint *v* onyesha

pint *n* painti

pioneer *n* mwasisi

P

pious *adj* tiifu

pipe *n* bomba

piracy *n* uharamia

pirate *n* haramia

pistol *n* bastola

pit *n* shimo

pitch-black *adj* nyeusi ti

pitiful *adj* -a kusikitisha

pity *n* huruma

placard *n* kabati

placate *v* tuliza

place *n* weka

placid *adj* mpole, tulivu

plague *n* tauni

plain *n* uwanda

plain *adj* -a kawaida

plainly *adv* waziwazi

plaintiff *n* mdai

plan *v* panga

plan *n* mpango

plane *n* ndege; hatua

planet *n* sayari

plant *v* otesha

plant *n* mmea

plaster *n* lipu

plaster *v* piga lipu

plastic *n* plastiki

plate *n* sahani

plateau *n* uwanda wa juu

platform *n* jukwaa

platinum *n* platinamu

plausible *adj* -a kueleweka

play *v* cheza

play *n* mchezo

player *n* wachezaji

playful *adj* changamfu

plea *n* ombi

plead *v* omba, sihi

pleasant *adj* -a kufurahisha

please *v* furahisha

pleasing *adj* -a kufurahisha

pleasure *n* furaha

pleat *n* rinda

pleated *adj* -enye marinda

pledge *v* ahidi; kula kiapo

pledge *n* ahadi; kiapo

plentiful *adj* -a wingi

plenty *n* nyingi

pliers *n* koleo

plot *v* kula njama

plot *n* njama

plow *v* lima kwa plau

ploy *n* hila

pluck *v* nyonyoa, donoa

plug *v* ziba

plug *n* kizibo

plum *n* plamu

plumber *n* fundi bomba

plummet *v* chubwi

plump *adj* nene

plunder *v* pora

plunge *v* tumbukiza

plunge *n* kujitosa, mbizi

plural *n* wingi

plus *adv* ongez

plush *adj* -a anasa

plutonium *n* plutoniamu

pneumonia *n* nimonia

pocket *n* mfuko

poem *n* shairi

poet *n* mshairi

poetry *n* ushairi

point *n* nukta; ncha

point *v* onyesha

pointed *adj* chongeka

pointless *adj* -sio na maana

poise *n* utulivu

poison *v* tia sumu

poison *n* sumu

poisonous *adj* -enye sumu

Poland *n* Poland

pole *n* nguzo

police *n* polisi

policeman *n* askari

policy *n* sera

Polish *adj* Kipolishi

polish *n* polishi

polish *v* piga polishi

polite *adj* mpole

politeness *n* adabu, murua

politician *n* mwanasiasa

politics *n* siasa

poll *n* kura

pollen *n* chavua

pollute *v* chafua

pollution *n* uchafuzi

pomegranate *n* komamanga

pomposity *n* majivuno

pond *n* bwawa

ponder *v* fikiri, tafakari

pontiff *n* askofu

pool *n* bwawa

pool *v* changa

poor *n* maskini

poorly *adv* kwa umaskini

popcorn *n* bisi

Pope *n* Papa

poppy *n* mpopi

populate *v* jaza watu

population *n* idadi ya watu

porcelain *n* kauri

porch *n* baraza**

P

porcupine *n* nungunungu

pore *n* unyeleo

pork *n* nguruwe

porous *adj* nywelevu

port *n* bandari

portable *adj* -a kubebeka

portent *n* ishara

porter *n* mchukuzi

portion *n* kipande

portrait *n* taswira

portray *v* toa taswira

Portugal *n* Ureno

Portuguese *adj* Mreno

pose *v* kaa mkao

posh *adj* -a kifahari

position *n* namna, nafasi

positive *adj* -a hakika

possess *v* miliki; pagawa

possession *n* umiliki; mali

possibility *n* uwezekano

possible *adj* yamkini

post *n* kitengo, nguzo

post office *n* posta

postage *n* stempu

postcard *n* posti-kadi

poster *n* bango

postman *n* msabazaji barua

postmark *n* mhuri wa posta

postpone *v* ahirisha

postponement *n* kuahirisha

pot *n* sufuria, chungu

potato *n* kiazi

potent *adj* -enye nguvu

potential *adj* -enye uwezekano

pothole *n* shimo

poultry *n* ufugaji wa ndege

pound *v* ponda, twanga

pound *n* ratili; zizi

pour *v* mimina

poverty *n* umaskini

powder *n* unga

power *n* nguvu; uwezo

powerful *adj* -enye nguvu

powerless *adj* dhaifu

practical *adj* -a kimatendo

practise *v* fanya mazoezi

practice *n* mazoezi; desturi

pragmatist *adj* myakinifu

prairie *n* mbuga

praise *v* sifu, pongeza

praise *n* sifa, pongezi

praiseworthy *adj* -a kusifika

prank *n* shere

prawn *n* kamba

pray *v* omba

prayer *n* maombi

preach v hubiri

preacher n mhubiri

preaching n kuhubiri

preamble n utangulizi

precarious adj -a mashaka

precaution n tahadhari

precede v tangulia

precedent n nondo

preceding adj -liotangulia

precept n agizo, fundisho

precious adj -a thamani

precipice n jabali

precipitate v harakisha

precise adj sahihi, hasa

precision n usahihi

precocious adj kiparamoto

precursor n ishara, dalili

predecessor n mtangulizi

predicament n hali ngumu

predict v tabiri, bashiri

prediction n utabiri

predilection n upendo

predominate v tawala

preempt v tangulia kufanya

preface n dibaji, utangulizi

prefer v pendelea

preference n upendeleo

prefix n kiambishi

pregnancy n ujauzito

pregnant adj mjamzito

preliminary adj -a awali

prelude n mwanzo

premature adj mapema mno

premeditate v dhamiria

premeditation n kudhamiria

premier adj -a kwanza

premise n dhana, tarajio

premises n maeneo

premonition n hisia

preoccupation n kushughulika

preoccupy v shughulisha

preparation n matayarisho

prepare v tayarisha

preposition n kihusishi

prerequisite n sharti

prerogative n haki, heshima

prescribe v agiza, amuru

prescription n agizo

presence n kuhudhuria

present adj -liokuwepo

present v toa, wasilisha

presentation n kukabidhi

preserve v hifadhi

preside v ongoza

presidency n uraisi

president n raisi

P

press *n* uhakiki
press *v* gandamiza
pressing *adj* -a haraka
pressure *v* weka shinikizo
pressure *n* shinikizo
prestige *n* hadhi
presume *v* dhani
presumption *n* dhana
presuppose *v* dhani
presupposition *n* dhana
pretend *v* jidai, jifanya
pretense *n* kujidai
pretension *n* ushaufu
pretty *adj* nzuri
prevail *v* tawala; shinda
prevalent *adj* -lioenea
prevent *v* zuia, kataza
prevention *n* kinga
preventive *adj* -a kukinga
preview *n* onyesha la awali
previous *adj* -a awali
previously *adv* kabla, awali
prey *n* windo
price *n* bei
pricey *adj* -enye bei
prick *v* choma
pride *n* majivuno; fahari
priest *n* padri, kasisi

priesthood *n* upadri
primacy *n* ukubwa; ubora
primarily *adv* haswa; kwanza
prime *adj* -a kwanza
primitive *adj* -a kizamani
principal *adj* mkuu
principle *n* kanuni; maadili
print *v* chapisha
printing *n* kuchapisha
prior *adj* kabla
priority *n* kipaumbele
prism *n* mche
prison *n* gereza, jela
prisoner *n* mfungwa
privacy *n* faragha
private *adj* -a binafsi
privilege *n* haki; upendeleo
prize *n* tunzo, zawadi
probability *n* uwezekano
probable *adj* -a kuwezekana
probe *v* chunguza
probing *n* kuchunguza
problem *n* tatizo
problematic *adj* -enye matatizo
procedure *n* utaratibu
proceed *v* endelea
proceedings *n* mashtaka
proceeds *n* mapato**

P

process *v* shughulikia
process *n* mfuatano
procession *n* maandamano
proclaim *v* tangaza, tamka
proclamation *n* tangazo
procrastinate *v* ahiri, chelewa
procreate *v* zaa, zaliana
procure *v* pata, nunua
prod *v* choma, chokoa
prodigious *adj* nyingi sana
prodigy *n* uweza wa ajabu
produce *v* zalisha
produce *n* mazao, bidhaa
product *n* bidhaa
production *n* uzalishaji
profane *adj* -a kufuru
profess *v* toa kauli
profession *n* kazi, shughuli
professional *adj* -a kikazi
professor *n* mwalimu
proficiency *n* utaalamu
profile *n* muhtasari
profit *v* nufaisha
profit *n* manufaa, faida
profitable *adj* -enye faida
profound *adj* -a kina, nzito
program *n* ratiba; programu
progress *v* endelea

progress *n* maendeleo
prohibit *v* zuia
prohibition *n* uzuizi
project *v* onyesha
project *n* mradi
prologue *n* dibaji
prolong *v* refusha, zidisha
prominent *adj* muhimu
promiscuous *adj* fasiki
promise *n* ahadi
promote *v* endeleza
promotion *n* kuendeleza
prompt *adj* himiza; uliza
prone *adj* kufudifudi
pronoun *n* kiwakilishi nomino
pronounce *v* tamka
proof *n* uthibitisho
propaganda *n* propaganda
propagate *v* eneza; zaliana
propel *v* endesha
propensity *n* hulka, tabia
proper *adj* hasa, barabara
properly *adv* sawasawa
property *n* mali, bidhaa
prophecy *n* ubashiri
prophet *n* mtume, nabii
proportion *n* uwiano
proposal *n* pendekezo

propose v pendekeza
proposition n pendekezo
prose n insha, nathari
prosecute v shtaki
prospect n matumaini
prosper v fanikiwa
prosperity n fanaka
prosperous adj -enye fanaka
prostate n tezi
prostrate adj -a kifudifudi
protect v linda
protection n uzinzi
protein n protini
protest v pinga
protest n kupinga
protocol n itifaki
prototype n mfano
protract v refusha
protracted adj -a muda mrefu
protrude v chomoza
proud adj -a kujivuna
proudly adv kwa kujivuna
prove v thibitisha
proven adj -liothibitishwa
proverb n methali
provide v patia
providence n Mungu
providing that c iwapo kama

province n jimbo
provision n sharti; utoaji
provisional adj -a muda
provocation n ufukufuku
provoke v ghadhabisha
prow n gubeti
proximity n ukaribu
proxy n wakala
prudence n uangalifu
prudent adj mwangalifu
prune v punguza
prune n plamu kavu
prurient adj asherati
pseudonym n jina la bandia
psychic adj -a utabiri
psychology n saikolojia
puberty n balehe
public adj -a umma
publication n chapisho
publicity n utangazaji
publicly adv hadharani
publish v chapisha
publisher n mchapishaji
pudding n kitindamlo
puerile adj ya kitoto
puff n pumzi
puffed adj -enye kukosa pumzi
pull v vuta

P

pull ahead *v* nenda mbele
pull down *v* bomoa
pull out *v* toka
pulley *n* kapi
pulp *n* nyama ya tunda
pulpit *n* madhabahu
pulsate *v* dunda, pwita
pulse *n* pigo la moyo
pulverize *v* saga
pump *v* jaza upepo
pump *n* pampu
pumpkin *n* boga
punch *v* pinga ngumi
punch *n* ngumi
punctual *adj* wakati upasao
puncture *n* toboa
punish *v* adhibu
punishable *adj* -a kuadhibiwa
punishment *n* adhabu
pupil *n* mwanafunzi
puppet *n* karagosi
puppy *n* kitoto cha mbwa
purchase *v* nunua
purchase *n* ununuzi
pure *adj* halisi
puree *n* rojo
purgatory *n* tohara
purge *n* kutakasa

purge *v* takasa, safisha
purification *n* utakaso
purify *v* takasa, safisha
purity *n* utakatifu, usafi
purple *adj* zambarau
purpose *n* makusudi
purposely *adv* kwa makusudi
purse *n* pochi
pursue *v* fuatilia
pursuit *n* kufuatilia
pus *n* usaha
push *v* sukuma
pushy *adj* -a kulazimisha
put *iv* weka
put aside *v* weka pembeni
put away *v* hifadhi, rudisha
put off *v* ahirisha
put out *v* sumbuliwa
put up *v* tundika, weka
put up with *v* vumilia
putrid *adj* -liooza
puzzle *n* chemshabongo
puzzling *adj* ya kitendawili
pyramid *n* haram
python *n* chatu

P

Q

quagmire *n* kinamasi
quail *n* tombo
quake *v* tetemeka
qualify *v* stahili
quality *n* ubora, sifa
qualm *n* mashaka
quandary *n* shaka
quantity *n* kiasi
quarrel *v* gombana
quarrel *n* ugomvi
quarrelsome *adj* mgomvi
quarry *n* mgodi
quarter *n* robo
quarterly *adj* -a miezi mitatu
quarters *n* malazi
quash *v* tangua; batilisha
queen *n* malikia
queer *adj* -a kibasha
quell *v* zima, komesha
quench *v* tosheleza; zima
quest *n* kutafuta
question *v* hoji, uliza
question *n* swali
questionable *adj* -a kushuku
questionnaire *n* hojaji

queue *n* mstari
quick *adj* haraka
quicken *v* harakisha
quickly *adv* kwa haraka
quicksand *n* mchanga didimizi
quiet *adj* kimya
quietness *n* ukimya
quilt *n* mfarishi
quit *iv* acha, ondoka
quite *adv* hasa, kabisa
quiver *v* tetemeka
quiz *v* fumbu
quotation *n* dondoo; kadirio
quote *v* dondoa; kadiria
quotient *n* hisa

R

rabbi *n* rabbi
rabbit *n* sungura
rabies *n* kichaa cha mbwa
race *v* shindana mbio
racism *n* ubaguzi wa rangi
racist *adj* mbaguzi wa rangi
racket *n* raketi

radar *n* rada

radiation *n* mnururisho

radiator *n* rejeta

radical *adj* wa siasa kali

radio *n* redio

radish *n* figili

radius *n* nusu kipenyo

raffle *n* bahati nasibu

raft *n* boya

rag *n* tambara

rage *n* hasira

ragged *adj* -liotatuka

raid *n* uvamizi

raid *v* shambulia

raider *n* mshabulizi

rail *n* reli

railroad *n* njia ya reli

rain *n* mvua

rain *v* nyesha

rainbow *n* upinde wa mvua

raincoat *n* koti la mvua

rainfall *n* mvua

rainy *adj* -a mvua

raise *n* mwinuko

raise *v* inua, ongeza

raisin *n* zabibu

rake *n* reki

rally *n* mkusanyiko

ram *n* kondoo dume

ram *v* gonga; lazimisha

ramification *n* matokeo

ramp *n* tuta, pa kushukia

rampage *v* fanya ghasia

rampant *adj* enea, wima

ranch *n* shamba la mifugo

rancor *n* kinyongo

randomly *adv* kwa mafamba

range *n* anuwai; masafa

rank *n* cheo, hadhi

rank *v* weka

ransack *v* pekua

ransom *v* koboa kwa fidia

ransom *n* fidia, malipo

rape *v* najisi, baka

rape *n* kubaka, kunajisi

rapid *adj* haraka

rapist *n* mbakaji

rapport *n* uhusiano

rare *adj* -a nadra

rarely *adv* kwa nadra

rascal *n* tapeli

rash *v* haraka ya pupa

rash *n* pupa; ukurutu

rat *n* panya

rate *n* kiasi, kima

rather *adv* nafuu, heri

R

ratification n kuidhinishwa
ratify v idhinisha
ratio n uwiano
ration v gawa
ration n mgao
rational adj -a uwiano
rationalize v tumia busara
rattle v bwabwaja
ravage v teketeza
ravage n uharibifu
raven n kunguru
ravine n korongo
raw adj mbichi
ray n mwonzi
raze v teketeza
razor n wembe
reach v fikia
reach n upeo; mwendeleo
react v jibu, itika
reaction n jibu, itiko
read iv soma
reader n msomaji
readiness n kuwa tayari
reading n kusoma
ready adj tayari
real adj -a kweli, halisi
realism n ukweli wa
reality n hali halisi

realize v fanikisha
really adv kweli
realm n ufalme
realty n ukweli
reap v vuna
reappear v tokezea tena
rear v fuga, lea
rear n nyuma, matako
rear adj -a nyuma
reason v fikiria, toa hoja
reason n kufikiri; sababu
reasonable adj -enye mantiki
reasoning n hoja
reassure v tuliza
rebate n punguzo
rebel v asi
rebel n mwasi
rebellion n maasi
rebirth n kuzaliwa upya
rebound v dunda
rebuff v kataa
rebuff n kukataa
rebuild v jenga tena
rebuke v gombeza
rebuke n kugombeza
rebut v kanusha, pinga
recall v rudisha, ita
recant v ruka, kataa

R

recap *v* toa muhtasari

recapture *v* kamata tena

recede *v* rudi nyuma

receipt *n* upokezi; risiti

receive *v* pokea

recent *adj* -a karibuni

reception *n* mapokezi; dhifa

receptive *adj* msikivu

recess *n* mapunziko

recharge *v* chaji tena

recipe *n* njia ya

reciprocal *adj* -a kutendeana

recital *n* kughani

recite *v* ghani

reckless *adj* -siomwangalifu

reckon *v* fikiri, hesabu

reckon on *v* tarajia

reclaim *v* dai tena

recline *v* egemea nyuma

recluse *n* mpweke

recognition *n* kutambua

recognize *v* tambua

recollect *v* kumbuka

recollection *n* kumbukumbu

recommend *v* pendekeza

recompense *v* fidia, lipa

recompense *n* malipo, fidia

reconcile *v* suluhisha

reconsider *v* fikiria tena

reconstruct *v* jenga tena

record *v* andika, onyesha

record *n* santuri

recorder *n* kinasa sauti

recording *n* kunasa sauti

recount *n* kuhesabu upya

recoup *v* fidia, lipa

recourse *v* tafua kimbilio

recourse *n* kimbilio

recover *v* pona

recovery *n* kupona

recreate *v* buni upya

recreation *n* burudani

recruit *v* ajiri; jiunga

recruit *n* askari mpya

recruitment *n* kujiunga

rectangle *n* mstatili

rectangular *adj* -a mstatili

rectify *v* sahihisha

rector *n* kasisi

rectum *n* puru, mkundu

recuperate *v* pata nafuu,

recur *v* tokea tena

recurrence *n* kurudia

recycle *v* tumia tena

red *adj* nyekundu

red tape *n* urasimu

R

redden v kuwa mwekundu
redeem v komboa
redemption n ukombozi
red-hot adj moto sana
redo v fanya tena
redouble v ongeza mara mbili
redress v sawadhisha, tibu
reduce v punguza
redundant adj -a ziada
reed n tete
reef n mwamba
reel n kibiringo
reelect v changua tena
reentry n kuingia tena
refer to v rejea kwenye
referee n mwamuzi
reference n marejeo
referendum n kura ya maoni
refill v jaza tena
refine v safisha
reflect v akisi
reflection n kuakisi
reflexive adj rejeshi
reform v rekebisha
reform n mabadiliko
refrain v jizuia
refresh v burudisha
refreshing adj -a kuburudisha

refreshment n viburudisho
refuel v jaza mafuta tena
refuge n kimbilio, hifadhi
refugee n mkimbizi
refund v lipa fidia
refund n fidia
refurbish v karabati
refusal n ukataaji
refuse v kataa
refuse n takataka
refute v kanusha, pinga
regain v pata tena
regal adj -a kifalme
regard v sharifu
regarding pre mintarafu
regardless adv bila kujali
regards n salaam
regent n mfalme
regime n siasa
regiment n kikosi
region n mkoa
regional adj -a mkoa
register v sajili
registration n usajili
regret v sikitika
regret n kusikitika
regrettable adj -a kusikitisha
regularity n tora

R

regularly *adv* mara kwa mara
regulate *v* rekebisha
regulation *n* kanuni
rehabilitate *v* karabati, fufua
rehearsal *n* zoezi
rehearse *v* fanya mazoezi
reign *v* tawala
reign *n* utawala
reimburse *v* fidia
reimbursement *n* kufidia
rein *v* dhibiti
rein *n* hatamu
reindeer *n* paa
reinforce *v* imarisha
reiterate *v* rudia
reject *v* kataa
rejection *n* kano
rejoice *v* furahia
rejoin *v* jiunge tena
rejuvenate *v* pata nguvu upya
relapse *n* kurudiwa
related *adj* husiana
relationship *n* uhusiano
relative *adj* -a undugu
relative *n* ndugu, jamaa
relax *v* jipumzisha
relax *n* pumzika
relaxing *adj* kupumzika

relay *v* tangaza
release *v* achia
relegate *v* agiza
relent *v* kubali
relentless *adj* -a kuendelea
relevant *adj* husika
reliable *adj* -a kuaminika
reliance *n* kutegemea
relic *n* masaa
relief *n* unafuu
relieve *v* saidia, pokea
religion *n* dini
religious *adj* -a dini
relinquish *v* achia
relish *v* furahia
relive *v* kumbukia
relocate *v* hama
relocation *n* kuhama
reluctant *adj* -a kusita
reluctantly *adv* kwa kusita
rely on *v* tegemea
remain *v* baki
remainder *n* salio
remaining *adj* -liobaki
remains *n* baki; uvumbi
remake *v* tengeneza tena
remark *v* nena, toa kauli
remark *n* neno, kauli

R

remarkable _adj_ -a ajabu

remarry _v_ oa tena

remedy _v_ sahihisha

remedy _n_ dawa, tiba

remember _v_ kumbuka

remembrance _n_ ukumbusho

remind _v_ kumbusha

reminder _n_ kumbusho

remission _n_ msamaha; ahueni

remit _v_ rudisha, lipa

remittance _n_ malipo

remnant _n_ baki, salio

remodel _v_ jenga upya

remorse _n_ majuto

remorseful _adj_ -enye na majuto

remote _adj_ -a mbali

removal _n_ kutoa

remove _v_ ondoa; fukuza

remunerate _v_ lipa fidia

renew _v_ karabati

renewal _n_ uanzishaji upya

renounce _v_ jitoa, kata tamaa

renovate _v_ karabati

renovation _n_ ukarabati

renowned _adj_ maarufu

rent _v_ kodisha

rent _n_ kodi

reorganize _v_ panga upya

repair _v_ karabati

reparation _n_ ukarabati

repatriate _v_ rejesha kwao

repay _v_ lipa

repayment _n_ malipo

repeal _v_ batilisha

repeal _n_ kutengua

repeat _v_ rudia

repel _v_ chukizwa

repent _v_ tubu

repentance _n_ kutubu

repetition _n_ kurudia

replace _v_ badilisha

replacement _n_ ubadilishaji

replay _n_ marudio

replenish _v_ jaza tena

replete _adj_ -enye kutosheka

replica _n_ nakala

replicate _v_ rudufu

reply _v_ jibu

reply _n_ jibu

report _v_ toa taarifa

report _n_ taarifa

repose _v_ pumzika

repose _n_ utulivu

represent _v_ wakilisha

repress _v_ komesha, zuia

repression _n_ uzuiaji

reprieve n msamaha
reprint v chapisha tena
reprint n kuchapisha tena
reprisal n kisasi
reproach v laumu
reproach n lawama
reproduce v toa upya
reproduction n nakala
reptile n reptilia
republic n jamhuri
repudiate v kana, kataa
repugnant adj -a maudhi
repulse v nyanyapaa
repulse n kuchukiza
repulsive adj -a kuchukiza
reputation n umaarufu
reputedly adv kwa kusemekana
request v omba
request n ombi
require v hitaji
requirement n hitaji
rescue v okoa
rescue n kuokoa
research v tafuta, chunguza
research n utafiti, uchunguzi
resemblance n kufanana
resemble v fanana
resent v chukia

resentment n chuki
reservation n hifadhi
reserve v tenga; hifadhi
reservoir n hodhi, bwawa
reside v kaa, ishi
residence n makazi
residue n mabaki, masalio
resign v jiuzulu
resignation n kujiuzulu
resilient adj imara
resist v pinga, kataa
resistance n upinzani
resolution n azimio
resolve v amua
resort v tegemea, ishia
resounding adj -enye kuvuma
resource n rasilimali; uwezo
respect v heshimu
respect n heshima
respectful adj jamhuri
respiration n pumzi
respite n nafuu
respond v jibu
response n jibu
responsibility n jukumu
rest v pumzika
rest n mapumziko
rest room n msalani

R

restaurant *n* hoteli
restful *adj* -a utulivu
restitution *n* fidia
restless *adj* -siotulia
restoration *n* kurudisha
restore *v* rudishia
restrain *v* zuia
restraint *n* uvumilivu
restrict *v* bana uhuru wa
result *n* matokeo
resume *v* anza tena
resumption *n* kuanza tena
resurface *v* zuka tena
resurrection *n* ufufuo
resuscitate *v* fufua
retain *v* zuia
retaliate *v* rudishia
retaliation *n* ulipizi
retarded *adj* taahira
retention *n* kushikilia
retire *v* staafu
retirement *n* kustaafu
retract *v* tangua, futa
retreat *v* rudi nyuma
retreat *n* kimbilio
retrieval *n* kupata tena
retrieve *v* ita, pata tena
return *v* rudi

return *n* kurudi
reunion *n* muungano
reveal *v* fichua, gundua
revealing *adj* -enye kufichua
revel *v* furahia
revelation *n* ufunuo
revenge *v* lipizia kisasi
revenge *n* kisasi
revenue *n* mapato
reverence *n* uchaji, heshima
reversal *n* utanguzi
reverse *n* kutangua
reversible *adj* -enye kupindulika
revert *v* rudia
review *v* pitia, hakiki
review *n* uhakiki, mapitio
revive *v* fufua
revoke *v* fusahi
revolt *v* asi
revolt *n* uasi
revolve *v* zunguka
revolver *n* bastola
revue *n* onyesho
revulsion *n* chuki kubwa
reward *v* zawadia, lipa
reward *n* zawadi, tuzo
rewarding *adj* -enye malipo
rheumatism *n* baridi yabisi

rhinoceros *n* kifaru

rhyme *n* kina

rhythm *n* mahadhi

rib *n* ubavu

ribbon *n* utepe

rice *n* mchele; wali

rich *adj* tajiri

rid of *iv* ondokana

riddle *n* kitendawili

ride *iv* panda, endesha

ridicule *v* cheka

ridicule *n* kucheka

ridiculous *adj* -a kipuuzi

rifle *n* bunduki

rift *n* ufa, mpasuko

right *adv* sawa, vema

right *adj* sahihi, sawa

right *n* kulia

rigid *adj* gumu, imara

rigor *n* msimamo

rim *n* ukingo; rimu

ring *iv* piga kengele, ita

ring *n* pete, mzunguko

rinse *v* suuza

riot *v* fanya fujo

riot *n* fujo, ghasia

rip *v* chana

rip apart *v* pasua

rip off *v* ibia, tapeli

ripe *adj* iva, komaa

ripen *v* kukomaa, kuiva

ripple *n* kiwimbi

rise *iv* simama, inuka

risk *v* hatarisha

risk *n* hatari

risky *adj* -a hatari

rite *n* kaida

rival *n* mpinzani

rivalry *n* ushindano

river *n* mto

rivet *v* piga ribiti

riveting *adj* -a kuvutia

road *n* barabara

roam *v* zurura

roar *v* nguruma

roar *n* ngurumo

roast *v* oka, banika

roast *n* nyama ya kuoka

rob *v* iba, ibia

robber *n* mwizi

robbery *n* uwizi

robe *n* gauni

robust *adj* -enye nguvu

rock *n* jiwe

rocket *n* kombora, roketi

R

rocky *adj* penye miamba
rod *n* fimbo, ufito
rodent *n* panya
roll *v* viringisha
romance *n* mahaba
roof *n* paa
room *n* chumba
roomy *adj* penye nafasi
rooster *n* jogoo, kikwara
root *n* mzizi
rope *n* kamba
rosary *n* tasbihi, rosari
rose *n* waridi
rot *v* oza
rot *n* uozo, uoza
rotate *v* zungusha
rotation *n* mzunguko
rotten *adj* bovu, viza
rough *adj* -a shida
round *adj* -a duara
roundup *n* kukusanya
rouse *v* amsha
rousing *adj* kuamsha
route *n* njia
routine *n* utaratibu
row *v* vuta masika
row *n* mstari
rowdy *adj* -enye kelele

R

royal *adj* -a kifalme
royalty *n* ukoo wa mfalme
rub *v* sugua
rubber *n* mpira; kifutio
rubbish *n* takataka
rubble *n* vifusi, kokoto
ruby *n* yakuti
rudder *n* usukani
rude *adj* fidhuli
rudeness *n* ufidhuli
rudimentary *adj* -a msingi
rug *n* jambi
ruin *v* haribu; angamiza
ruin *n* mabaki; kufilisika
rule *v* tawala
rule *n* sheria, kanuni
ruler *n* mtawala
rum *n* pombe ya rum
rumble *v* nguruma
rumble *n* mgurumo
rumor *n* uvumi, tetesi
run *iv* kimbia
run away *v* toroka
run into *v* kutana na
run out *v* ishiwa
run over *v* kanyaga, gonga
run up *v* panda
runner *n* mkimbiaji

rupture *n* kupasuka
rupture *v* pasuka
rural *adj* -a shamba
ruse *n* ujanja, hila
rush *v* harakisha
Russia *n* Urusi
Russian *adj* Mrusi
rust *v* Ingia kutu
rust *n* kutu
rustic *adj* -a kishamba,
rust-proof *adj* -sio pata kutu
rusty *adj* -enye kutu
ruthless *adj* katili
rye *n* ngano nyekundu

S

sabotage *v* hujumu
sabotage *n* hujuma
sack *v* fukuza kazi
sack *n* mfuko
sacrament *n* sakramenti
sacred *adj* takatifu
sacrifice *n* sadaka
sacrilege *n* kufuru

sad *adj* huzuni
sadden *v* huzunisha
saddle *n* saruji
sadist *n* mkatili
sadness *n* huzuni
safe *adj* salama
safeguard *n* linda
safety *n* usalama
sail *v* tweka
sail *n* tanga
sailor *n* baharia
saint *n* mtakatifu
salad *n* kachumbari
salary *n* mshahara
sale *n* mauzo, uuzaji
sale slip *n* stakabadhi
salesman *n* muuzaji
saliva *n* mate
saloon *n* ukumbi
salt *n* chumvi
salty *adj* -a chumvi
salvage *v* okoa
salvation *n* kuokoka
same *adj* ile ile; sawa
sample *n* sampuli
sanctify *v* fanya takatifu
sanction *v* idhinisha
sanction *n* idhini

R
S

sanctity *n* utakatifu

sanctuary *n* kimbilio

sand *n* mchanga

sandal *n* kubadhi

sandpaper *n* msasa

sandwich *n* sandwichi

sane *adj* timamu

sanity *n* akili timamu

sap *n* utomvu

sap *v* dhoofisha

saphire *n* yakuti

sarcasm *n* kejeli

sarcastic *adj* -enye kukejeli

sardine *n* dagaa

satanic *adj* -a kishetani

satellite *n* satelaiti, mwezi

satire *n* tashtiti

satisfaction *n* kuridhika

satisfactory *adj* -a kuridhisha

satisfy *v* ridhisha

saturate *v* kifu

Saturday *n* Jumamosi

sauce *n* mchuzi

saucepan *n* sufuria

saucer *n* kisosi

sausage *n* soseji

savage *adj* mshenzi

savagery *n* ukatili; ukali

save *v* okoa

save *v* weka akiba

savings *n* akiba

savior *n* mwokozi

savor *v* ona raha ya

saw *iv* piga msumeno

saw *n* msumeno

say *iv* sema

saying *n* usemi

scaffolding *n* dungu, jukwaa

scald *v* babua

scale *v* panda

scale *n* mzani

scalp *n* ngozi ya kichwa

scam *n* utapeli

scan *v* angalia, tazama

scandal *n* junaa, fedheha

scandalize *v* fedhehesha

scapegoat *n* msingiziwa

scar *n* jeraha

scarce *adj* hadimu

scarcely *adv* kwa nadra

scarcity *n* uhaba

scare *v* ogopesha, tisha

scare *n* tishio

scare away *v* kurupusha

scarf *n* kitambaa

scary *adj* -a kuogopesha

S

scatter v sambaza

scenario n muhtasari

scene n mandhari

scenery n mandhari

scent n harufu

sceptic adj -enye shaka

schedule v panga ratiba

schedule n ratiba

scheme n mpango

schism n mfarakano

scholar n msomi

school n shule

science n sayansi

scientific adj -a kisa-ansi

scientist n mwanasayansi

scissors n mkasi

scoff v tania, kejeli

scold v gombeza

scolding n kugombeza

scooter n pikipiki; skuta

scope n upeo

scorch v unguza

score n korija; matokeo

score v funga goli; kwaruza

scorn n dharau

scornful adj -a dharau

scorpion n nge

scoundrel n ayari

scour v sugua

scourge n mjeledi, kiboko

scout n skauti

scramble v vuruga

scrambled adj -liovurugwa

scrap n mabaki

scrap v tupa, acha

scrape v komba

scratch v kuna

scratch n mkwaruzo

scream v piga kelele

scream n yowe, ukelele

screen n pazia

screen v ficha

screw v tia scrubu

screw n skrubu

screwdriver n bisibisi

scribble v andika haraka

script n mwandiko

scroll n msokoto

scrub v sugua sana

scruples n maadili

scrupulous adj adilifu

scuffle n ugonvi

sculptor n msanii

sculpture n sanaa

sea n bahari

seagull n shakwe

S

seal *v* funga
seal *n* muhuri, nembo
seal off *v* zuia njia
seam *n* pindo
seamless *adj* -sio na pindo
seamstress *n* mshonaji wa kike
search *v* tafuta
search *n* msako
seashore *n* ufukwe
seasick *adj* kulewa bahari
seaside *adj* ufukwe
season *n* majira, msimu
seasonal *adj* -a msimu
seasoning *n* viungo
seat *n* kiti, nafasi
seated *adj* -enye kukaa
secede *v* jitoa, jitenga
secluded *adj* -enye kutengwa
seclusion *n* kutengwa
second *n* secunde, kaimu
secondary *adj* -a pili
secrecy *n* siri
secret *n* siri
secretary *n* karani
secretly *adv* kwa siri
sect *n* faraka, dhehebu
section *n* sehemu
sector *n* upande

secure *v* imarisha
secure *adj* -a usalama
security *n* usalama
sedate *v* tuliza kwa dawa
seduce *v* tongoza
seduction *n* kutongoza
see *iv* ona
seed *n* mbegu
seedless *adj* -sio na mbegu
seedy *adj* dhalili
seek *iv* tafuta
seem *v* onekana kama
segment *n* kipande
segregate *v* tenga
segregation *n* kutenga
seize *v* fanya taflisi
seizure *n* taflisi
seldom *adv* kwa nadra
select *v* chagua
selection *n* uchaguzi
self-concious *adj* kujibaini
self-esteem *n* kujiheshimu
self-evident *adj* dhairi, wazi
selfish *adj* -enye ubinafsi
selfishness *n* ubinafsi
self-respect *n* kujiheshimu
sell *iv* uza
seller *n* muuzaji**

S

sellout *n* saliti

semblance *n* mfano wa

semester *n* muhula

seminary *n* seminari

senate *n* bunge; senati

senator *n* mbunge, senata

send *iv* tuma

sender *n* mtumaji

senile *adj* zulufu

senior *adj* mkuu,kuu

seniority *n* ukubwa

sensation *n* kuhisi

sense *v* hisi

sense *n* hisia; akili

senseless *adj* bila fahamu

sensible *adj* -enye hekima

sensitive *adj* -enye hisia

sensual *adj* wa kutamanisha

sentence *v* hukumu

sentence *n* sentensi

sentiment *n* hisia; akili

sentry *n* askari, mlinzi

separate *v* tenganisha

separate *adj* mbalimbali

separation *n* kutengana

September *n* Semptemba

sequel *n* tokep

sequence *n* mfuatano

serene *adj* tulivu

serenity *n* utulivu

sergeant *n* sagenti

series *n* mfuatano

serious *adj* -a makini

seriousness *n* uzito

sermon *n* mahubiri

serpent *n* nyoka

serum *n* dawa ya sindano

servant *n* mtumishi

serve *v* tumikia, hudumia

service *n* huduma

service *v* toa huduma

session *n* kikao; muhula

set *n* kundi, seti

set *iv* weka, panga

set about *v* shambulia

set off *v* anza safari

set out *v* dhamiria

set up *v* anzisha

setback *n* kizuizi

setting *n* kutua

settle *v* tua

settle down *v* tulia

settle for *v* kubali

settlement *n* suluhu

settler *n* mhamiaji

setup *n* mpangilio**

S

seven *adj* saba
seventeen *adj* kumi na saba
seventh *adj* -a saba
seventy *adj* sabini
sever *v* kata, vunja
several *adj* baadhi
severance *n* kuvunja
severe *adj* kali
severity *n* ukali
sew *v* shona
sewage *n* maji machafu
sewing *n* kushona
sex *n* jinsia
sexuality *n* ujinsia
shabby *adj* hovyo
shack *n* kibanda
shackle *n* pingu, kikuku
shade *n* kivuli
shadow *n* kivuli
shady *adj* -enye kivuli
shake *iv* tingisha
shaken *adj* -liotingishwa,
shaky *adj* -a kutetemesha
shallow *adj* haba, kina kifupi
sham *n* bandia, uongo
shambles *n* vurumai, vurugu
shame *v* aibisha
shame *n* aibu

shameful *adj* -a aibu
shameless *adj* bila aibu
shape *v* tengeneza
shape *n* umbo
share *v* gawana
share *n* sehemu
shareholder *n* -enye hisa
shark *n* papa
sharp *adj* kali
sharpen *v* noa
sharpener *n* kinoleo
shatter *v* vunja, pasua
shattering *adj* -a kuvunja
shave *v* nyoa
she *pro* yeye (mke)
shear *iv* kata kwa mkasi
shed *iv* pukusa; mwaga
sheep *n* kondoo
sheets *n* mashuka
shelf *n* rafu
shell *n* gamba
shellfish *n* kombe
shelter *v* hifadhi, hami
shelter *n* makazi, hifadhi
shelves *n* rafu
shepherd *n* mchungaji
shield *v* kinga
shield *n* ngao

shift *n* zamu; mgeuko

shift *v* geuka, hamisha

shine *iv* ng'aa

shiny *adj* -a kung'aa

ship *n* meli

shipment *n* mzigo, bidhaa

shipwreck *n* mabaki ya meli

shipyard *n* bunta

shirk *v* kwepa

shirt *n* shati

shiver *v* tetemeka

shiver *n* mtetemeko

shock *v* shtua

shock *n* mshtuko

shocking *adj* -a kushtua

shoddy *adj* puluki

shoe *n* kiatu

shoelace *n* kamba ya kiatu

shoepolish *n* dawa ya viatu

shoestore *n* duka la viatu

shoot *iv* tungua

shoot down *v* piga na bunduki

shop *v* nunua

shop *n* duka

shoplifting *n* iba dukani

shore *n* ufukweni

short *adj* fupi

shortage *n* uhaba

shortcoming *n* dosari

shortcut *n* mkato

shorten *v* fupisha

shorthand *n* hatimkato

shortlived *adj* -a muda mfupi

shortly *adv* kwa ufupi

shorts *n* kaptura

shortsighted *adj* -sioona mbali

shot *n* sindano; risasi

shotgun *n* bunduki

shoulder *n* bega

shout *n* kelele

shouting *n* kupiga kelele

shove *v* sukuma

shove *n* kikumbo

shovel *n* beleshi

show *iv* onyesha

show off *v* jionyesha

show up *v* onekana

showdown *n* pambano

shower *n* mvua, kuoga

shrapnel *n* marisawa

shred *v* katakata

shred *n* kipande

shrewd *adj* mjanja

shriek *v* piga ukelele

shriek *n* ukelele

shrimp *n* kamba

S

shrine *n* ulili, ziara
shrink *iv* sinyaa, nywea
shroud *n* sanda
shrouded *adj* -liogubikwa
shrub *n* kichaka
shrug *v* inua mabega
shudder *n* kiusisimka
shudder *v* sisimka
shuffle *v* changa
shun *v* jitenga na
shut *iv* funga
shut off *v* zuia
shut up *v* nyamaza
shuttle *v* nenda na kurudi
shy *adj* -enye haya
shyness *n* aibu, haya
sick *adj* mgonjwa
sicken *v* ugua
sickening *adj* -a kukifu
sickle *n* mundu, upamba
sickness *n* ugonjwa
side *n* pembe, upande
sideburns *n* sharafa
sidestep *v* kwepa
sideways *adv* kwa pembeni
siege *n* kuzingirwa
siege *v* zingira
sift *v* chekecha

sigh *n* kushusha pumzi
sigh *v* shusha pumzi
sight *n* uwezo wa kuona
sign *v* tia saini
sign *n* saini, ishara
signal *n* ishara
signature *n* saini
significance *n* umuhimu
significant *adj* muhimu
signify *v* maanisha
silence *n* ukimya
silence *v* nyamazisha
silent *adj* kimya
silhouette *n* kivuli cha umbo
silk *n* hariri
silly *adj* -a upuuzi
silver *n* fedha
silversmith *n* sonara
similar *adj* -enye kufanana
similarity *n* ufananaji
simmer *v* chemka
simple *adj* rahisi
simplicity *n* urahisi
simplify *v* rahisisha
simply *adv* kwa urahisi
simulate *v* jidai, jifanya
simultaneous *adj* -a pamoja
sin *v* fanya dhambi**

S

sin *n* dhambi

since *c* tangu, toka

since *pre* tokea, toka

since then *adv* tokea hapo

sincere *adj* -a kweli

sincerity *n* uaminifu, ukweli

sinful *adj* -a dhambi

sing *iv* imba

singer *n* mwibaji

single *n* moja

single *adj* pekee, moja tu

singlehanded *adj* peke yake

singular *adj* -a namna yake

sinister *adj* mbaya, ovu

sink *iv* zama

sink in *v* zama ndani

sinner *n* mkosefu

sip *v* kunywa kidogo

sip *n* unywaji kidogo

sir *n* mzee; ndugu

siren *n* king'ora

sirloin *n* salala

sister *n* dada

sister-in-law *n* wifi; shemeji

sit *iv* kaa

site *n* eneo

sitting *n* kukaa

situated *adj* ilipo

situation *n* hali

six *adj* sita

sixteen *adj* kumi na sita

sixth *adj* -a sita

sixty *adj* sitini

sizable *adj* nyingi kiasi

size *n* kiasi, ukubwa

size up *v* pima

skate *n* reli za barafu

skeleton *n* kiunzi cha mifupa

sketch *v* mchoro

sketch *n* mchoro

sketchy *adj* -siokamilifu

skill *n* ufundi, ustadi

skillful *adj* stadi, bingwa

skim *v* engua

skin *v* chuna

skin *n* ngozi

skinny *adj* mwembamba

skip *v* ruka

skip *n* kuruka

skirmish *n* vita vidogo

skirt *n* sketi

skull *n* fuvu la kichwa

sky *n* mbingu, anga

skylight *n* dirisha la darini

skyscraper *n* ghorofa

slab *n* ubamba

S

slack *adj* -enye kulegea

slacken *v* legeza

slacks *n* suruali

slam *v* bamiza

slander *n* kashfa

slanted *adj* -lioupande

slap *n* kofi

slap *v* piga kofi

slash *n* mpasuo; uchale

slash *v* kata, chanja

slate *n* kigae

slaughter *v* chinja

slaughter *n* kuchinja

slave *n* mtumwa

slavery *n* utumwa

slay *iv* ua

sleazy *adj* dhalili

sleep *iv* lala

sleep *n* kulala, usingizi

sleeve *n* mkono

sleeveless *adj* bila mikono

slender *adj* nyembamba

slice *v* kata, chanja

slice *n* kipande; slesi

slightly *adv* kidogo

slim *adj* mwembamba

slip *v* teleza, ponyoka

slip *n* kuteleza

slipper *n* malapa

slippery *adj* -a kuteleza

slit *iv* chana, gema

slob *adj* baradhuli

slogan *n* wito, msomo

slope *n* mteremko

sloppy *adj* ovyo

slot *n* nafasi

slow *adj* -a polepole

slow down *v* punguza mwendo

slow motion *n* mwendopole

slowly *adv* polepole

sluggish *adj* -a polepole

slum *n* nyumba duni

slur *v* kokoteza maneno

sly *adj* -a kijanja

smack *n* pigo

smack *v* piga kofi

small *adj* ndogo

small print *n* chapa ndogo

smallpox *n* ndui

smart *adj* mwerevu, stadi

smash *v* vunja

smear *n* kashfa, kupaka

smear *v* paka

smell *iv* nuka

smelly *adj* -a kunuka

smile *v* tabasamu

S

smile *n* tabasamu

smith *n* mhunzi, mfuaji

smoke *v* vuta

smoked *adj* -a moshi

smoker *n* mvutaji

smoking gun *n* ushaidi dhahiri

smooth *v* nyoosha

smooth *adj* ororo

smoothly *adv* sawa, shwari

smoothness *n* ororo

smother *v* kaba

smuggler *n* mfanya magendo

snail *n* konokono

snake *n* nyoka

snapshot *n* picha

snare *v* tega

snare *n* mtego

snatch *v* nyakua

sneak *v* penyeza

sneeze *v* piga chafya

sneeze *n* chafya

sniff *v* nusa

snitch *v* dokoa

snooze *v* sinzia

snore *v* koroma

snore *n* kukoroma

snow *v* anguka theluji

snow *n* theluji

snub *v* dharau, beza

snub *n* bezo, dharau

soak *v* loweka

soak in *v* loweka kwenye

soak up *v* fyonza

soar *v* paa angani

sob *v* kikweukweu

sob *n* mamia

sober *adj* mzima

sociable *adj* changamfu

socialism *n* ujamaa

socialist *adj* mjamaa

society *n* jamii

sock *n* soksi

sod *n* mpumbavu

soda *n* soda

sofa *n* kochi

soft *adj* laini

soften *v* lainisha

softly *adv* taratibu

softness *n* ulaini

soggy *adj* chepechepe

soil *v* chafua

soil *n* udongo

soiled *adj* -liochafuka

solace *n* faraja

solar *adj* -a jua

solder *v* lehemu

S

soldier *n* askari

sole *n* soli

sole *adj* -a pekee

solely *adv* pekee, tu

solemn *adj* -a dhati

solicit *v* omba, sihi

solid *adj* gumu

solidarity *n* umoja

solitary *adj* -a peke -ake

solitude *n* upweke

soluble *adj* -enye kuyeyuka

solution *n* ufumbuzi

solve *v* tatua

solvent *adj* kiyeyusho

somber *adj* -a giza

some *adj* kadhaa, kiasi

somebody *pro* mtu

someday *adv* siku moja

someone *pro* mtu

something *pro* kitu

sometimes *adv* wakati mwingine

someway *adv* kwa kiasi fulani

somewhat *adv* kiasi

son *n* mwana wa kiume

song *n* wimbo

son-in-law *n* mkwe

soon *adv* muda si mrefu

soothe *v* bembeleza

sorcerer *n* mchawi

sorcery *n* uchawi

sore *n* kidonda

sore *adj* -enye kuuma

sorrow *n* huzuni

sorrowful *adj* -enye huzuni

sorry *adj* sikitika

sort *n* aina, jinsi

sort out *v* tatua

soul *n* nafsi

sound *n* sauti

sound *v* piga, vuma

sound out *v* vumisha

soup *n* supu

sour *adj* chachu

source *n* chanzo

south *n* kusini

southern *adj* -a kusini

southerner *n* wa kunisi

souvenir *n* kumbukumbu

sovereign *adj* -a ufalme

sovereignty *n* ufalme

soviet *adj* -a kirusi

sow *iv* panda, pandikiza

spa *n* chemchemi

space *n* nafasi, uwanda

space out *v* tawanyisha

spacious *adj* -enye nafasi

S

spade *n* sepeto
Spain *n* Spain
span *v* vuka, dumu
span *n* shubiri
Spaniard *n* Mspanish
Spanish *adj* -a Kispanish
spank *v* chapa
spanking *n* kuchapa
spare *v* gombana
spare *adj* -a ziada
spare part *n* kipuli
sparingly *adv* kwa ubanifu
spark *n* cheche
spark off *v* chokoza
spark plug *n* plagi
sparkle *v* metameta
sparrow *n* jurawa
sparse *adj* hadimu, haba
spasm *n* mshtuko
speak *iv* ongea
speaker *n* spika
spear *n* mkuki
spearhead *v* ongoza, anzisha
special *adj* maalum
specialize *v* taalimu
specialty *n* utaalamu
species *n* spishi
specific *adj* maalum; dhahiri

specimen *n* sampuli
speck *n* chembe, kidoto
spectacle *n* onyesho
spectator *n* mtazamaji
speculate *v* kisia, otea
speculation *n* makisio
speech *n* hotuba
speechless *adj* duwaa
speed *iv* nenda kasi
speed *n* kasi
speedily *adv* kwa kasi
speedy *adj* kasi
spell *iv* taja herufi, andika
spell *n* kipindi
spelling *n* tahajia
spend *iv* tumia
spending *n* kutumia
sperm *n* shahawa
sphere *n* tufe; fani
spice *n* kiungo
spicy *adj* -enye viungo
spider *n* buibui
spiderweb *n* tandu ya buibui
spill *iv* mwaga
spill *n* kumwaga
spin *iv* zungusha
spine *n* uti wa mgongo
spineless *adj* mwoga

S

spinster *n* mseja

spirit *n* roho

spiritual *adj* -a kiroho

spit *iv* tema

spite *n* chuki, inda

spiteful *adj* -enye chuki

splash *v* rushia maji

splendid *adj* bora, -a fahari

splendor *n* ufahari; utukufu

splint *n* kitata

splinter *n* kibanzi

splinter *v* vunjavunja

split *n* mpasuo

split *iv* pasua

split up *v* achana

spoil *v* haribu

spoils *n* ngawira

sponge *n* sifongo, buga

sponsor *n* mfadhili

spontaneous *adj* -a papo hapo

spooky *adj* -a kutisha

spool *n* kibiringo

spoon *n* kijiko

spoonful *n* kijiko kizima

sporadic *adj* -a hapa na pale

sport *n* michezo

sporty *adj* -a michezo

spot *v* ona, tambua

spot *n* kidoti, kidoa

spotless *adj* bila doa

spotlight *n* kivutio

spouse *n* mke; mume

sprain *v* teguka

sprawl *v* jibwaga

spray *v* pulizia

spread *iv* sambaza

spring *iv* ruka

spring *n* chemchemi

springboard *n* ubao wa kurukia

sprinkle *v* nyunyizia

sprout *v* chipua

spruce up *v* maridadisha

spur *v* himiza

spur *n* kikwaru; tuta

spy *v* peleleza

spy *n* jasusi

squalid *adj* dhalili, chafu

squander *v* fuja, tapanya

square *adj* -a pembe mraba

square *n* mraba

squash *v* ponda

squeamish *adj* -enye uoga

squeeze *v* kamua

squeeze in *v* penyeza

squeeze up *v* banana

squid *n* ngisi

squirrel *n* kidiri

stab *v* choma

stab *n* jeraha la kuchoma

stability *n* uthabiti

stable *adj* imara

stable *n* zizi

stack *v* rundika

stack *n* lundo

staff *n* wafanyakazi

stage *n* jukwaa

stage *v* andaa, panga

stagger *v* pepesuka

staggering *adj* -a kushangaza

stagnant *adj* yaliyo tuama

stagnate *v* tuama

stagnation *n* kutuama

stain *v* tia doa, chafua

stain *n* doa

stair *n* ngazi

staircase *n* ngazi

stairs *n* ngazi

stake *n* kiguzo

stake *v* tia dau

stale *adj* -a zamani

stalk *v* nyatia, nyemelea

stalk *n* shina

stall *n* kibanda

stall *v* chelewesha

stammer *v* gugumia

stamp *v* piga mhuri

stamp *n* stempu

stamp out *v* komesha

stampede *n* mkurupuko

stand *iv* simama

stand *n* kusimama

stand for *v* wakilisha

stand out *v* jitokeza

stand up *v* simama

standard *n* kawaida

standing *n* kusimama

standpoint *n* msimamo

standstill *adj* -siosogea

staple *v* bana

staple *n* bidhaa kuu

star *n* nyota

starch *n* wanga

starchy *adj* -enye wanga

stare *v* kodolea macho

stark *adj* wazi

start *v* anza

start *n* kuanza

startle *v* shtua, gutusha

startled *adj* -enye kushtuka

starvation *n* njaa

starve *v* kaa na njaa

state *n* hali; jimbo

S

state *v* sema, tamka

statement *n* maelezo

station *n* kituo

stationary *adj* -liosimama

stationery *n* vifaa vya ofisi

statistic *n* takwimu

statue *n* sanamu

status *n* hali

statute *n* sheria

staunch *adj* thabiti, imara

stay *v* baki, kaa

stay *n* kukaa, kamba

steady *adj* imara

steak *n* mnofu wa nyama

steal *iv* iba

stealthy *adj* -a kunyatia

steam *n* mvuke

steel *n* chuma

steep *adj* -a mwinuko mkali

stem *n* shina

stem *v* anzia

stench *n* harufu mbaya

step *n* hatua

step down *v* achia ngazi

step out *v* toka

step up *v* jitokeze mbele

stepbrother *n* kaka wa kambo

step-by-step *adv* hatua kwa hatua

stepdaughter *n* binti wa kambo

stepfather *n* baba wa kambo

stepladder *n* ngazi

stepmother *n* mama wa kambo

stepsister *n* dada wa kambo

sterile *adj* tasa; safi kabisa

sterilize *v* safisha kabisa

stern *n* tezi

stern *adj* kali

sternly *adv* kwa ukali

stew *n* mchuzi

stick *v* ganda, gandisha

stick *iv* choma

stick around *v* baki

stick out *v* tokezea

stick to *v* ng'ang'ania

sticker *n* kibandiko

sticky *adj* -enye gundi

stiff *adj* -liokakamaa

stiffen *v* kaza

stiffness *n* ugumu

stifle *v* kaba

still *adj* -liosimama

still *adv* kimya

stimulant *n* kiamshi

stimulate *v* amsha

stimulus *n* kiamshi

sting *iv* choma, washa

S

sting *n* uchungu, kuuma

stinging *adj* -a kuwasha

stingy *adj* bahili

stink *iv* nuka

stink *n* kunuka

stinking *adj* -a kunuka

stipulate *v* eleza

stir *v* koroga, amsha

stir up *v* anzisha

stitch *v* shona

stitch *n* mshono

stock *v* jaza, weka

stock *n* bidhaa; mchuzi

stocking *n* kuweka, kujaza

stockroom *n* ghala

stoic *adj* kakamavu

stomach *n* tumbo

stone *n* jiwe

stone *v* piga na mawe

stool *n* choo, kigoda

stop *v* acha

stop *n* kuacha

stop by *v* pitia

stop over *v* simama

storage *n* kuhifadhi

store *v* hifadhi

store *n* ghala

stork *n* korongo

storm *n* dhoruba

stormy *adj* -a dhoruba

story *n* hadithi

stove *n* jiko

straight *adj* nyooka

straighten out *v* nyoosha

strain *v* chuja

strain *n* mvuto; mbegu

strained *adj* -a kulazimisha

strainer *n* kichujio

strait *n* njia

stranded *adj* kwama

strange *adj* -a ajabu

stranger *n* mgeni

strangle *v* kaba

strap *n* ukanda

strategy *n* mkakati

straw *n* nyasi

stray *adj* -liopotea

stray *v* tangatanga

stream *n* mto mdogo

street *n* njia, barabara

streetcar *n* gari

streetlight *n* taa za barabarani

strength *n* nguvu

strengthen *v* imarisha, kaza

strenuous *adj* -a kuhitaji bidii

stress *n* kanineno; msisitizo

S

stressful *adj* -a kuchokesha

stretch *n* kujinyoosha

stretch *v* nyoosha

stretcher *n* machela

strict *adj* kali

stride *iv* piga hatua ndefu

strife *n* ugomvi, mapigano

strike *n* mgomo

strike *iv* goma

strike back *v* rudishia kipigo

strike out *v* futa

strike up *v* anza

striking *adj* kugoma

string *n* kamba, uzi

stringent *adj* kali

strip *n* kishoroba, upapi

strip *v* vua

stripe *n* mistari

striped *adj* -enye mistari

strive *iv* lenga, jitahidi

stroke *n* dhoruba, pigo

stroll *v* tembea tembea

strong *adj* -enye nguvu

structure *n* jengo, muundo

struggle *v* pambana

struggle *n* mapambano

stub *n* kisiki; kichungi

stubborn *adj* mbishi

student *n* mwanafunzi

study *v* soma, jifunza

stuff *n* vitu

stuff *v* jaza, shindilia

stuffing *n* vijazio

stuffy *adj* -enye hewa nzito

stumble *v* jikwaa

stun *v* zubaisha

stunning *adj* nzuri sana

stupendous *adj* kubwa sana

stupid *adj* mjinga

stupidity *n* ujinga

sturdy *adj* imara

stutter *v* gugumia

style *n* mtindo, namna

subdue *v* shinda

subdued *adj* -liohafifu

subject *v* tegemea

subject *n* raia; mada

sublime *adj* utukufu

submerge *v* zamisha

submissive *adj* nyenyekevu

submit *v* kubali; wasilisha

subpoena *v* ita mahakamani

subscribe *v* changa

subsequent *adj* -a kufuatia

subsidiary *adj* tanzu

subsidize *v* saidia**

subsidy *n* msaada

subsist *v* jikimu, ishi

substance *n* kitu; maudhui

substantial *adj* -a muhimu

substitute *v* badili

substitute *n* badala

subtle *adj* -enye hila

subtract *v* ondoa, toa

subtraction *n* kutoa

suburb *n* kiunga

succeed *v* fanikiwa

success *n* mafanikio

successful *adj* -liofanikiwa

successor *n* mrithi

succumb *v* shindwa

such *adj* kama

suck *v* nyonya

sucker *adj* chipukizi

sudden *adj* -a ghafla

suddenly *adv* kwa ghafla

sue *v* shitaki

suffer *v* teseka, taabika

suffer from *v* sumbuliwa na

suffering *n* kuteseka

sufficient *adj* -a kutosha

suffocate *v* kosa hewa

sugar *n* sukari

suggest *v* shuri

suggestion *n* ushauri, oni

suggestive *adj* -a kuashiria

suicide *n* kujiua

suit *n* suti

suitable *adj* -a kufaa

suitcase *n* sanduku

sullen *adj* -enye kununa

sulphur *n* salfa

sum *n* jumla, idadi

sum up *v* toa muhtasari

summarize *v* eleza kwa ufupi

summary *n* muhtasari

summer *n* kiangazi

summit *n* kilele

summon *v* ita

sumptuous *adj* nzuri sana

sun *n* jua

sunburn *n* kuungua na jua

Sunday *n* Jumapili

sundown *n* machweo

sunglasses *n* miwani ya jua

sunken *adj* -liozama

sunny *adj* -a jua

sunrise *n* macheo

sunset *n* kuchwa jua

superb *adj* nzuri sana

superfluous *adj* -siohitajika

superior *adj* bora zaidi; kuu

S

superiority *n* ubora

supermarket *n* duka kubwa

superpower *n* taifa kubwa

supersede *v* shika nafasi ya

superstition *n* ushirikina

supervise *v* simamia

supervision *n* usimamizi

supper *n* mlo wa jioni

supple *adj* laini

supplier *n* mgawaji

supplies *n* mahitaji, vifaa

supply *v* toa, patia

support *v* unga mkono

supporter *n* muunga mkono

suppose *v* dhani, waza

supposing *c* iwapo, kama

supposition *n* dhana

suppress *v* zima, komesha

sure *adj* -a hakika

surely *adv* kwa hakika

surf *v* rambaza

surface *n* uso

surge *n* wimbi

surgeon *n* daktari mpasuaji

surgical *adv* -a upasuaji

surname *n* jina la ukoo

surpass *v* zidi

surplus *n* ziada

surprise *v* shangaza

surprise *n* mshangao

surrender *v* jisalimisha

surrender *n* kujisalimisha

surround *v* zunguka

surroundings *n* mazingira

surveillance *n* uchunguzi

survey *n* ukaguzi

survival *n* kuishi

survive *v* ishi

survivor *n* -enye kunusurika

suspect *v* shuku

suspect *n* mtuhumiwa

suspend *v* ahirisha

suspense *n* wasiwasi

suspension *n* kusimamishwa

suspicion *n* shaka

suspicious *adj* -enye shuku

sustain *v* himili, mudi

sustenance *n* riziki, ulaji

swallow *v* meza

swamp *n* kinamasi

swamped *adj* zidiwa na,

swan *n* bata maji

swap *v* badilishana

swap *n* kubadilishana

swarm *n* kundi

sway *v* pepesuka

S

swear *iv* apa

sweat *n* jasho

sweat *v* toka jasho

sweater *n* sweta

Sweden *n* Sweden

Sweedish *adj* Swideni, Uswidi

sweep *iv* fagia

sweet *adj* tamu

sweeten *v* fanya tamu

sweetheart *n* kipenzi

sweetness *n* utamu

sweets *n* pipi

swell *iv* vimba

swelling *n* uvimbe

swift *adj* haraka

swim *iv* ogelea

swimmer *n* mwogeleaji

swimming *n* kuogelea

swindle *v* tapeli

swindle *n* utapeli

swindler *n* tapeli, mtapeli

swing *iv* bembea

swing *n* bembea

Swiss *adj* Mswisi

switch *v* badilisha; washa

switch *n* swichi

switch off *v* zima

switch on *v* washa

Switzerland *n* Uswisi

swivel *v* zunguka

swollen *adj* -a kuvimba

sword *n* jambia

swordfish *n* nduwari

syllable *n* silabi

symbol *n* alama, ishara

symbolic *adj* -a mfano

symmetry *n* mlingano pacha

sympathize *v* hurumia, hani

sympathy *n* huruma

symptom *n* dalili

synagogue *n* sinagogi

synchronize *v* sawazisha

synthesis *n* uunganishaji

syphilis *n* kaswende

syringe *n* bomba

syrup *n* shira

system *n* mfumo

systematic *adj* -a utaratibu

S

table 174

T

table *n* meza
tablet *n* kidonge
tack *n* bandi; msumari
tackle *v* shughulika na
tact *n* busara
tactful *adj* -a adabu
tactical *adj* -a mbinu
tactics *n* mbinu
tag *n* kibandiko
tail *n* mkia
tail *v* fuata
tailor *n* mshoni
tainted *adj* najisiwa
take *iv* chukua
take apart *v* bomoa
take away *v* ondoa
take back *v* rudisha
take in *v* pokea
take off *v* vua, toa
take out *v* toa, chukua
take over *v* twaa, miliki
tale *n* hadithi
talent *n* kipaji
talk *v* ongea
tall *adj* ndefu

tame *v* fuga
tangerine *n* chenza
tangible *adj* -a kushikika
tangle *n* fundo, msokoto
tank *n* kifaru; tangi
tantamount to *adj* sawa na
tantrum *n* ghadhabu
tap *n* bomba
tap into *v* tumia nguvu za
tape *n* kanda
tar *n* lami
tarantula *n* bui wa sumu
tardy *adv* kwa kuchelewa
target *n* lengo
tariff *n* gharama
tarnish *v* fifisha mg'ao
tart *n* pai
tartar *n* ukoga
task *n* kazi, shughuli
taste *v* onja
taste *n* ladha
tasteful *adj* -enye ladha nzuri
tasteless *adj* -sio na ladha
tasty *adj* -enye ladha nzuri
tavern *n* mgahawa wa vileo
tax *n* ushuru
tea *n* chai
teach *iv* fundisha

teacher *n* mwalimu

team *n* kikosi, timu

teapot *n* birika la chai, buli

tear *iv* chana

tear *n* mpasuo, mpasuko

tearful *adj* -a kulia

tease *v* tania

teaspoon *n* kijiko cha chai

technical *adj* -a kiufundi

technicality *n* mbinuufundi

technician *n* fundi

technique *n* ujuzi

technology *n* teknologia

tedious *adj* -a kuchosha

tedium *n* uchovu

teenager *n* kijana

teeth *n* meno

telegram *n* telegramu

telephone *n* simu

telescope *n* darubini

television *n* runinga

tell *iv* sema, simulia

teller *n* mhesabu kura

telling *adj* -a nguvu

temper *n* hasira

temperature *n* halijoto

tempest *n* dhoruba

temple *n* hekalu

temporary *adj* -a muda

tempt *v* shawishi

temptation *n* ushawishi

tempting *adj* -a kushawishi

ten *adj* kumi

tenacity *n* kunata

tenant *n* mpangaji

tendency *n* mazoea

tender *adj* zabuni

tenderness *n* upendo; maumivu

tennis *n* tenisi

tense *adj* -a kukakamaa

tension *n* mvuto

tent *n* hema

tentacle *n* mnyiri

tentative *adj* -a majaribio

tenth *adj* -a kumi

tenuous *adj* hafifu

tepid *adj* vuguvugu

term *n* muhula

terminate *v* maliza, koma

terminology *n* istilahi

termite *n* mchwa

terms *n* vigezo

terrace *n* baraza

terrain *n* ardhi

terrestrial *adj* -a nchi kavu

terrible *adj* mabaya sana

T

terrific *adj* nzuri sana
terrify *v* tisha
terrifying *adj* -a kutisha
territory *n* eneo, sehemu
terror *n* vitisho
terrorism *n* ugaidi
terrorist *n* gaidi
terrorize *v* tishia kikatili
terse *adj* fupi
test *v* jaribu, pima
test *n* mtihani; jaribio
testament *n* agano, usia
testify *v* toa ushaidi
testimony *n* ushaidi
text *n* maandishi
textbook *n* kitabu
texture *n* mfumo
thank *v* shukuru
thanks *n* ahsante
that *adj* ile; kwamba
thaw *v* yeyuka
theft *n* wizi
theme *n* dhamira
themselves *pro* wenyewe
then *adv* wakati huo
theologian *n* mwanatheologia
theology *n* theologia
theory *n* nadharia

therapy *n* matibabu, tiba
there *adv* pale
therefore *adv* kwa hivyo
thermometer *n* pimajoto
these *adj* hizi
thesis *n* tasnifu
they *pro* wao
thick *adj* nene
thicken *v* fanya kuwa nzito
thickness *n* unene
thief *n* mwizi
thigh *n* paja
thin *adj* nyembamba
thing *n* kitu
think *iv* fikiria, fikiri
thinly *adv* kwa wembamba
third *adj* -a tatu
thirst *v* kuwa na kiu
thirsty *adj* -enye kiu
thirteen *adj* kumi na tatu
thirty *adj* thelathini
this *adj* hii
thorn *n* mwiba
thorny *adj* -enye miiba
thorough *adj* kamilifu, fasaha
those *adj* zile
though *c* hata kama
thought *n* fikra**

thoughtful *adj* wa kufikiri

thousand *adj* elfu

thread *v* weka uzi

thread *n* uzi

threat *n* tishio, hatari

threaten *v* tisha, tishia

three *adj* tatu

thresh *v* pukuchua

threshold *n* kizingiti

thrill *v* sisimua

thrill *n* msisimko

thrive *v* neemeka, kua

throat *n* koo

throb *n* mapigo, mpwito

throb *v* pwita

throne *n* kiti cha enzi

throng *n* umati

through (thru) *pre* kutokana

throw *iv* rusha

throw away *v* tupa

throw up *v* tapika

thug *n* jambazi

thumb *n* dole gumba

thumbtack *n* pini

thunder *n* mngurumo

thunderbolt *n* radi

Thursday *n* Alhamisi

thus *adv* hivyo

thwart *v* zuia

thyroid *n* kikoromeo

tickle *v* tekenya

tickle *n* kutekenya

ticklish *adj* anayetekenyeka

tidal wave *n* wimbi kubwa

tide *n* bamvua

tidy *adj* nadhifu, safi

tie *v* funga

tie *n* tai

tiger *n* chui mwenye milia

tight *adj* -liokazwa

tighten *v* kaza

tile *n* vigae

till *adv* mpaka

till *v* lima

tilt *v* shambulia

timber *n* mbao

time *n* muda, saa

time *v* pima muda

timely *adj* -a kuwahi

times *n* nyakati

timetable *n* ratiba

timid *adj* chachili

timidity *n* tahayari

tin *n* kopo

tiny *adj* kiduchu

tip *n* kilele, ncha

T

tiptoe n nyemelea

tired adj choko

tiredness n uchovu

tireless adj bila kuchoka

tiresome adj -a kuchoka

tissue n shashi

title n kichwa

to pre kwa

toad n chura

toast v banika mkate

tobacco n tumbaku

today adv leo

toddler n chekechea

toe n kidole cha mguuni

together adv pamoja

toil v vumaika

toilet n msala, choo

token n ishara

tolerable adj -enye kuvumilika

tolerance n uvumilivu

tolerate v vumilia

toll n ushuru

toll v gonga kengele

tomato n nyanya, tungule

tomb n kaburi

tombstone n jiwe la kaburi

tomorrow adv kesho

ton n tani

tone n sauti

tongs n koleo

tongue n ulimi

tonic n kichangamshi

tonight adv usiku huu

tonsil n tukwa

too adv pia

tool n kifaa

tooth n jino

toothache n maumivu ya jino

top n kilele; kifuniko

topic n mada; somo

topple v pindua, anguka

torch n tochi

torment v tesa

torment n mateso

torrent n maji kimbizi

torrid adj -a jazba

torso n pingiti

tortoise n kobe

torture v sulubu

torture n suluba

toss v rusha

total adj jumla

totality n kamilifu, ujumla

touch n kugusa

touch v gusa

touch on v gusia

touch up v karabati

touching adj kugusa

tough adj ngumu

toughen v fanya imara

tour n safari ya kitalii

tourism n utalii

tourist n mtalii

tow v vuta

towards pre kuelekea

towel n taulo

tower n mnara

towering adj refu mno

town n mji

town hall n mamlaka ya mji

toxic adj -a sumu

toxin n sumu ya nyoka

toy n sesere

trace v fuatilia

track n nyayo

track v fuata nyayo

traction n mng'ang'anio

tractor n trekta

trade n biashara

trade v fanya biashara

trademark n nembo

trader n mfanyabiashara

tradition n mila, desturi

traffic v fanya magendo

tragedy n janga

tragic adj -a kusikitisha

trail v fuata, saka

trail n njia, nyayo

trailer n trela

train n treni

train v fanya mazoezi

trainee n mwanafunzi

trainer n mkufunzi

training n mafunzo

trait n sifa

traitor n msaliti, haini

trajectory n mtupo

trample v kanyaga kanyaga

trance n duwaa

tranquility n utulivu

transcend v vuka mipaka

transcribe v nakili

transfer v hamisha

transfer n uhamisho

transform v badilisha

transformation n badiliko

transfusion n kuwekewa damu

transient adj -a kupita

transit n kupita

transition n mpito

translate v tafsiri

translator n mfasiri

T

transmit *v* sambaza

transplant *v* hamisha

transport *v* safirisha

trap *n* mtego

trash *n* takataka

trash can *n* pipa

travel *v* safiri

traveler *n* msafiri

tray *n* sinia

treacherous *adj* -a kisaliti

treachery *n* usaliti

tread *iv* tembea

treason *n* uhaini

treasure *n* mali, hazina

treasurer *n* mweka hazina

treat *v* tendea

treat *n* karamu

treatment *n* matibabu

treaty *n* mkataba

tree *n* mti

tremble *v* vinya

tremendous *adj* kubwa sana

tremor *n* mtetemeko

trench *n* handaki

trend *n* mwelekeo

trespass *v* ingilia eneo

trial *n* kesi, jaribio

triangle *n* pembetatu

tribe *n* kabila

tribulation *n* taabu

tribunal *n* mahakama

tribute *n* shukrani

trick *v* fanya hila

trick *n* ujanja

trickle *v* mchiriziko

tricky *adj* ngumu

trigger *v* anzisha

trim *v* punguza

trimester *n* muhula

trimmings *n* marupurupu

trip *n* safari

trip *v* jikwaa

triple *adj* mara tatu

triumph *n* shinda

triumphant *adj* kiushindi

troop *n* kikosi

trophy *n* kombe

tropic *n* tropiki

tropical *adj* -a tropiki

trouble *n* matatizo

trouble *v* sumbua

troublesome *adj* -a matatizo

trousers *n* suruali

trout *n* trauti

truce *n* kusitisha ugomvi

truck *n* lori

trucker *n* dereva lori
trumped-up *adj* -a uzushi
trumpet *n* tarumbeta
trunk *n* shina
trust *v* amini
trust *n* imani
truth *n* ukweli
truthful *adj* mkweli
try *v* jaribu
tub *n* beseni, pipa
tuberculosis *n* kifua kikuu
Tuesday *n* Jumanne
tuition *n* mafunzo
tumble *v* anguka
tummy *n* tumbo
tumor *n* uvimbe
tumult *n* ghasia, vurugu
tumultuous *adj* -a ghasia
tuna *n* jodari
tune *n* melodia
tune *v* linganisha
tune up *v* linganisha milio
tunic *n* kanzu
tunnel *n* handaki
turbine *n* rafadha
turbulence *n* dharuba
Turk *adj* Mturuki
Turkey *n* Uturuki

turmoil *n* ghasia
turn *n* kona
turn *v* geuka
turn back *v* rudi
turn down *v* kataa
turn in *v* lala
turn off *v* zima
turn on *v* washa
turn out *v* fukuza
turn over *v* geuza
turn up *v* tokezea
turret *n* mnara mdogo
turtle *n* kasa
tusk *n* pembe
tutor *n* mwalimu
tweezers *n* koleo
twelfth *adj* -a kumi na mbili
twelve *adj* kumi na mbili
twentieth *adj* -a ishirini
twenty *adj* ishirini
twice *adv* mara mbili
twin *n* pacha
twinkle *v* metameta
twist *v* sokota, viringisha
twist *n* mgeuzo
twisted *adj* -liosokotwa
twister *n* tapeli, laghai
two *adj* mbili

T

tycoon *n* bepari
type *n* aina
type *v* chapa
typical *adj* -a mfano hasa
tyranny *n* udhalimu
tyrant *n* mdhalimu

U

ugliness *n* ubaya
ugly *adj* mbaya
ulcer *n* kidonda
ultimate *adj* -a mwisho
ultimatum *n* sharti la mwisho
umbrella *n* mwavuli
umpire *n* mwamuzi
unable *adj* kutoweza
unanimity *n* umoja
unarmed *adj* bila silaha
unattached *adj* -siooa, -sioolewa
unavoidable *adj* -siozuilika
unaware *adj* bila kujua
unbeatable *adj* -sioshindwa
unbelievable *adj* -sioaminika
unbroken *adj* haikuvunjika

unbutton *v* fugua vifungo
uncertain *adj* bila uhakika
uncle *n* mjomba
uncommon *adj* -sio ya kawaida
unconscious *adj* kosa fahamu
uncover *v* gundua
undecided *adj* -sioamua
undeniable *adj* -siopingika
under *pre* chini
undercover *adj* -a siri
underdog *n* mlalahoi
undergo *v* pitia
underground *adj* -a siri
underlie *v* -wa chini ya
underlying *adj* -wa chini
undermine *v* dhoofisha
underneath *pre* chini ya
understand *v* elewa
understanding *adj* kuelewa
undertake *v* ahidi
underwear *n* nguo za ndani
underwrite *v* kubali kugharimia
undeserved *adj* -sio stahili
undesirable *adj* -siotakiwa
undo *v* batilisha
undoubtedly *adv* bila shaka
undress *v* vua
undue *adj* -liopita kisasi**

unearth *v* fukua, zua

uneasiness *n* wasiwasi

uneasy *adj* -a wasiwasi

uneducated *adj* -sioelimika

unemployed *adj* bila ajira

unemployment *n* ukosefu wa kazi

unending *adj* -sioisha

unequivocal *adj* -a wazi

uneven *adj* -siolingana

uneventful *adj* -sio na matukio

unexpected *adj* bila kutegemea

unfailing *adj* bila kukosa

unfair *adj* -siosawa

unfairly *adv* bila ya haki

unfairness *n* ukosefu wa haki

unfaithful *adj* -siomwaminifu

unfamiliar *adj* -a kigeni

unfasten *v* fugua

unfavorable *adj* -siotumainiwa

unfit *adj* -siofaa

unfold *v* kunjua

unforeseen *adj* -siotegemewa

unforgettable *adj* -siosahaulika

unfounded *adj* -sio na msingi

unfriendly *adj* -sio ya kirafiki

unfurnished *adj* -sio na samani

ungrateful *adj* -sio na shukurani

unhappiness *n* huzuni

unhappy *adj* -enye huzuni

unharmed *adj* bila kuumia

unhealthy *adj* dhaifu

unhurt *adj* bila kuumia

unification *n* muungano

uniform *n* sare

uniformity *n* mlingano

unify *v* unganisha

unilateral *adj* upande mmoja

union *n* muungano

unique *adj* ghamma

unit *n* kitu kimoja

unite *v* ungana

unity *n* umoja

universal *adj* -a fani zote

universe *n* ulimwengu

university *n* chuo kikuu

unjust *adj* -sio haki

unjustified *adj* bila sababu

unknown *adj* -sio julikana

unlawful *adj* -a kukiuka sheria

unleash *v* achia, achilia

unless *c* ila, isipokuwa

unlike *adj* tofauti

unlikely *adj* -sioelekea

unlimited *adj* bila mpaka

unload *v* pakua, toa

unlock *v* fungua

U

unlucky *adj* -sio na bahati

unmarried *adj* mseja

unmask *v* fichua

unmistakable *adj* wazi

unnecessary *adj* -sio ya lazima

unnoticed *adj* bila kuonekana

unoccupied *adj* wazi

unofficially *adv* si rasmi

unpack *v* fungua mizigo

unpleasant *adj* -siofurahisha

unplug *v* chomoa

unpopular *adj* -siopendwa

unpredictable *adj* -siotabirika

unprofitable *adj* -sio na faida

unprotected *adj* -sio lindwa

unravel *v* fumua, kunjua

unreal *adj* -sio ya kweli

unrealistic *adj* -sio aminika

unreasonable *adj* -sio na busara

unrelated *adj* tofauti

unrest *n* machafuko

unsafe *adj* -sio ya usalama

unselfish *adj* bila ubinafsi

unspeakable *adj* -siosemeka

unstable *adj* -sio imara

unsteady *adj* -sio imara

unsuccessful *adj* bila mafanikio

unsuitable *adj* -siofaa

unthinkable *adj* -siowazika

untie *v* fungua

until *pre* mpaka

untouchable *adj* -siogusika

untrue *adj* -sio kweli

unusual *adj* -sio ya kawaida

unveil *v* tangaza

unwillingly *adv* bila kutaka

unwind *v* kunjua; pumzika

unwise *adj* -sio ya busara

unwrap *v* fungua

upbringing *n* malezi

upcoming *adj* karibuni

update *v* rekebisha

upgrade *v* pandisha daraja

upheaval *n* mapinduzi

uphill *adv* ngumu

uphold *v* dumisha

upon *pre* juu; hapo

upper *adj* -a juu

upright *adj* mwaminifu

uprising *n* maasi

uproar *n* vurumai, fujo

uproot *v* ng'oa

upset *v* kasirisha; vuruga

upside-down *adv* juu chini

upstairs *adv* juu

up-to-date *adj* -a hivi sasa

upturn *n* maendeleo

upwards *adv* kwa juu

urban *adj* -a mjini

urge *n* kuhimiza

urge *v* sihi

urgency *n* haraka

urgent *adj* -a haraka

urinate *v* kojoa

urine *n* mkojo

urn *n* dumu

us *pro* sisi

usage *n* matumizi

use *v* tumia

use *n* utumiaji

used to *adj* zoea

useful *adj* -enye manufaa

usefulness *n* manufaa

useless *adj* -sio na manufaa

user *n* mtumiaji

usher *n* bawabu

usual *adj* kawaida

usurp *v* chukua kwa nguvu

utensil *n* kifaa

uterus *n* kizazi

utilize *v* tumia

utmost *adj* -a juu kabisa

utter *v* sema, tamka

V

vacancy *n* nafasi wazi

vacant *adj* tupu, wazi

vacate *v* ondoka, hama

vacation *n* likizo

vaccinate *v* chanja

vaccine *n* chanjo

vacillate *v* kosa msimamo

vagrant *n* anaye randaranda

vague *adj* -a mashaka

vain *adj* bure; jiona

vainly *adv* bure

valiant *adj* shujaa, jasiri

valid *adj* -liohalali

validate *v* halalisha

validity *n* uhalali

valley *n* bonde

valuable *adj* -enye thamani

value *n* thamani; maadili

valve *n* kilango

vampire *n* mnyonya damu

van *n* behewa

vandalize *v* haribu makusudi

vanguard *n* uongozi

vanish *v* toweka

vanity *n* majivuno

U
V

vanquish v shinda

variable adj geugeu

varied adj -a namna nyingi

variety n tofauti, jamii

various adj mbalimbali

varnish v paka vanishi

varnish n vanishi

vary v tofautiana

vase n chombo cha maua

vast adj kubwa mno

veal n nyama ya ndama

veer v badili mweleko

vegetable v mboga

vegetation n uoto, mmea

vehicle n gari, motokaa

veil n shela

vein n mshipa

velocity n kasi

velvet n bahameli

venerate v heshimu sana

vengeance n kisasi

venison n nyama ya pori

venom n sumu ya nyoka

vent n tundu la hewa

ventilate v ingiza hewa safi

ventilation n uingizaji wa hewa

venture v thubutu

venture n mradi; jaribio

verb n kitenzi

verbally adv kwa maneno

verbatim adv neno kwa neno

verdict n hukumu

verge n ukingo

verification n uthibitisho

verify v hakikisha

verse n ushairi, ubeti

versed adj -enye maarifa

version n toleo

versus pre dhidi

vertebra n vetebra

very adv sana, kabisa

vessel n chombo

vest n fulana

vestige n masaa, alama

veteran n askari mstaafu

veto v piga kura ya turufu

viaduct n daraja refu

vibrant adj changamfu

vibrate v tikisika

vibration n mtikisiko

vice n tabia mbaya; vice

vicinity n maeneo ya karibu

vicious adj ovu

victim n mwathirika

victimize v onea, athiri

victor n mshindi

V

victorious *adj* -a ushindi

victory *n* ushindi

view *n* mwonekano

view *v* tazama, angalia

viewpoint *n* mtazamo

vigil *n* mkesha

village *n* kijiji

villager *n* mwanakijiji

villain *n* mhalifu

vindicate *v* halalisha; tetea

vine *n* mzabibu

vinegar *n* siki

violate *v* vunja; haramisha

violence *n* jefule

violent *adj* dhalimu

violet *n* urujuani

violin *n* fidla

violinist *n* mpiga fidla

viper *n* nyoka, kifutu

virgin *n* bikira

virginity *n* ubikira

virility *n* nguvu za kiume

virtually *adv* kama vile

virtue *n* wema, uadilifu

virtuous *adj* tawa

virus *n* virusi

visibility *n* upeo wa kuona

visible *adj* -a kuonekana

vision *n* kuona, mtazamo

visit *n* ziara, matembezi

visit *v* tembelea

visitor *n* mgeni

visual *adj* -a kuona

visualize *v* bainisha

vital *adj* muhimu

vitality *n* uzima, nguvu

vitamin *n* vitamini

vivacious *adj* changamfu

vivid *adj* -a wazi; ng'aavu

vocabulary *n* msamiati

vocation *n* wito; taaluma

vogue *n* mtindo, fasheni

voice *n* sauti

void *adj* tupu, batili

volatile *adj* -a hatari

volcano *n* volkeno

volleyball *n* mpira wa wavu

voltage *n* volteji

volume *n* wingi; juzuu

volunteer *n* mtu anaejitolea

vomit *v* tapika

vomit *n* matapishi

vote *v* piga kura

vote *n* kura

voting *n* upigaji kura

voucher *n* vocha, hati

V

vow *v* apa
vowel *n* irabu
voyage *n* safari
voyager *n* msafiri
vulgar *adj* -a kihuni
vulgarity *n* matule
vulnerable *adj* -a udhaifu
vulture *n* tai mzoga

W

wag *v* tingisha, tikisa
wage *n* mshahara, ujira
wagon *n* behewa; gari
wail *v* piga kite
wail *n* kite; mlio
waist *n* kiuno
wait *v* subiri
waiter *n* mhudumu
waiting *n* kusubiri
waitress *n* mhudumu
waive *v* tangua; samehe
wake up *iv* amka
walk *v* tembea
walk *n* matembezi

walkout *n* mgomo
wall *n* ukuta
wallet *n* pochi ya pesa
wander *v* zurura
wanderer *n* mzururaji; msafiri
wane *v* fifia, pungua
want *v* taka
war *n* vita
ward *n* kata; wodi
warden *n* mlezi
wardrobe *n* mavazi
warehouse *n* ghala, bohari
warfare *n* vita, mapigano
warm *adj* -a joto
warm up *v* changamkia
warmth *n* ukunjufu
warn *v* toa tahadhari
warning *n* ilani
warp *v* potosha
warped *adj* -liopotoshwa
warrant *v* halalisha; amuru
warrant *n* hati; uhalalishaji
warranty *n* dhamana
warrior *n* mpiganaji
warship *n* manowari
wart *n* sugu, chunjua
wary *adj* -a makini
wash *v* osha**

V
W

washable *adj* -a kuosheka
wasp *n* nyigu
waste *v* haribu, poteza
waste *n* uharibifu,
waste basket *n* pipa la karatasi
wasteful *adj* uharibifu
watch *n* saa
watch *v* tazama
watch out *v* chunga
watchful *adj* -enye hadhari
water *n* maji
water *v* mwagilia maji
water down *v* zimua
waterheater *n* hodhi
watermelon *n* tikiti
waterproof *adj* -siopitisha maji
watershed *n* tengamaji
watertight *adj* thabiti
watery *adj* -a maji maji
watt *n* wati
wave *n* wimbi
waver *v* sitasita; yumba
wavy *adj* -enye mawimbi
wax *n* nta
way *n* njia
way in *n* njia ya kuingilia
way out *n* njia ya kutokea
we *pro* sisi

weak *adj* mnyonge, mdhaifu
weaken *v* dhoofisha
weakness *n* unyonge, udhaifu
wealth *n* utajiri
wealthy *adj* tajiri
weapon *n* silaha
wear *n* vazi; uchakavu
wear *iv* vaa
wear down *v* chakaza
wear out *v* chosha
weary *adj* kwa uchovu
weather *n* hali ya hewa
weave *iv* fuma; tunga
web *n* mtandao
web site *n* tovuti
wed *iv* oa
wedding *n* harusi
wedge *n* kabari
Wednesday *n* jumatano
weed *n* gugu
weed *v* palilia
week *n* wiki, juma
weekday *adj* siku ya kazi
weekend *n* mwisho wa wiki
weekly *adv* kwa wiki
weep *iv* lia
weigh *v* pima uzito
weight *n* uzito

W

weird _adj_ -sio ya kawaida
welcome _v_ karibisha
welcome _n_ mapokezi
weld _v_ tambuza
welder _n_ mtambuzaji
welfare _n_ ustawi
well _n_ kisima
well-known _adj_ anaye fahamika
well-to-do _adj_ -enye uwezo
west _n_ magharibi
western _adj_ -a magharibi
wet _adj_ lowa
whale _n_ nyangumi
wharf _n_ gati
what _adj_ nini
whatever _adj_ yoyote
wheat _n_ ngano
wheel _n_ gurudumu
wheelbarrow _n_ toroli
when _adv_ lini
whenever _adv_ kila
where _adv_ wapi
whereabouts _n_ mahali alipo
whereas _c_ ambapo
whereupon _c_ ndipo
wherever _c_ popote, kokote
whether _c_ kama
which _adj_ ipi

while _c_ wakati
whim _n_ wazo la ghafla
whine _v_ nung'unika
whip _v_ chapa mjeledi
whip _n_ mjeledi
whirl _v_ mzunguko wa kasi
whirlpool _n_ mzunguko
whiskers _n_ masharubu
whisper _v_ nong'ona
whisper _n_ kunong'ona
whistle _v_ piga mluzi
whistle _n_ mluzi
white _adj_ nyeupe
whiten _v_ fanya nyeupe
whittle _v_ chonga
who _pro_ nani
whoever _pro_ yeyote
whole _adj_ yote
wholesale _n_ mauzo ya jumla
whom _pro_ yupi, nani
why _adv_ kwa nini
wicked _adj_ mwovu
wickedness _n_ uovu
wide _adj_ pana
widely _adv_ kwa wingi
widen _v_ panua
widespread _adj_ -liosambaa
widow _n_ mjane

widower *n* mjane mwanaume

width *n* upana

wield *v* tumia

wife *n* mke

wig *n* wigi

wiggle *v* tikisatikisa

wild *adj* -a pori, -a mwitu

wild boar *n* ngiri

wilderness *n* msitu, pori

wildlife *n* wanyama pori

will *n* hiari, matakwa

willfully *adv* kwa makusudi

willing *adj* -enye nia

willingly *adv* kwa hiari

willingness *n* kuwa tayari

wily *adj* mjanja

wimp *adj* kifefe

win *iv* shinda

win back *v* shinda tena

wind *n* upepo

wind *iv* zungusha

wind up *v* ishia

windmill *n* kinuupepo

window *n* dirisha

windpipe *n* koo

windy *adj* -a upepo

wine *n* mvinyo

wing *n* bawa

wink *n* kukonyeza

wink *v* konyeza

winner *n* mshindi

winter *n* kipupwe

wipe *v* futa, kausha

wipe out *v* angamiza

wire *n* waya

wireless *adj* bila waya

wisdom *n* busara, hekima

wise *adj* -enye busara

wish *v* nuiza, tamani

wish *n* matakwa

wit *n* akili

witch *n* mchawi

witchcraft *n* uchawi

with *pre* na

withdraw *v* ondoa, futa

withdrawal *n* kuondoa

withdrawn *adj* kujitenga

wither *v* sinyaa

withhold *iv* zuia

within *pre* kwa ndani

without *pre* bila

withstand *v* stahimili

witness *n* shahidi

witty *adj* mcheshi

wives *n* wake

wizard *n* mchawi

wobble *v* yumbayumba

woes *n* masikitiko

wolf *n* mbwa mwitu

woman *n* mwanamke

womb *n* kizazi

women *n* wanawake

wonder *v* staajabu

wonder *n* kustaajabu

wonderful *adj* nzuri sana

wood *n* mbao

wooden *adj* -a mbao

wool *n* sufu

woollen *adj* -a sufu

word *n* neno

work *n* kazi

work *v* fanya kazi

work out *v* fanya mazoezi

workable *adj* -enye kutendeka

worker *n* mfanyakazi

workshop *n* karakana; warsha

world *n* dunia, ulimwengu

worldly *adj* -a dunia

worm *n* mnyoo

worn-out *adj* chakaa

worrisome *adj* -a kutia hofu

worry *v* hofia

worry *n* hofu

worse *adj* mbaya zaidi

worsen *v* tibua zaidi

worship *n* abudu

worst *adj* mbaya kuliko zote

worthless *adj* -sio na thamani

worthwhile *adj* -enye manufaa

worthy *adj* -enye kustahili

would-be *adj* mtarajiwa

wound *n* jeraha

wound *v* jeruhi

woven *adj* fumwa

wrap *v* funga

wrap up *v* maliza

wrapping *n* cha kufungia

wrath *n* ghadhabu

wreath *n* shada

wreck *v* haribu; vunja vunja

wreckage *n* gofu

wrench *n* kwapua

wrestle *v* shindana mieleka

wrestling *n* pigana mieleka

wretched *adj* nyonge

wring *iv* kamua

wrinkle *v* kunja kunja

wrinkle *n* kunyanzi

wrist *n* kifundo cha mkono

write *iv* andika

write down *v* andika

writer *n* mwandishi

W

writhe *v* tapatapa
writing *n* maandishi
written *adj* andikwa
wrong *adj* -a makosa

X

X-mas *n* krismasi
X-ray *n* eksrei

Y

yacht *n* mashua ya anasa
yam *n* gimbi
yard *n* uwanja
yarn *n* uzi; hadithi ndefu
yawn *n* mwayo
yawn *v* piga mwayo
year *n* mwaka
yearly *adv* kwa mwaka
yearn *v* tamani
yeast *n* hamira
yell *v* piga kelele
yellow *adj* njano
yes *adv* ndio

yesterday *adv* jana
yet *c* hata
yield *v* toa
yield *n* mapato
yoke *n* nira
yolk *n* kiini
you *pro* wewe
young *adj* mdogo
youngster *n* mtoto, kijana
your *adj* yako
yours *pro* yako
youth *n* kijana
youthful *adj* kijana

Z

zeal *n* shauku
zealous *adj* -enye shauku
zebra *n* punda milia
zero *n* sufuri
zest *n* shauku
zinc *n* zinki
zip code *n* msimbo wa posta
zipper *n* zipu
zone *n* eneo
zoology *n* zuologia

W
X
Y
Z

Swahili-English

Bilingual Dictionaries, Inc.

Abbreviations

English - Swahili

a - article - kibainishi
adj - adjective - kivumishi
adv - adverb - kielezi
c - conjunction - kiunganishi
e - exclamation - kiingizi
n - noun - nomino
pre - preposition - kihusishi
pro - pronoun - kiwakilishi
v - verb - kitenzi

A

abiri *v* navigate
abiria *n* passenger
abjadi *n* alphabet
abudu *n* worship
acha *v* cease, stop
acha kutumika *n* disuse
acha njia ya reli *v* derail
achana *v* break up
achia *v* let go, release
achia huru *n* acquittal
achia huru *v* free, let out
achia ngazi *v* step down
achiliwa *adj* exempt
achisha kazi *v* lay off
adabu *n* courtesy
adapta *n* adapter
adhabu *n* punishment
adhibu *v* punish
adhimisha *v* commemorate
adhiri *v* denigrate
adhuhuri *n* noon
adilifu *adj* impartial
admeri *n* admiral
adui *n* enemy

afisa *n* officer
afya *n* health
afya! kwaheri *n* cheers
afyuni *n* opium
agano *n* testament
agiza *v* prescribe
agizo *n* prescription
Agosti *n* August
ahadi *n* promise
ahidhi *v* undertake
ahidi *v* offer, pledge
ahiri *v* procrastinate
ahirisha *v* postpone
ahsante *n* thanks
ahueni *n* remission
aibisha *v* embarrass
aibu *n* disgrace
aina *n* brand, make
ajali *n* accident
ajenda *n* agenda
ajira *n* employment
ajiri *v* employ, hire
akaunti *n* account
akiba *n* savings
akili *n* sense, mind
akili timamu *n* sanity
akisi *v* reflect
akustika *adj* acoustic

alafu *adj* next
alama *n* mark, vestige
alama ya kidole *n* fingerprint
alama ya mguu *n* footprint
alama ya nyota *n* asterisk
alfabeti *n* alphabet
alfajiri *n* dawn
Alhamisi *n* Thursday
alika *v* click
aljebra *n* algebra
almasi *n* diamond
aloi *n* alloy
aluminiamu *n* aluminum
ama *adv* either
amali *n* career
amana *n* deposit
amani *n* peace
ambapo *c* whereas
ambatanisha *v* attach
ambia siri *v* confide
ambukiza *v* infect
ambukzizo *n* infection
amini *v* believe, trust
amiri *n* commander
amka *v* awake
amkia *v* greet
amonia *n* ammonia
amplifaya *n* amplifier

amri *n* decree
amsha *v* arouse, evoke
amua *v* determine
amuru *v* ordain, dictate
analojia *n* analogy
anasa *n* luxury
andaa *v* equip
andika *v* write, record
andikiana *v* correspond
andikisha *v* matriculate
andiko *n* inscription
andikwa *adj* written
anga *n* sky
anga ya nchi *n* airspace
angakewa *n* atmosphere
angalia *v* observe
angamia *v* perish
angamiza *v* destroy
angamizwa *adj* doomed
angaza *v* illuminate
Anglikana *adj* Anglican
anguka *v* fall, tumble
anguka ghafla *v* slump
anguka theluji *v* snow
anguko *n* downfall
angusha *v* drop, cut down
anuwai *n* diversity, range
anwani *n* address

anza *v* begin, start
anza safari *v* set off
anza tena *v* resume
anza upya *v* rebuild
anzia *v* stem
anzisha *v* initiate
anzisha ukoloni *v* colonize
apa *v* vow, swear
apostrofi *n* apostrophe
Aprili *n* April
aproni *n* apron
ardhi *n* ground, land
arieli *n* antenna
arifia *v* bid
arki *n* essence
arobaini *adj* forty
asa *n* cane
asali *n* honey
asenia *n* arsenic
aseniki *n* arsenic
asheni *n* vogue
asherati *adj* prurient
ashiki *n* admirer, lust
ashiria *v* gesticulate
ashiya *n* curfew
asi *v* rebel, revolt
asili *n* origin, nature
asilimia *n* percentage

askari *n* cop, soldier
askari mpya *n* recruit
askari mstaafu *n* veteran
askofu *n* bishop, pontiff
askofu mkuu *n* archbishop
asparaga *n* asparagus
aspirini *n* aspirin
asubuhi *n* morning
athari *n* fallout, impact
athiri *v* affect, impact
atomu *n* atom
au *c* or
au *adv* either
auwali *n* inception
awali *adv* previously
aya *n* paragraph
ayari *n* scoundrel
azima *v* borrow, lend
azimio *n* resolution
azimisha *v* ram

B

baa *n* bar

baada *pre* after

baadae *adv* afterwards

baadaye *adv* later

baadhi *adj* several

baba *n* dad, father

baba mkwe *n* father-in-law

baba wa kambo *n* stepfather

babaika *v* falter

babu *n* grandfather

babu na bibi *n* grandparents

babua *v* corrode, scald

badala *adv* instead

badala *n* substitute

badhiri mali *v* embezzle

badili *adj* avaricious

badili *v* substitute

badili mada *v* digress

badili mweleko *v* veer

badilika *v* change, distort

badiliko *n* transformation

badilisha *v* alter, modify

badilishana *v* exchange

bafu *n* bath, bathtub

bafuni *n* bathroom

bagua *v* discriminate

bahameli *n* velvet

bahari *n* sea, ocean

baharia *n* crew, sailor

baharia *adj* navy blue

bahasha *n* envelope

bahati *n* destiny, luck

bahati mbaya *adj* accidental

bahati nasibu *n* lottery, raffle

bahatika *adj* lucky

bahili *n* miser

bahili *adj* stingy

bainisha *v* visualize

baiskeli *n* bicycle

bajeti *n* budget

baka *v* rape, molest

baki *v* remain, stay

baki *n* remains, remnant

bakoli *n* buckle

bakora *n* crook

bakshishi *n* bonus

bakteria *n* bacteria

bakuli *n* bowl

balaa *n* misfortune, disaster

balasi *n* jug

balbu *n* bulb

balehe *n* puberty

Balozi *n* ambassador

balozi mdogo *n* consul

balungi *n* grapefruit

bamiza *v* bang, slam

bamizo *n* knock

bamvua *n* tide

bana *v* clinch, staple

bana komeo *v* bolt

bana uhuru wa *v* restrict

banana *v* squeeze up

bandari *n* harbor, port

bandi *n* tack

bandia *adj* artificial, fake

bandia *n* imitation

bandia ghushi *adj* counterfeit

bandika *v* affix

bandua *v* detach

bangi *n* hashish

bangili *n* bracelet

bango *n* banner, poster

banika *v* broil, grill, roast

banika mkate *v* toast

bano *n* bracket

bao *n* goal

bara *n* mainland

barabara *n* avenue, road

barabara kuu *n* freeway

baradhuli *adj* slob

barafu *n* frost, ice

baraka *n* benediction

barakoa *n* mask

baraza *n* patio, porch

baridi *n* chill

baridi *adj* chilly

baridi sana *adj* ice-cold

baridi yabisi *n* rheumatism

bariki *v* anoint, bless

barometa *n* barometer

barua *n* letter, mail

barua ya ndege *n* airmail

baruti *n* gunpowder

bashasha *adj* affable

bashiri *v* predict

basi *n* bus

bastola *n* handgun

bata *n* duck

bata bukini *n* goose

bata maji *n* swan

batalioni *n* battalion

batili *n* invalid, null

batilisha *v* repeal, nullify

batiza *v* baptize

bawa *n* wing

bawaba *n* hinge

bawabu *n* usher

bayana *adj* positive

beba *v* haul, cart

bechi *n* batch

bega *n* shoulder

behewa *n* van, wagon

bei *n* price

beji *n* badge

beleshi *n* shovel

bemba *v* flirt

bembea *n* hammock

bembea *v* swing

bembeleza *v* soothe

benchi *n* bench, pew

bendeji *n* bandage

bendera *n* flag

bendi *n* band

benki *n* bank

benki ya data *n* database

bepari *n* tycoon

bereti *n* beret

beseni *n* basin, tub

besi *n* base

betri *n* battery

bezo *n* cynicism, snub

bia *n* beer

biashara *n* business

bibi *n* grandmother

bibi harusi *n* bride

biblia *n* bible

bibliografia *n* bibliography

bidhaa *n* product, stock

bidhaa kuu *n* staple

bidi *v* ought to

bidii *n* dedication, drive

bidika *v* have to

bikira *n* virgin

bila *pre* without

bilauri *n* chalice

bili *n* bill

biliadi *n* billiards

bilioni *n* billion

bima *n* assurance

binadamu *n* mankind

binafsi *pre* oneself

binamu *n* cousin

bingwa *n* champion

bingwa *adj* skillful

binti *n* daughter, lady

biolojia *n* biology

biri *n* cigar

birika *n* kettle

birika la chai *n* teapot

bisha *v* dispute

bishana *v* argue

bishana bei *v* haggle

bisi *n* popcorn

bisibisi *n* screwdriver

biskuti _n_ biscuit, cookie
bitana _n_ lining
blanketi _n_ blanket
blauzi _n_ blouse
boflo _n_ loaf
bofya _v_ click
boga _n_ pumpkin
boksi _n_ box
boma _n_ enclosure
bomba _n_ faucet, pipe
bombwe _n_ pattern
bomoa _v_ dismantle
bomoka _v_ cave in
bomu _n_ bomb
bonde _n_ valley
bondia _n_ boxer
bonge _n_ bulk, lump
bonyeza _v_ press
bora _adj_ better
bora sana _adj_ excellent
bora zaidi _adj_ superior
boresha _v_ improve
boriti _n_ boom
bosi _n_ boss
botania _n_ botany
boti _n_ boat
bovu, viza _adj_ rotten
boya _n_ buoy, raft

brandi _n_ brandy
brashi _n_ brush
breki _v_ brake
brigedi _n_ brigade
bubu _adj_ mute, dumb
bucha _n_ butcher
budi _n_ alternative
buga _n_ sponge
bugia _v_ devour, gobble
bui wa sumu _n_ tarantula
buibui _n_ spider
bukua _v_ cram
buli _n_ teapot
bulunda _v_ mess up
buluu _v_ bleach
bundi _n_ owl
bunduki _n_ gun, rifle
bunge _n_ congress
buni _v_ concoct, invent
buni upya _v_ recreate
bunta _n_ shipyard
bunzi _n_ cob
bure _adj_ barren
bure _adv_ vainly
burudani _adj_ amusing
burudisha _v_ refresh
buruji _n_ cornet
burura _v_ manhandle

B
C

busara *n* discretion
bustani *n* garden, park
busu *n* kiss
busu *v* kiss
busu *v* kiss
buti *n* boot
butu *adj* dull, blunt
bwabwaja *v* rattle
bwalo *n* mess
bwana *n* mister, lord
bwana harusi *n* groom
bwawa *n* pool, pond
bweha *n* jackal
bweka *v* bark
bweni *n* dormitory

C

chacha *v* ferment
chache *adj* few
chache zaidi *adj* fewer
chachili *adj* timid
chachu *adj* sour
chafu *adj* dirty, filthy

chafua *v* stain, soil
chafua jina *v* defile
chafya *n* sneeze
chagua *v* choose, elect
chaguo *n* choice
chaguzi *adj* choosy
chai *n* tea
chaji tena *v* recharge
chakaa *adj* worn-out
chakavu *adj* derelict
chakaza *v* wear down
chaki *n* chalk
chakula *n* diet, food
chale *n* clown
chama *n* party
chambo *n* bait
chambua *v* analyze
chamgamfu *adj* gregarious
chana *v* rip, tear
changa *adj* immature
changa *v* contribute
changamfu *adj* playful
changamka *v* cheer up
changamkia *v* warm up
changamoto *n* challenge
changamsha *v* animate
changanya *v* mix, blend
changanyika *v* integrate

changarawe *n* pebble

changia *v* contribute

chango *n* colic

changua tena *v* reelect

chanika *v* come apart

chanja *v* immunize

chanjo *n* vaccine

chanua *v* blossom, flourish

chanuo *n* comb

chanzo *n* cause

chapa *v* spank, lash

chapa mjeledi *v* whip

chapa ndogo *n* small print

chapisha *n* edition

chapisha *v* publish

chapisha tena *v* reprint

chapisho *n* publication

chati *n* chart

chatu *n* python

chavua *n* pollen

chawa *n* lice

chaza *n* oyster, clam

cheche *n* spark

chechemea *v* limp

cheka *v* ridicule

cheka chinichini *v* chuckle

chekecha *v* sift

chekechea *n* toddler

chekelea *v* giggle

chekesha *v* entertain

chelewa *v* miss

chelewesha *v* delay

chembe *n* shred, particle

chembechembe *n* crumb

chemchem *n* fountain

chemchemi *n* spa, spring

chemka *v* simmer

chemsha *v* boil

chemshabongo *n* puzzle

chenga *n* chip

chengeu *n* lampshade

chenza *n* tangerine

cheo *n* rank

chepechepe *adj* soggy

chepusha *v* divert

chesi *n* chess

cheti *n* certificate

cheua *v* belch, burp

cheuzi *n* burp

chewa *n* cod

cheza *v* dance

cheza kamari *v* gamble

chezea *v* manipulate

chimba *v* excavate

chimbuko *n* essence

chini *adv* below, under

C

chini chini *adj* lowkey

chini ya *pre* below

chini zaidi *adj* lower

chinja *v* slaughter

chipsi *n* fries

chipua *v* germinate

chipukizi *n* bud, graft

chiriku *n* canary

chochea *v* fuel, goad

chochea ugomvi *v* embroil

chocheleza *v* indoctrinate

chochote *pro* anything

choka *adj* fed up

chokaa *n* mortar

choko *adj* tired

chokoa *v* prod

chokoleti *n* chocolate

chokoza *v* goad

choma *v* prick, sting

choma maiti *v* cremate

chombo *n* container, dish

chomboni *adv* aboard

chomoa *v* unplug

chomoza *n* breakthrough

chomoza *v* protrude

chonga *v* carve, whittle

chongea *v* denounce

chongeka *adj* pointed

choo *n* lavatory

chora *v* illustrate

chora picha *v* portray

chosha *v* exasperate

choshwa *adj* bored

choyo *adj* mean

chua *v* massage

chubua *v* bruise

chubwi *v* plummet

chuchu *n* comforter

chuchumaa *v* crouch

chui *n* leopard

chui mweusi *n* panther

chuja *v* filter, strain

chujio *n* filter

chuki *n* distaste

chuki kubwa *n* revulsion

chukia *v* abhor, despise

chukiza *v* embitter

chukizwa *v* repel

chukua *v* get, take

chukua hatua *v* institute

chuma *n* metal, steel

chumba *n* chamber, room

chumba kidogo *n* compartment

chumbia *v* court

chumbiwa *n* engagement

chumo la ziada *n* by-product**

chumvi *n* salt
chuna *v* skin
chunga *v* look after, mind
chungu *n* pot
chungulia *v* peep
chunguza *v* investigate
chungwa *n* orange
chunusi *n* pimple
chuo *n* college
chuo kikuu *n* university
chupa *n* bottle
chupi *n* pants
chura *n* frog, toad
chusa *n* harpoon

D

dada *n* sister
dada wa kambo *n* stepsister
dadisi *v* sound out
dadu *n* dice
daftari *n* notebook
dagaa *n* sardine
dai *v* allege, claim

dai tena *v* reclaim
daima *adv* always
daiwa *v* owe
dakika *n* minute
dakiza *v* meddle
daktari *n* physician
daktari mpasuaji *n* surgeon
dalili *n* symptom, clue
damu *n* blood
danganya *v* delude, dupe
danganyika *adj* gullible
danguro *n* brothel
dansi *n* dance
daraja *n* bridge
daraja la pili *n* coach
daraja refu *n* viaduct
darasa *n* classroom
dari *n* attic, ceiling
darubini *n* binoculars
data *n* data
datsi *n* dart
dau *n* cutter
dawa *n* cure, medicine
dawa ya kuboresha *n* conditioner
dawa ya madoa *n* bleach
dawa ya sindano *n* serum
dawa ya viatu *n* shoepolish
dawati *n* desk, bureau

C
D

dayosisi *n* diocese

dazeni *n* dozen

dekeza *v* pamper

demokrasia *n* democracy

dengu *n* lentil

deni *n* debt

Denmark *n* Denmak

dereva *n* driver

dereva lori *n* trucker

desimali *adj* decimal

desturi *n* custom, norm

dhahabu *n* gold

dhahiri *adj* exact, distinct

dhahiri iliyo wazi *adj* obvious

dhaifu *adj* unhealthy

dhairi *adj* self-evident

dhairi kabisa *adj* clear-cut

dhalili *adj* sleazy

dhalilika *v* condescend

dhalilisha *v* demean

dhalimu *adj* violent

dhamana *n* guarantee

dhambi *n* sin

dhamini *v* guarantee

dhamira *n* theme

dhamiri *n* conscience

dhamiria *v* intend

dhana *n* assumption

dhani *v* assume

dhania *v* attribute

dharau *n* defiance, snub

dharau *v* defy, scorn

dharuba *n* impact

dharura *n* emergency

dhehebu *n* sect

dhibiti *v* control, rein

dhidi *pre* against

dhifa *n* banquet

dhihaka *n* gag

dhihaki *n* mockery, irony

dhihakia *v* mock

dhihirisha *v* authenticate

dhima *n* liability

dhoofika *v* deteriorate

dhoofisha *v* weaken, sap

dhoruba *n* storm, tempest

dhuluma *n* injustice

dhuru *v* afflict

dibaji *n* preface

dini *n* religion

diplomasia *n* diplomacy

dira *n* compass

dirisha *n* window

dirisha la darini *n* skylight

Disemba *n* December

doa *n* blemish, stain

dokeza v hint, infer
dokezo n hint, allusion
dokoa v snitch
dola n dollar
dole gumba n thumb
dondoa v quote
dondoo n excerpt, item
donge n dough
donge la damu n clot
donoa v peck, pluck
doria n patrol
dosari n imperfection
duara n circle
duara dufu adj oval
dubu n bear
dufu adj insipid
duka n shop
duka kubwa n supermarket
duka la dawa n pharmacy
duka la sonara n jewelry store
duka la viatu n shoestore
duka la vitabu n bookstore
dume n ace, bull
dumisha v uphold
dumu v last, span
dumu n urn
dumu kuliko v outlast
dunda v rebound

dunga v inject
dungu n scaffolding
duni adj cheap, petty
dunia n earth, world
duwaa adj speechless
duwaa n trance

E

egemea v lean
egemea nyuma v recline
egemeo n linchpin
egesha v park
Eire n Ireland
eka n acre
ekolojia n ecology
ekseli n axle
eksrei n X-ray
kwa kuelea adv adrift, afloat
elea v drift, float
elekea adj bound for
elekea v drive at
elekeza v direct, guide
elewa v comprehend

D
E

elewa vibaya *v* misconstrue
elewa visivyo *v* misinterpret
eleweka *adj* coherent
eleza *v* brief, explain
eleza kwa kifupi *v* outline
eleza kwa ufupi *v* summarize
eleza maana *v* define
elfu *adj* thousand
elimisha *v* educate
elimu *n* knowledge
elimu kale *n* archaeology
elimu mwili *n* anatomy
elimu ya vitabu *adj* pedantic
endekeza *v* indulge, pander
endelea *v* carry on
endelea kukua *v* evolve
endeleza *v* keep up
endesha *v* propel, drive
endesha vibaya *v* mismanage
enea *v* fit
enea *adj* rampant
eneo *n* area, site
eneo la maduka *n* mall
eneza *v* propagate
engua *v* skim
epuka *v* avoid, elude
epukika *adj* avoidable

F

faa *v* get by
fadhaa *n* bombshell
fadhaika *adj* frantic
fadhaisha *adj* distraught
fadhila *n* favor, charity
fafanua *v* clarify, illustrate
fagia *v* sweep
fahali *n* bull, ox
fahamiana *v* acquaint
fahamu *adj* aware
faharasa *n* glossary
fahari *n* pride, luxury
faharisi *n* index
faida *n* advantage
faini *n* fine
falaki *n* astronomy
falsafa *n* philosophy
faluda *n* custard
familia *n* family
fanaka *n* prosperity
fanana *v* resemble
fani *n* sphere
fanicha *n* furniture
fanikisha *v* realize

F

fanikiwa v accomplish

fanya v act, carry out

fanya biashara v trade, deal

fanya fujo v riot

fanya ghasia v rampage

fanya giza v darken

fanya hila v trick

fanya imara v toughen

fanya juhudi v exert

fanya kampeni v campaign

fanya kazi v work

fanya kiziwi v deafen

fanya magendo v traffic

fanya masihara v mess around

fanya mawimbi v curl

fanya mazoezi v exercise

fanya muafaka v compromise

fanya ngumu v harden

fanya nyeupe v whiten

fanya rasmi v formalize

fanya takatifu v sanctify

fanya tamu v sweeten

fanya tashihisi v embody

fanya tena v redo

fanya ufa v crack

fanya ukatili v brutalize

fanya urafiki v befriend

fanya utundu v misbehave

fanyia shari v malign

faragha n privacy

faraja n comfort

faraka n sect

farasi n horse

farasi jike n mare

fariji v console

fariki v die, pass away

fasaha adj thorough

fasihi n literature

fasiki adj immoral

fasiri v deduce

fataki n fireworks, fuse

faulu v pass

Februari n February

fedha n money, cash

fedheha n scandal

fedhehesha v scandalize

feli v flunk

feni n fan

feri n iron

ficha v conceal, hide

fichua v debunk, expose

fidhuli adj cheeky, rude

fidia n compensation

fidia v indemnify

fidla n fiddle, violin

fifia adj blurred

fifia _v_ dwindle, fade
fifisha _v_ attenuate, dim
fifisha mg'ao _v_ tarnish
figili _n_ celery, radish
figo _n_ kidney
fika _v_ arrive
fika mwisho _v_ expire
fikia _v_ amount to
fikia matarajio _v_ live up
fikiri _v_ think, ponder
fikiri vibaya _v_ misjudge
fikiria _v_ reason
fikiria kuhusu _v_ consider
fikiria tena _v_ reconsider
fikra _n_ concept
filamu _n_ film
filimbi _n_ flute
filisika _v_ bankrupt
fimbo _n_ rod
finya _v_ pinch
finyanga _v_ mold
fisi _n_ hyena
fisi maji _n_ otter
fizikia _n_ physics
fomula _n_ formula
forodha _n_ customs
foronya _n_ pillowcase
fosforasi _n_ phosphorus

fremu _n_ frame
friza _n_ freezer
fua bila maji _v_ dryclean
fua vyuma _v_ forge
fuata _v_ follow, imitate
fuata desturi _v_ conform
fuata nyayo _v_ track
fuatilia _v_ trace, monitor
fuawe _n_ anvil
fufua _v_ rehabilitate
fuga _v_ tame, rear
fugua _v_ unfasten
fugua vifungo _v_ unbutton
fuja _v_ squander
fujo _n_ chaos, riot
fukara _adj_ penniless, destitute
fukiza _v_ fumigate
fuko _n_ mole
fukua _v_ unearth
fukuza _v_ banish, dismiss
fukuza kazi _v_ sack
fukuza nchini _v_ deport
fulana _n_ vest
fulani _adj_ certain
fululiza _v_ persevere
fuma _v_ knit, weave
fumbo _n_ innuendo
fumbu _v_ quiz

F

fumbua *v* decipher

fumua *v* unravel

fumuka *v* erupt

fumwa *adj* woven

fundi *n* mechanic

fundi bomba *n* plumber

fundi miwani *n* optician

fundi umeme *n* electrician

fundisha *v* teach, instruct

fundisho *n* precept

fundistadi *n* craftsman

fundo *n* knot, tangle

funga *v* lock, fasten

funga bendeji *v* bandage

funga choo *adj* constipated

funga goli *v* score

funga jela *v* imprison

funga pingu *v* handcuff

fungasha *v* bundle, pack

fungate *n* honeymoon

fungia *v* confine, enclose

fungu *n* bunch, cluster

fungua *v* open, unlock

fungua mizigo *v* unpack

fungulia *v* let out

fungwa *adj* closed

funika *v* cover

fununu *n* inkling

funza *v* learn

fupi *adj* brief, short

fupisha *v* abridge, shorten

furaha *n* happiness, joy

furaha kubwa *n* euphoria

furahi *adj* glad, happy

furahia *v* enjoy, relish

furahisha *v* amuse, please

furika *v* flood, inundate

furiko *n* glut

fursa *n* occasion

furushi *n* bundle

fusahi *v* revoke

futa *v* delete, erase

futa kabisa *v* obliterate

futia dhambi *v* absolve

fuvu la kichwa *n* skull

fuwele *n* crystal

fyeka *v* mow

fyonza *v* absorb, drain

fyuzi *n* fuse

G

gadhabisha *v* enrage
gaidi *n* terrorist
galoni *n* gallon
gamba *n* crust, shell
ganda *v* freeze, coagulate
gandamiza *v* oppress, crush
gandisha *v* paste, stick
gange *n* limestone
gango *n* clamp
gari *n* automobile, car
gari la jeneza *n* hearse
gari nyumba *n* caravan
gati *n* pier, wharf
gauni *n* gown, robe
gavana *n* governor
gawa *v* hand out
gawa kati *v* intersect
gawana *v* share
gawanya *v* divide
gawanya nusu *v* halve
gawia *v* allocate
gawio *n* dividend
gazeti *n* newspaper
gego *n* molar

gema *v* slit
genge *n* kiosk
gereji *n* garage
gereza *n* detention, jail
gesi *n* gas
geugeu *adj* variable
geuka *v* avert, shift
geukia *v* backfire
geuza *v* turn over
ghadhabisha *v* provoke
ghadhabu *n* tantrum
ghafla *adv* abruptly
ghala *n* warehouse
ghala la silaha *n* arsenal
ghamma *adj* unique
ghani *v* recite
gharama *n* cost, expense
gharimia *v* fund, cost
ghasia *n* insurgency
ghorofa *n* skyscraper
ghuba *n* gulf, bay, creek
ghushi *v* falsify, forge
gia *n* gear
gimbi *n* yam
gita *n* guitar
giza *adj* dark
giza *n* darkness
glavu *n* glove

glukozi *n* glucose
godoro *n* mattress
gofu *n* wreckage
gogo *n* log
goigoi *adj* clumsy
goka *v* gag
goli *n* goal
golikipa *n* goalkeeper
goma *v* strike
gombana *v* quarrel, fight
gombeza *v* rebuke, chide
gome *n* bark
gomea *v* boycott
gonga *v* knock, batter
gonga kengele *v* toll
gongana *v* clash, collide
gongo *n* crutch
goti *n* knee
gramu *n* gram
grisi *n* grease
gubeti *n* prow
guda *v* dock
gudi *n* dock
gudulia *n* barrel
gugu *n* weed
gugumia *v* stammer
guguna *v* gnaw
gumba *adj* childless

gumu *adj* solid, rigid
guna *v* groan, growl
gundi *n* glue, paste
gundisha *v* glue
gundua *v* disclose, reveal
gurudumu *n* wheel
guruto *v* mangle
gusa *v* touch
gusia *v* touch on
gutusha *v* startle
gwaride *n* march, parade

H

haba *adj* sparse, shallow
habari *n* information
hadharani *adv* publicly
hadhi *n* dignity, rank
hadhira *n* audience
hadi sasa *adv* hitherto
hadimu *adj* scarce, sparse
hadithi *n* fable, story
hadithi ya kidini *n* parable
hadithia *v* narrate

G
H

hadubini *n* microscope
hafifu *adj* benign, tenuous, faint
hai *adj* active, alive
haiba *n* charm
haidrojeni *n* hydrogen
haidroliki *adj* hydraulic
haikosi *adv* surely
haikuvunjika *adj* unbroken
haisomeki *adj* illegible
haitekelezeki *adj* impractical
haiwezekani *adj* impossible
haja *n* fad
haji *n* pilgrim
hajiri *v* emigrate
haki *n* prerogative
hakiki *v* review
hakikisha *v* ascertain
hakikishia *v* guarantee
hakikisho *n* guarantee
hakimiliki *n* copyright
hakimu *n* magistrate
hakuna *pre* none
hakuna *adj* neither
hakuna kitu *n* nothing
halalisha *v* justify
hali *n* mood, situation
hali hafifu *v* break down
hali halisi *n* reality

hali ngumu *n* predicament
hali ya hatari *n* crisis
hali ya hewa *n* climate
hali ya usununu *adj* moody
halijoto *n* temperature
halisi *adj* actual, real
halmashauri *n* council
haluli *adj* laxative
hama *v* evacuate
hamasa *n* ardor
hamasisha *v* mobilize
hami *v* insulate
hamia *v* immigrate
hamira *n* yeast
hamisha *v* shift, transfer
hamsini *adj* fifty
hamu kubwa *n* craving
hamu ya kula *n* appetite
handaki *n* bunker, tunnel
hani *v* sympathize
hanithi *adj* impotent
hapa *adv* here
haradali *n* mustard
harage *n* bean
haraka *n* haste, urgency
haraka *adj* quick, swift
haraka ya pupa *v* rash
harakisha *v* hasten, hurry

haram *n* pyramid

haramia *n* pirate

haramisha *v* violate

haramu *adj* illicit, illegal

haribika *v* decompose

haribika *n* disrepair

haribika tabia *v* degenerate

haribu *v* adulterate

haribu makusudi *v* vandalize

haribu mimba *v* miscarry

haribu sura *v* damage

hariri *v* edit

hariri *n* silk

harufu *n* odor, scent

harufu mbaya *n* stench

harusi *n* wedding

hasa *adv* chiefly, quite

hasa *adj* literal, precise

hasara *n* deficit

hasi *adj* negative

hasira *n* anger, rage

haswa *adv* especially, mainly

haswa *adj* main, definite

hata *adv* neither

hata *c* yet

hata hivyo *c* however, nonetheless

hata hivyo *adv* nevertheless

hata kama *c* even if, though

hatamu *n* bridle, rein

hatari *n* danger, peril

hatarisha *v* risk

hati *n* warrant, voucher

hati ya madai *n* invoice

hatia *n* guilt

hatimkato *n* shorthand

hatua *n* footstep

hawala *n* money order

hawilisha *v* convey

haya *n* shyness

hazina *n* fund

hedhi *n* menstruation

heka heka *adj* hectic

hekalu *n* temple

hekaya *n* legend

hekima *n* wisdom

helikopta *n* helicopter

helmeti *n* helmet

hema *n* tent

hendeli *n* crank

henzirani *n* cane

hereni *n* earring

heri *adv* rather

herufi kubwa *n* capital letter

herufi ndogo *n* fine print

hesabu *n* math

hesabu *v* count, reckon

H

heshima *n* homage
heshimu *v* respect
heshimu sana *v* esteem
hewa *n* air
hiari *n* will
hifadhi *n* asylum, shelter
hifadhi *v* shelter
hifadhi mkebeni *v* can
hii *adj* this
hija *n* pilgrimage
hila *n* ploy
himiza *v* lean on, sustain
hirimu *n* peer
hisa *n* quotient
hisi *v* sense, feel
hisia *n* feeling, hunch
hisia mapema *n* foretaste
historia *n* antecedents, history
hitaji *v* need, require
hitaji *n* requirement
hitilafu *n* discrepancy
hitimisha *v* infer
hitimisho *n* conclusion
hitimu *v* graduate
hivi *adv* incidentally
hivi karibuni *adv* lately
hivi sasa *adv* hereby
hivyo *adv* hence, thus, therefore

hizi *adj* these
hodari *adj* audacious
hodhi *n* boiler
hofia *v* apprehend; worry
hofisha *adj* alarming
hofiwa *adj* dreaded
hofu *n* panic, worry
hoja *n* reasoning
hojaji *n* questionnaire
hoji *v* interrogate
holela *adj* arbitrary
homa *n* fever, malaria
homa *adj* feverish
homa ya mafua *n* influenza
honga *v* bribe, buy off
hongera *n* congratulations
hongo *n* bribe, graft
hori *n* creek, estuary
hospitali *n* hospital
hoteli *n* hotel, inn
hotuba *n* speech
hovyo *adj* shabby
hubiri *v* preach
hudhuria *v* attend
hudhurio *n* participation
huduma *n* service
hudumia *v* cater to
hujaji *n* pilgrim

hukumu *n* judgment
hukumu *v* condemn
hulka *n* propensity
huru *adj* independent
huruma *n* mercy, pity
hurumia *v* sympathize
husiana *adj* related
husika *v* concern
husika *adj* relevant
husisha *v* implicate
husu *v* consist, pertain
husudu *n* admiration
husudu *v* admire
husuni *n* castle
hususan *adv* notably
hutubia *v* address
huzuni *adj* sad
huzuni *n* sadness
huzunisha *v* sadden

I

iba *v* rob, steal
iba dukani *n* shoplifting
iba kidogo *v* pilfer
ibia *v* cheat, rip off
ibuka *v* emerge
idadi *n* count, sum
idadi kubwa *n* multitude
idadi ya watu *n* population
idara *n* department
idhini *n* permission
idhinisha *v* authorize
ifia *v* ebb
iga *v* imitate
igiza *v* fake
igiza tamthilia *v* dramatize
ijayo *adj* forthcoming
Ijumaa *n* Friday
iko *adj* located
ikweta *n* equator
ila *c* barring, unless
ilani *n* warning
ile *adj* that
ile ile *adj* same
imani *n* belief, faith

imara *adj* rigid, sturdy
imarisha *v* strengthen
imba *v* embezzle
inama *v* bend down
inamaanisha *n* means
inapatikana *adj* located
inavyodaiwa *adv* allegedly
inchi *n* inch
inda *n* spite
ingia *v* come in, enter
Ingia kutu *v* rust
ingilia *v* intrude, meddle
ingilia eneo *v* trespass
ingilia kati *v* intervene
ingilia mali ya *v* encroach
ingilika *adj* approachable
ingine *adj* another
ingiza *v* insert, let in
ingiza hewa safi *v* ventilate
ingizo *n* input
ini *n* liver
injili *n* gospel
injini *n* engine
insha *n* essay
inua *v* elevate, lift
inua mabega *v* shrug
inuka *v* get up, rise
iodini *n* iodine

ipasavyo *adv* duly
ipi *adj* which
irabu *n* vowel
irabu unganifu *n* diphthong
irishi *adj* Irish
ishara *n* gesture, sign
ishi *v* inhabit, dwell
ishi katika *v* occupy
ishi kuliko *v* outlive
ishi kwa *v* live off
ishi pamoja *v* coexist
ishia *v* end up
ishirini *adj* twenty
ishiwa *v* run out
isiotumika *adj* idle
isipokuwa *pre* barring
isitoshe *adv* furthermore
istiara *n* allegory
istilahi *n* terminology
ita *v* recall, summon
ita mahakamani *v* subpoena
Italia *n* Italy
italiki *adj* italics
itifaki *n* protocol
itika *v* react
itikadi *n* ideology
itiko *n* reaction
itisha *v* convene

iva *adj* ripe
iva uso *v* flush
iwapo *c* supposing
iwapo kama *c* providing that

J

jaa *adj* full
jaa tele *v* abound
jabali *n* precipice, cliff
jadili *v* discuss
jadiliana *v* negotiate
jagi *n* jug
jahanamu *n* hell
jaji *n* judge
jaketi *n* jacket
jalada *n* dossier, file
jali *v* care
jamaa *n* relative
jambazi *n* attacker, thug
jambi *n* rug
jambia *n* dagger, sword
jambo *n* event
jambo la pekee *n* exception

jamhuri *n* republic
jamii *n* community
jamii shinani *adj* grassroots
jamu *n* conserve
jamvi *n* carpet
jana *adv* yesterday
jana usiku *adv* last night
janga *n* calamity
jangili *n* bandit
jangwa *n* desert
jani *n* leaf
jani dogo *n* leaflet
janja *adj* astute
Januari *n* January
japokuwa *c* although
jaribio *n* attempt
jaribu *v* test, try
jarida *n* magazine
jarida la habari *n* newsletter
jasho *n* sweat
jasiri *adj* bold, brave, daring
jasusi *n* spy
jawabu *n* answer
jaza *v* fill, cram, load
jaza tena *v* replenish
jaza upepo *v* pump
jaza watu *v* populate
jazia vitu laini *v* pad

I
J

jefule n violence
jela n jail, prison
jemadari n marshal
jemu n jam
jenerata n generator
jeneza n coffin
jenga v build
jenga tena v rebuild
jenga upya v remodel
jengo n construction
jengo kubwa n edifice
jeraha n bruise, wound
jeraha la moto n burn
jeruhi v wound
jeshi n army
jeuri n arrogance
jibanza v lurk
jibini n cheese
jibu v answer, reply
jibu n respond, reply
jibwaga v sprawl
jicho n eye
jidai v pretend
jifanya v feign, pretend
jifanya kama v pose
jificha v lurk
jihadhari v beware
jiji n city

jikimu v subsist
jiko n cuisine, stove
jikoni n kitchen
jikwaa v falter, stumble
jimbo n county, province
jina n name
jina la bandia n pseudonym
jina la ukoo n surname
jina la utani n nickname
jinamizi n nightmare
jino n tooth
jino chonge n fang
jinsi n sort; mode
jinsia n gender, sex
jinyima v abstain
jinzi n jeans
jiografia n geography
jiologia n geology
jiometri n geometry
jiona adj vain
jiondoe v log off
jioni n evening
jionyesha v show off
jipatia v avail
jipendekeza v ingratiate
jipumzisha v relax
jirani n neighbor
jisalimisha v surrender

jisifu *v* boast

jitayarishe *v* brace for

jitenga *v* drop out

jitenga na *v* shun

jitihada *n* endeavor

jitoa *v* renounce

jitoa mhanga *v* devote

jitokeza *v* stand out

jitokeze mbele *v* step up

jitu *n* giant, monster

jiunga *v* enlist

jiunge tena *v* rejoin

jiuzulu *v* abdicate

jivu *n* cinder

jivuna *v* boast

jiwe *n* rock, stone

jiwe la kaburi *n* tombstone

jiweke huru *v* break free

jizuia *v* refrain, desist

jkikwara *n* rooster

jodari *n* tuna

jogoo *n* cock, rooster

joho *n* cassock, cloak

joko *n* furnace, oven

jokofu *n* icebox

jongea *v* loom

jongo *n* gout

joto *n* heat

joto *adj* hot

jozi *n* pair

jua *v* know

jua *n* sun

juhudi *n* effort

juhudi ya kazi *n* diligence

jukumu *n* commitment

jukwaa *n* platform

Julai *n* July

Jumamosi *n* Saturday

Jumanne *n* Tuesday

Jumapili *n* Sunday

jumatano *n* Wednesday

Jumatatu *n* Monday

jumba kubwa *n* mansion

jumla *n* general

jumla *adj* total, gross

jumlisha *n* addition

jumuisha *v* encompass

junaa *n* scandal

Juni *n* June

jurawa *n* sparrow

jutia *v* lament

juu *pre* above, over

juu *adj* high

juu *pre* upon

juu chini *adv* upside-down

K

kaa *v* reside, stay
kaa kinyumba *v* cohabit
kaa mkao *v* pose
kaa na njaa *v* starve
kaa vibaya *adj* misfit
kaakaa *n* palate
kaanga *v* fry
kaba *v* smother, stifle
kababu *n* meatball
kabati *n* cabinet, closet
kabati la vitabu *n* bookcase
kabichi *n* cabbage
kabidhi *v* hand over
kabila *n* tribe
kabiliana *v* confront
kabisa *adv* entirely
kabla *adv* before
kabla *adj* prior
kabureta *n* carburetor
kaburi *n* grave, tomb
kachumbari *n* salad
kadhaa *adj* some
kadhalika *adv* likewise
kadi *n* card

kadibodi *n* cardboard
kadiria *v* appraise
kadirio *n* estimation
kagua *v* audit, inspect
kahawa *n* coffee
kaida *n* rite
kaidi *v* disobey
kaimu *n* exorcist
kaka *n* brother
kaka wa kambo *n* stepbrother
kakamaa *n* cramp
kakamaa *adj* tense
kakamavu *adj* stoic
kakao *n* cocoa
kalamu *n* pencil
kalamu ya wino *n* pen
kalenda *n* calendar
kali *adj* strict, stern
kalibu *n* foundry, mold
kalori *n* calorie
kama *adj* akin, such
kama *c* if, whether
kama *pre* like
kama vile *adv* virtually
kamanda *n* commander
kamari ya dadu *n* crap
kamasi *n* mucus
kamata *v* capture, grasp

kamata tena _v_ recapture
kamati _n_ committee
kamba _n_ cord, rope
kambi _n_ camp
kame _adj_ arid
kamera _n_ camera
kamili _adj_ intact
kamilifu _adj_ thorough
kamilifu _n_ totality
kamilisha _v_ conclude
kampeni _n_ campaign
kampuni _n_ company, firm
kamsa _n_ alarm
kamua _v_ squeeze, wring
kamusi _n_ dictionary
kamusi elezo _n_ encyclopedia
kamwe _adv_ never
kana _v_ repudiate
kanali _n_ colonel
kanda _n_ tape
kandili _n_ lantern
kando ya _pre_ beside
kangaga _n_ brake
kanineno _n_ stress
kanisa _n_ church
kanisa dogo _n_ chapel
kanisa kuu _n_ cathedral
kano _n_ rejection

kansa _n_ cancer
kanseli _n_ consulate
kantini _n_ canteen
kanuni _n_ doctrine
kanuni za imani _n_ creed
kanusha _v_ refute, rebut
kanya _v_ censure
kanyaga _v_ run over
kanzu _n_ tunic
kapera _n_ bachelor
kapi _n_ pulley
kapteni _n_ captain
kaptura _n_ shorts
karabati _v_ refurbish, renew
karagosi _n_ puppet
karaha _n_ discomfort
karakana _n_ workshop
karamu _n_ treat
karanga _n_ peanut
karani _n_ clerk, secretary
karatasi _n_ paper
karatasi ya kura _n_ ballot
karate _n_ karate
karati _n_ carat
karibia _v_ approach
karibia _adj_ imminent
karibia _adv_ nearly
karibisha _v_ welcome

K

karibu na *pre* close to, near
karibuni *adj* upcoming
kariri *v* memorize
karne *n* century
karo *n* fee
karoti *n* carrot
kasa *n* turtle
kasha *n* box
kashfa *n* insult
kashifu *v* insult
kasi *n* speed
kasia *n* oar
kasino *n* casino
kasirika *adj* angry, upset
kasirisha *v* infuriate
kasisi *n* priest, rector
kaskazini *n* north
kasoro *n* defect
kasri *n* palace
kasuku *n* parrot
kasumba *n* opium
kaswende *n* syphilis
kata *v* amputate
kata kata *v* chop
kata kichwa *v* behead
kata kwa mkasi *v* shear
kata mti *v* log
kata rufaa *v* appeal

kata tamaa *v* give up
kataa *v* deny, disclaim
katakata *v* hack, shred
katalogi *n* catalog
kataza *v* ban, forbid
katekisimu *n* catechism
kati *n* center
kati ya *pre* among
katia bima *v* insure
katiba *n* constitution
katika *pre* in
katikati *pre* amid
katikati *n* middle
katili *adj* ruthless
katisha tamaa *v* disappoint
katiza *v* interrupt
katoliki *adj* catholic
katuni *n* cartoon
kauka *adj* dried
kaukau *adj* crisp
kauli *n* remark
kaunta *n* counter
kauri *n* ceramic
kausha *v* dry, wipe
kausha maji *v* dehydrate
kavu *adj* dry
kawaida *adj* normal, usual
kawaida *n* standard

kawaida *adv* normally

kawaida sana *n* banality

kawiza *v* hold up

kaza *v* strengthen

kaza sana *v* clench

kazi *n* career, job, task

kazi bora *n* masterpiece

kazi maalum *n* assignment

kazi ya msingi *n* groundwork

kazi ya ukarani *n* paperwork

kazi ya ziada *adv* overtime

kazi za ndani *n* housework

kebo *n* cable

kebu *n* cab

kefya *v* nag

kejeli *n* irony, sarcasm

kekee *n* drill

keki *n* cake

kelele *n* noise, shout

kemea *v* rebuke

kemia *n* chemistry

kemikali *adj* chemical

kengele *n* bell, buzzer

kera *v* annoy, irritate

keshia *n* cashier

kesho *adv* tomorrow

kiambatanisho *n* annex

kiambato *n* ingredient

kiambishi *n* prefix

kiamshi *n* stimulant

kiangazi *n* summer

kiango *n* bracket

kiapo *n* oath, pledge

Kiarabu *adj* Arabic

kiasi *n* amount

kiasi cha chini *n* minimum

kiasi cha juu *adj* maximum

kiatu *n* shoe

kiazi *n* potato

kiazisukari *n* beet

kibaka *n* hoodlum

kibali *n* approval

kibanda *n* booth, stall

kibandiko *n* sticker, tag

kibanio *n* clamp

kibanzi *n* splinter

kibaraka *n* henchman

kibarua *n* laborer

kiberiti *n* lighter

kibiblia *adj* biblical

kibiolojia *adj* biological

kibiongo *n* hump

kibiringo *n* reel, spool

kibodi *n* keyboard

kiboko *n* scourge

kibonge *n* pat

K

kibonyeo *n* dent
kiburudisho *n* amusement
kibwanyenye *adj* bourgeois
kichaa *n* craziness
kichaa *adj* crazy, insane
kichaka *n* bush, shrub
kichangamshi *n* tonic
kichapuzi *n* accelerator
kichefuchefu *n* disgust
kichekesho *n* farce, joke
kicheko *n* laugh
kichujio *n* strainer
kichumba *n* cabin
kichungi *n* butt, stub
kichwa *n* title, heading
kichwani *adv* mentally
kidahizo *n* catchword
kidani *n* pendant
kidau *n* cartridge
kidevu *n* chin
kidimbwi *n* ditch
kidiri *n* squirrel
kidoa *n* spot
kidoa cha ngozi *n* freckle
kidogo *adj* less, little
kidogo *adv* slightly
kidogo kidogo *adv* little by little
kidole *n* finger, digit

kidole tumbo *n* appendicitis
kidonda *n* injury, sore
kidonge *n* capsule, pill
kidoti *n* spot
kidoto *n* speck
kiduchu *adj* tiny
kielelezo *n* pattern
kielezi *n* adverb
kielezo *n* illustration
kifaa *n* appliance
kifafa *n* epilepsy
kifani *v* duplicate
kifaranga *n* chick
kifaru *n* rhinoceros
kifefe *adj* wimp
kifereji *n* duct
kifo *n* death
kifu *adj* fed up
kifua *n* bosom, bust
kifua kikuu *n* tuberculosis
kifumba mbegu *n* ovary
kifungo *n* confinement
kifungoni *n* captivity
kifungua kinywa *n* breakfast
kifungua mlo *n* entree
kifuniko *n* hood
kifupi *n* abbreviation
kifurushi *n* package

kifusi *n* debris
kifutio *n* rubber
kifuto *n* eraser
kifutu *n* viper
kiga *n* ham
kigae *n* slate
kiganja *n* palm
kigari *n* cart
kigeugeu *adj* fickle
kigezo *n* criterion
kigoda *n* stool
kigori *n* chick
kiguzo *n* stake
kihalisi *adv* literally
kihami *n* insulation
kihusishi *n* preposition
kiingilio *n* entrance
kiini *n* core, focus
kiinimacho *n* hypnosis
kiinitete *n* embryo
kiinjili *adj* apostolic
kiinua mgongo *n* pension
kiitikio *n* chorus
kijaluba *n* casket
kijana *n* adolescent
kijana mhalifu *adj* delinquent
kijani *adj* green
kijarida *n* leaflet

kijasiri *adv* bravely
kijazilizo *n* complement
kijazio *n* filling
kijembe *n* innuendo
kijidudu *n* microbe
kijiji *n* hamlet
kijiko *n* spoon
kijiko cha chai *n* teaspoon
kijiko kizima *n* spoonful
kijitabu *n* booklet
kijivu *adj* gray
kijumbe *n* informant
kikaangio *n* frying pan
kikafiri *adj* godless
kikao *n* session
kikapu *n* basket
kikasha *n* casket
kikatili *adj* atrocious
kiko *n* elbow
kikokotoo *n* calculator
kikoloni *adj* colonial
kikombe *n* cup
kikomo *n* limit
kikoromeo *n* thyroid
kikosi *n* brigade
kikuku *n* shackle
kikumbo *n* shove
kikwaru *n* spur**

K

kikwazo *n* hurdle
kikweukweu *v* sob
kila *adj* every
kila mmoja *adj* each
kila moja *adv* apiece
kila moja *adj* each
kila mtu *pro* everyone
kila mwaka *adj* annual
kila saa *adv* hourly
kila siku *adv* daily
kilango *n* valve
kilele *n* peak, top
kilema *adj* cripple
kilema *n* deformity
kileo *adj* alcoholic
kileo *n* booze
kilicho fichuliwa *adj* exposed
kilima *n* hill
kilimani *n* hillside
kilimo *n* agriculture
kilio *n* funeral
kilipulio *n* detonator
kilogramu *n* kilogram
kilometa *n* kilometer
kilowati *n* kilowatt
kima *n* mincemeat
kimada *n* mistress
kimalaika *adj* angelic

kimanda *n* omelette
kimbia *v* flee, run
kimbilio *n* recourse
kimbiza *v* chase
kimbunga *n* hurricane
kimelea *n* parasite
kimia *n* lace
kimondo *n* comet
kimori *n* apron
kimsingi *adj* basic
kimulimuli *n* beacon
kimwili *adj* bodily
kimya *adj* quiet, silent
kina *n* depth
kina kifupi *adj* shallow
kina kirefu *n* abyss
kinamasi *n* quagmire
kinanda *n* keyboard
kinasa sauti *n* recorder
kinasaba *n* gene
kindugu *adj* brotherly
kinene *adj* chubby
kinga *v* cushion
kinga *n* prevention
kingama *v* criss-cross
king'ora *n* siren
kinoleo *n* sharpener
kinu *n* mill**

kinuupepo *n* windmill
kinyama *adj* bestial
kinyambuo *adj* derivative
kinyesi *n* dung
kinyongo *n* grudge
kinyozi *n* barber
kinyume *adj* contrary
kinyume *adv* backwards
kinyunga *n* dough
kinywaji *n* beverage
kinza *v* counteract
kiongozi *n* guide, leader
kioo *n* glass, mirror
kiota *n* nest
kiowevu *n* liquid
kipaji *n* genius, talent
kipaji *adj* gifted
kipandauso *n* migraine
kipande *n* bit, part
kipande kidogo *n* little bit
kipara *adj* bald
kiparamoto *adj* precocious
kipaumbele *n* priority
kipaza sauti *n* loudspeaker
kipengee *n* detour
kipenyo *n* diameter
kipenzi *adj* favorite
kipenzi *n* sweetheart

kipeo *adj* ideal
kipepeo *n* butterfly
kipimo *n* dimension
kipindi *n* period, era
kipindi kifupi *adv* momentarily
kipindupindu *n* cholera
kipingamizi *n* obstruction
kipipa *n* keg
kipodozi *n* cosmetic
kipofu *adj* blind
Kipolishi *adj* Polish
kiporo *n* backlog
kipuli *n* spare part
kipupwe *n* autumn
kiraka *n* patch
kiri *v* confess
kiroboto *n* flea
kirungu *n* baton, knob
kisa *n* anecdote
kisahani *n* disk
kisanamu *n* miniature
kisasi *n* revenge
kisasili *n* myth
kishale *n* dart
kishawishi *n* enticement
kishazi *n* clause
kishetani *n* fairy
kishoka *n* hatchet

K

kishoroba *n* strip
kishubaka *n* recess
kisia *v* speculate
kisigino *n* heel
kisiki *n* stub
kisima *n* well
kisingizio *n* excuse
kisio *n* guess
kisiwa *n* island, isle
kisosi *n* saucer
kistariungio *n* hyphen
kisu *n* knife
kisukari *n* diabetes
kisukuku *n* fossil
kitaaluma *adj* academic
kitabu *n* book
kitambaa *n* handkerchief
kitana *n* comb
kitanda *n* bed, berth
kitangulizi *n* antecedent
kitani *n* linen
kitanzi *n* noose
kitasa *n* latch, lock
kite *n* moan, wail
kitendawili *n* riddle
kitendo *n* feat
kitendo kiovu *n* outrage
kitengo *n* post

kitenzi *n* verb
kitezi *n* gerund
kiti *n* chair, seat
kiti cha enzi *n* throne
kitindamlo *n* dessert
kitisho *n* horror
kititia *n* bunch
kitivo *n* faculty
kito *n* gem, jewel
kitobosha *n* pastry
kitoto cha paka *n* kitten
kitoto wa mbwa *n* puppy
kitovu *n* navel, hub
kitu *n* thing, item
kitu cha kufungia *n* wrapping
kitu kimoja *n* unit
kituguta *n* cheekbone
kitundu *n* loophole
kitunguu *n* onion
kitunguu swaumu *n* garlic
kitwana *adj* brat
kiuasumu *n* antidote
kiuavijasumu *n* antibiotic
kiulaini *adv* softly
kiumbe *n* being
kiunga *n* outskirts
kiunganishi *n* conjunction
kiungo *n* condiment

kiungulia *n* heartburn
kiuno *n* hip, waist
kiunzi *n* mount, hull
kiushindi *adj* triumphant
kiusisimka *n* shudder
kivinjari *n* browser
kivuko *n* crossing
kivuli *n* shadow
kivuli cha umbo *n* silhouette
kivumishi *n* adjective
kivutio *n* attraction
kiwanda *n* factory
kiwango *n* level
kiwango rasmi *n* parity
kiwashio *n* lighter
kiwavi *n* caterpillar
kiweo *n* ham
kiwimbi *n* ripple
kiyeyusho *adj* solvent
kizazi *n* womb, birth
kizembe *adj* lax
kizibo *n* cork, plug
kizidishi *n* coefficient
kiziduo *n* infusion
kizimba *n* cage
kizingiti *n* threshold
kizio *n* hemisphere
kiziwi *adj* deaf

kizuio *n* curb
kizuizi *n* obstacle
kizuizini *n* banishment
kizunguzungu *n* dizziness
klabu *n* club
kliniki *n* clinic
kobe *n* tortoise
koboa kwa fidia *v* ransom
kocha *n* coach
koche *n* lobster
kochi *n* couch, sofa
kodi *n* rent, lease
kodiani *n* accordion
kodisha *v* rent
kodolea macho *v* stare
kofi *n* slap
kofia *n* cap, hat
kohoa *v* cough
kojoa *v* urinate
kokein *n* cocaine
kokote *c* wherever
kokoteza maneno *v* slur
kokoto *n* gravel
kokotoa *v* calculate
kokteli *n* cocktail
kokwa *n* nut-shell
kola *n* collar
koleo *n* pincers, pliers

K

kolesteroli n cholesterol

koliflawa n cauliflower

koloni n colony

koma n comma

komaa adj mature

komamanga n pomegranate

komba v scrape

kombamwiko n beetle

kombe n trophy

komboa v redeem

kombora n rocket, missile

komeo n bolt

komesha v abolish

kompyuta n computer

komunisti adj communist

komunyo n communion

kona n corner, turn

kondakta n conductor

kondoo n lamb

kondoo dume n ram

kongomana v agglomerate

kongosho n pancreas

kongwe adj ancient

koni n cone

konokono n snail

konsonanti n consonant

kontua n contour

konyeza v wink

koo n throat

kope n eyelash

kopesha v loan

koplo n corporal

kopo n canister, can

korija n score

koroga v stir

koroma v snore

korongo n ravine, gorge

kosa n error, fault

kosa dogo n misdemeanor

kosa fahamu adj unconscious

kosa heshima n disrespect

kosa hewa v suffocate

kosa kazi adj jobless

kosa kuona v overlook

kosa msimamo v vacillate

kosa subira n impatience

kosea v err, goof

kosefu adj devoid

kosoa v criticize

kote kote adv about

koti n coat, jacket

koti kubwa n overcoat

koti la mvua n raincoat

kotmiri n parsley

kozi n course

Krisimasi n Christmas

krismasi *n* X-mas
kua *v* evolve, thrive
kuabiri *n* navigation
kuabudu sanamu *n* idolatry
kuacha *n* omission
kuahirisha *n* postponement
kuakisi *n* reflection
kuamini *adj* confident
kuaminika *adj* believable
kuamka *n* awakening
kuamsha *adj* rousing
kuandika *n* engraving
kuanguka *n* collapse
kuanza *n* start
kuanza tena *n* resumption
kuasi *n* defection
kuba *n* dome
kubadhi *n* sandal
kubadilisha *n* interchange
kubadilishana *n* swap
kubahatisha *n* conjecture
kubainisha *n* highlight
kubaka *n* rape
kubali *v* accept
kubaliana *v* concur
kubalika *v* get by
kubatilisha *n* blowout
kubomoa *n* demolition

kubuni upya *n* recreation
kubuniwa *n* fiction
kuburudisha *adj* balmy
kubwa *adj* astronomic
kubwa mno *adj* enormous
kucha *n* fingernail
kuchacha *adj* broke
kuchapa *n* spanking
kuchapisha *n* printing
kuchechemea *n* limp
kucheka *n* ridicule
kuchelewa *n* delay
kucheua *n* belch
kucheza *n* dancing
kuchinja *n* slaughter
kuchonga *adj* arduous
kuchosha *adj* boring
kuchua *n* massage
kuchukiza *n* repulse
kuchunguza *n* probing
kuchwa jua *n* sunset
kudhamiria *n* premeditation
kudonoa *n* peck
kuelekea *pre* towards
kuelekea chini *adv* downstairs
kuelewa *adj* understanding
kueleweka *n* clearness
kuendelea *n* continuation

K

kuendeleza *n* promotion
kuepuka *n* avoidance
kufa *v* die
kufa ganzi *adj* numerous
kufaa *adj* beneficial
kufaa *n* effectiveness
kufanana *n* likeness
kufariki *adj* dying
kufaulu *n* pass
kuficha *n* coverup
kufidia *v* compensate
kufika mwisho *n* expiration
kufikia *adj* accessible
kufilisi *n* liquidation
kufilisika *adj* bankrupt
kufilisika *n* bankruptcy
kufiwa *adj* bereaved
kufuatana na *pre* according to
kufuatilia *n* pursuit
kufudifudi *adj* prone
kufuga *adj* close
kufukuza *v* brush aside
kufukuzwa *n* removal
kufuli *n* padlock
kufundisha *n* coaching
kufundisha mtu *v* coach
kufunga *adj* binding
kufunga choo *n* constipation

kufungwa *adj* bound
kufurahia *n* gusto
kufurahisha *n* delight
kufurika *n* flooding
kufuru *v* desecrate
kufuru *n* sacrilege
kufuta *n* cancellation
kufyonza *n* assimilation
kuganda ngozi *n* frostbite
kughani *n* recital
kughushi *n* forgery
kugoma *adj* striking
kugombeza *n* rebuke
kugongana *n* clash
kugugumia *n* gulp
kugusa *n* touch
kugusa *adj* touching
kuhama *n* relocation
kuhani mkuu *n* pontiff
kuharibika *n* breakdown
kuharisha *n* diarrhea
kuhesabu upya *n* recount
kuhifadhi *n* storage
kuhimiza *n* urge
kuhisi *n* sensation
kuhitaji *n* need
kuhonga *n* bribery
kuhubiri *n* preaching

kuhudhuria *n* presence
kuhusika *n* involvement
kuhusu *pre* about
kuidhinisha *n* endorsement
kuidhinishwa *n* ratification
kuiga *n* imitation
kuingia *n* admission
kuingia tena *n* reentry
kuingilia *n* access
kuingilia kati *n* intervention
kuishi *n* survival
kuishi milele *n* immortality
kuiva *v* ripen
kuja *n* coming
kujali *adj* caring
kujamiiana *n* intimacy
kujaza *n* stocking
kujibaini *adj* self-concious
kujidai *n* pretense
kujifanya *n* guise
kujifunza *n* learning
kujigeuza *v* disguise
kujiheshimu *n* self-esteem
kujinyima *n* abstinence
kujinyoosha *n* stretch
kujisalimisha *n* surrender
kujitawala *n* autonomy
kujitenga *adj* withdrawn

kujitokeza *n* appearance
kujitosa *n* plunge
kujiua *n* suicide
kujiunga *n* recruitment
Kujiuzulu *n* abdication, resignation
kukaa *n* sitting, stay
kukaa uchi *n* nudism
kukabidhi *n* presentation
kukamata *n* arrest
kukamilika *n* completion
kukana Mungu *n* atheism
kukaribia *n* approach
kukata *n* clipping
kukata kiungo *n* amputation
kukata nywele *n* haircut
kukata tamaa *n* despair
kukataa *n* rebuff
kukatika *n* break
kukatisha *pre* across
kukemea *n* rebuke
kukera *adj* annoying
kukiri *n* confession
kukohoa *n* cough
kukoma hedhi *n* menopause
kukomaa *v* ripen
kukonyeza *n* wink
kukoroma *n* snore
kukosa *n* miss

K

kukosa pumzi *n* asphyxiation
kukosa raha *adj* miserable
kukosekana *adj* absent
kukosoa *n* critique
kuku *n* chicken, hen
kukubali *n* acceptance
kukufuru *n* blasphemy
kukumbatia *n* embrace
kukunja uso *n* grimace
kukusanya *n* roundup
kukutana *n* encounter
kukuza ubaya *n* aggravation
kula *v* eat, consume
kula kiapo *v* pledge
kula njama *v* conspire
kulaghai *n* hustle
kulala *adj* asleep
kulalai *n* sleep
kulazimisha *n* coercion
kulegalega *n* breach
kuleta utata *adj* controversial
kulewa *adj* drunk
kulewa bahari *adj* seasick
kulia *n* crying
kumbatia *v* embrace, hug
kumbuka *v* remember
kumbukia *v* relive
kumbukumbu *n* memory

kumbusha *v* remind
kumbusho *n* reminder
kumega *n* bite
kumi *adj* ten
kumi na mbili *adj* twelve
kumi na moja *adj* eleven
kumi na nane *adj* eighteen
kumi na nne *adj* fourteen
kumi na saba *adj* seventeen
kumi na sita *adj* sixteen
kumi na tano *adj* fifteen
kumi na tatu *adj* thirteen
kumi na tisa *adj* nineteen
kumwaga *n* spill
kuna *v* scratch
kunajisi *n* rape
kunakili *n* duplication
kunasa sauti *n* recording
kunata *n* tenacity
kundi *n* flock, group
kundi la ghasia *n* mob
kundi la nyota *n* galaxy
kung'ang'ania *n* persistence
kung'ara *adj* dazzling
kunguni *n* bug
kunguru *n* crow, raven
kuni *n* fuel
kunja *v* flex, fold

kunja kunja *v* wrinkle

kunja uso *v* frown

kunjo *n* crease

kunjua *v* unfold

kunjufu *adj* cordial

kunong'ona *n* whisper

kunuka *n* stink

kunyakua *n* clutch

kunyanzi *n* wrinkle

kunyima *n* deprivation

kunywa *v* drink

kunywa kidogo *v* sip

kuoa wake wengi *n* polygamy

kuoga *n* shower

kuogelea *n* swimming

kuokoa *n* rescue

kuokoka *n* salvation

kuomba *adj* appealing

kuomba lifti *n* hitchhike

kuona *n* vision

kuona aibu *adj* ashamed

kuona mbele *n* foresight

kuondoa *n* clearance

kuondoka *n* departure

kuonea *adj* bully

kuoza *n* decay

kupaa *n* lift-off

kupagawa *adj* hysterical

kupaka *n* smear

kupakana *adj* adjoining

kupamba *n* garnish

kupanda *n* ascendancy

kupandisha *n* hoist

kupanga *n* adoption

kupasuka *n* rupture

kupata *adj* catching

kupata afueni *adj* convalescent

kupata tena *n* retrieval

kupatana *n* bargaining

kupatikana *adj* attainable

kupatwa *n* eclipse

kupauka *n* paleness

kupenda kitu *n* penchant

kupenda mno *adv* dearly

kupenya *n* infiltration

kupiga kelele *n* shouting

kupiga mbizi *n* diving

kupiga msasa *v* brush up

kupiga rangi *n* painting

kupika *n* cooking

kupindua *n* overthrow

kupinga *n* protest

kupita *n* passage

kupita kiasi *adv* exceedingly

kupita kwa maji *n* drainage

kupitisha macho *n* glimpse

K

kupitiwa *n* oversight

kupona *n* recovery

kuponi *n* coupon

kupooza *n* paralysis

kuporomoka *n* flop

kupoteza *n* loss

kupotoka *n* lapse

kupumua *n* breathing

kupumzika *adj* relaxing

kupungua *n* decrease

kupwa *v* ebb

kura *n* vote, poll

kura ya maoni *n* referendum

kuremba *n* garnish

kuridhika *n* satisfaction

kuridhisha *n* appeasement

kurudi *n* return

kurudi ulingoni *n* comeback

kurudia *n* repetition

kurudisha *n* restoration

kurudiwa *n* relapse

kuruka *n* skip

kurunzi *n* flashlight

kurupusha *v* scare away

kusadikisha *adj* convincing

kusafisha *n* clearance

kusahauliwa *n* oblivion

kusamehe *n* pardon

kusanya *v* collect

kusanyika *v* congregate

kushangaza *adj* astonishing

kushauri *v* advise

kushawishi *n* persuasion

kushika *adj* catching

kushikilia *n* retention

kushikwa *n* fit

kushindwa *n* defeat, failure

kushiriki *n* share

kushirikiana *adj* cooperative

kushona *n* sewing

kushua chombo *n* launch

kushughulika *n* preoccupation

kushuka *v* descend

kushuka *n* downturn

kushusha pumzi *n* sigh

kusifu mno *n* adulation

kusikia *n* hearing

kusikitika *n* regret

kusimama *n* stand

kusimamishwa *n* suspension

kusimika *n* inauguration

kusini *n* south

kusinzia *n* nap

kusita *n* hesitation

kusitisha *n* cancellation

kusitisha ugomvi *n* truce

kusoma *n* reading
kustaafu *n* retirement
kustaajabu *n* wonder
kustahimili *adj* bearable
kusubiri *n* waiting
kusudio *n* determination
kusujudu *n* adoration
kuta *v* overtake
kutafuta *n* quest
kutahiri *n* circumcision
kutaja *n* mention
kutakasa *n* purge
kutambua *n* recognition
kutamka *n* articulation
kutana *v* encounter
kutana na *v* run into
kutangaza *n* advertising
kutangua *n* reverse
kutatua *n* solution
kutawaliwa *n* addiction
kutawazwa *n* coronation
kutegemea *n* reliance
kuteka *n* capture, hijack
kuteka nyara *n* kidnapping
kutekenya *n* tickle
kuteketeza *n* annihilation
kutekwa *n* captive
kutekwa nyara *n* abduction

kuteleza *n* slip
kuteleza barafu *v* ice skate
kutembea *n* hike
kutenga *n* segregation
kutengana *n* separation
kutengua *n* repeal
kutengwa *n* isolation
kuteseka *n* suffering
kuthubutu *n* dare
kutisha *adj* awful
kutiwa hatiani *n* conviction
kutoa *n* removal
kutoa dawa *n* dispensation
kutoa mkono *n* handshake
kutoamini *n* distrust
kutoboa *n* piercing
kutofautisha *n* distinction
kutojali *n* neglect
kutojisika vizuri *adj* indisposed
kutoka *n* exit
kutoka *pre* from
kutoka *adv* off
kutokana *adj* consequent
kutokea *n* happening
kutokujua *n* ignorance
kutolingana *n* imbalance
kutomudu *n* incompetence
kutongoza *n* seduction**

K

kutoona mbali *adj* nearsighted
kutopata *n* miss
kutopatana *n* discord
kutopenda *n* antipathy
kutoridhika *n* disapproval
kutoridhika *adj* dissatisfied
kutoweza *n* inability
kutoweza *adj* unable
kutowezekana *n* impossibility
kutu *n* rust
kutua *n* setting
kutuama *n* stagnation
kutubu *n* repentance
kutukuza *n* consecration
kutulia *n* calm
kutumbukiza *n* immersion
kutumia *n* spending
kutumia vibaya *n* misuse
kutupa *n* disposal
kutupa jicho *n* glance
kuu *adj* major, senior
kuukuu *adj* antiquated
kuuma *n* sting
kuumbika *n* formation
kuumwa sikio *n* earache
kuunga mkono *n* backing
kuungana *adj* allied
kuungua na jua *n* sunburn

kuvaa *n* dressing
kuvimba gesi *adj* bloated
kuvimbiwa *n* indigestion
kuvu *n* mildew, mold
kuvuja *n* leak
kuvuja damu *n* hemorrhage
kuvumwani *n* moss
kuvunja *n* severance
kuvunjika *adj* broken
kuvuta mawazo *n* distraction
kuvutia *adj* alluring
kuvutiwa *adj* interested
kuwa *v* be, become
kuwa kuzidi *v* outgrow
kuwa mfano *v* personify
kuwa mfano wa *v* epitomize
kuwa mwekundu *v* redden
kuwa na *v* have
kuwaka *n* combustible
kuwashwa *n* itchiness
kuwasili *n* arrival
kuwasilisha *n* delivery
kuweka *n* stocking
kuwekewa damu *n* transfusion
kuwepo *v* exist
kuwepo *n* presence
kuweza *adj* capable
kuwinda *n* hunting

kuza _v_ magnify, enlarge
kuza sauti _v_ amplify
kuza ubaya _v_ aggravate
kuzaa _n_ reproduction
kuzaliwa _v_ be born
kuzaliwa upya _n_ rebirth
kuzidisha _n_ multiplication
kuzimia _n_ blackout
kuzingirwa _n_ siege
kuzirai _n_ collapse
kuziua _n_ meditation
kuzuia _n_ retention
kuzuia _v_ incapacitate
kuzuka _n_ outbreak
kuzunguka _pro_ around
kwa _pre_ at, by, per, to
kwa ghafla _adv_ suddenly
kwa heri _e_ bye, farewell
kwa nini _adv_ why
kwa sababu _c_ because
kwa sababu ya _pre_ because of
kwa uchafu _adv_ grossly
kwa vyovyote _pro_ anyhow
kwale _n_ pheasant
kwama _adj_ stranded
kwamisha _v_ foil
kwanza _adj_ first
kwanza _adv_ primarily

kwapa _n_ armpit
kwapua _n_ wrench
Kwaresma _n_ Lent
kwaruza _v_ score
kwato _n_ hoof
kwaya _n_ choir
kweli _adj_ frank
kweli _adv_ really
kwenye _pre_ at, in, on
kwenye kopo _adj_ canned
kwepa _v_ dodge, duck
kwikwi _n_ hiccup

K
L

L

laana _v_ curse
laana _n_ damnation
laani _v_ damn
labda _adv_ perhaps
ladha _n_ flavor, taste
lafudhi _n_ accent
laghai _v_ deceive
laghai _n_ twister
lahaja _n_ dialect

laini *adj* mellow, soft
lainisha *v* soften
lala *v* lie, sleep
lalamika *v* complain
lalamiko *n* complaint
lamba *v* lick
lami *n* asphalt, tar
lango *n* gate
latitudo *n* latitude
laumu *v* blame
lawama *n* blame
laza *v* flatten, lay
laza hospitali *v* hospitalize
lazima *v* must
lazimisha *v* force, impose
lazimu *v* obligate
lea *v* foster, nurture
lebo *n* label
legea *v* loose
legeza *v* loosen, slacken
lehemu *v* solder
leja *n* ledger
lemaza *v* maim, mutilate
lenga *v* aim, aspire
lengo *n* objective
leo *adv* today
leseni *n* licence
leta *v* cause, bring

leta hisia *v* evoke
levya na dawa *v* drug
lewa *adj* intoxicated
leza *n* laser
lia *v* weep, cry
licha ya *c* despite
lifti *n* elevator
ligi *n* league
lika *v* eat away
likizo *n* holiday
lilia *v* grieve
lima *v* cultivate, till
lima kwa plau *v* plow
limau *n* lemon
linda *v* protect
linda *n* safeguard
linganisha *v* align, match
linganisha milio *v* tune up
linganishi *adj* comparative
lini *adv* when
lipa *v* disburse, pay
lipa fidia *v* refund
lipia *v* defray, finance
lipiza kisasi *v* avenge
lipizia *v* pay back
lipizia kisasi *v* revenge
lipu *n* plaster
lipua *v* detonate**

lipua bomu *v* bomb
lipuka *v* erupt, explode
lipukia *v* backfire
lisha *v* nourish, feed
lishe *n* nourishment
lita *n* liter
litania *n* litany
liturujia *n* liturgy
liwaza *v* console
lodi *adj* nobleman
loga *v* bewitch
longitudo *n* longitude
lori *n* truck
losheni *n* lotion
lowa *adj* wet
loweka *v* soak
loweka kwenye *v* soak in
lowesha *v* moisten
lozi *n* almond
lugha *n* language
lulu *n* pearl
lundika pamoja *v* lump together
lundikwa *v* heap
lundo *n* heap, pile
lundo la nyasi *n* haystack
lungula *v* blackmail
luteni *n* lieutenant

M

maabara *n* lab
maadili *n* principle
maadili ya hekima *n* maxim
maafikiano *n* pact
maagizo *n* order
maajabu *n* marvel
maalum *adj* specific
maalumu *adj* particular
maalumu hasa *adv* particularly
maana *n* definition
maandamano *n* procession
maandishi *n* text, writing
maangamizi *n* devastation
maanisha *v* mean
maanisha *n* meaning
maarifa *n* ingenuity
maarufu *adj* renowned
maasi *n* rebellion
maasumu *adj* impeccable
mabadiliko *n* change
mabaki *n* leftovers
mabaki ya meli *n* shipwreck
mabaya sana *adj* terrible
mabishano *n* argument

L
M

M

machachari *adj* boisterous
machafuko *n* unrest
machela *n* stretcher
macheo *n* sunrise
Machi *n* March
machweo *n* sundown
mada *n* subject, theme
madaha *n* elegance
madai *n* claim, lawsuit
madanganyo *n* delusion
madhabahu *n* pulpit
madhabahuni *n* altar
madhara *n* disadvantage
madhehebu *n* cult
madhubuti *adj* efficient
madini *n* mineral, ore
maduka ya soko *n* bazaar
maegesho *n* parking
maelekezo *n* guidelines
maelezo *n* statement
maendeleo *n* progress
maeneo *n* premises
mafanikio *n* achievement
maficho *n* hideaway
mafla *n* muffler
mafua *n* flu
mafunzo *n* training, tuition
mafuriko *n* deluge

mafuta *n* oil, fuel
mafuta ghafi *n* petroleum
maganda *n* peel
magendo *n* contraband
magharibi *n* dusk
maguno *n* groan
mahaba *adj* adorable
mahaba *n* romance
mahadhi *n* rhythm
mahafali *n* graduation
mahakama *n* courthouse
mahali *n* location
mahali alipo *n* whereabouts
mahame *adj* derelict
mahari *n* dowry
maharusi *adj* newlywed
mahiri *adj* clever
mahitaji *n* supplies
mahubiri *n* sermon
mahudhurio *n* attendance
maili *n* mile
maisha *n* life
maisha yote *adj* lifetime
maiti *n* corpse
majadiliano *n* debate
majaliwa *n* fate
majani *n* grass
majeruhi *n* casualty

maji *n* water
maji kimbizi *n* torrent
maji machafu *n* sewage
maji ya limau *n* lemonade
maji ya matunda *n* juice
majili *n* gallows
Majilio *n* Advent
majini *adj* aquatic
majira *n* season
majivu *n* ash
majivuno *n* pride, vanity
majonzi *n* grief, distress
majuto *n* remorse
makabiliano *n* confrontation
makaburini *n* cemetery
makala *n* article, feature
makao makuu *n* capital
makato *n* debit
makazi *n* residence
makazi ya mjini *n* hometown
makelele *v* clamor
makini *n* alert
makisio *n* speculation
makofi *n* applause
makombo *n* scrap
maktaba *n* library
makubaliano *n* accord, deal
makusudi *n* purpose

makwa *n* groove
malai *n* ice cream
malaika *n* angel
malalamiko *n* grievance
malapa *n* slipper
malaria *n* malaria
malazi *n* quarters
malengelenge *n* blister
malezi *n* upbringing
malhamu *n* ointment
mali *n* asset, goods
mali kwa mali *v* barter
mali ya *n* belongings
mali ya wizi *n* booty, loot
malikia *n* queen
malipizi *n* retaliation
malipo *n* payment
malishoni *n* pasture
maliza *v* deplete, end
malizikia *v* culminate
mama *n* mother, mom
mama mkwe *n* mother-in-law
mama wa kambo *n* stepmother
mamajusi *n* astronomer
mamalia *n* mammal
mamba *n* alligator
mamia *n* sob
mamlaka *n* authority

M

mamlaka ya mji *n* town hall
mandhari *n* scene
mandhari yote *n* panorama
mandharimbele *n* foreground
maneno *n* lyrics
maneno mengi *adj* garrulous
mango *n* milestone
manowari *n* warship
mantiki *n* logic
manufaa *n* benefit
manukato *n* perfume
manyunyu *n* drizzle
maombi *n* prayer
maombolezo *n* mourning
maongezi *n* dialogue
maoni *n* feelings
maoni rejea *n* feedback
maonyesho *n* display, fair
mapambano *n* struggle
mapambo *n* furnishings
mapatano *n* bond
mapato *n* income
mapema *adv* early
mapema mno *adj* premature
mapenzi *n* fondness
mapigano *n* battle
mapigo *n* assault
mapinduzi *n* upheaval

mapitio *n* review
mapokezi *n* welcome
mapunziko *n* recess, rest
mara *c* once
mara kwa mara *adj* frequent
mara kwa mara *adv* often
mara mbili *adv* twice
mara moja *adv* immediately
mara moja moja *adv* occasionally
mara tatu *adj* triple
marashi *n* cologne
marejeo *n* reference
marekebisho *n* adaptation
marhamu *n* balm
maridadi *adj* classy
maridadisha *v* spruce up
marisawa *n* pellet
Mars *n* Mars
marudio *n* repetition
marufuku *n* ban
marumaru *n* marble
marupurupu *n* trimmings
masaa *n* relic, vestige
masafa *n* range
masahihisho *n* amendment
masalio *n* leftovers
mashaka *n* predicament
mashariki *n* east, orient

M

masharubu *n* mustache

mashindano *n* contest

mashine *n* machine

mashtaka *n* proceedings

mashua *n* barge

mashua ya anasa *n* yacht

mashua ya tanga *n* sailboat

mashuhuri *adj* well-known, famous

mashuka *n* bedding

mashuku *n* misgivings

masikitiko *n* woes

Masiya *n* Messiah

masizi *n* grime

maskini *adj* indigent

maskini *n* poor

mastaajabu *n* amazement

masumbwi *n* boxing

matako *n* bottom, rear

matakwa *n* desire, wish

matangazo *n* announcement

matapishi *n* vomit

matarajio *n* prospect

matatizo *n* trouble

matayarisho *n* preparation

mate *n* saliva

mategemeo *n* aspiration

mategu *n* misprint

mateka *n* hostage

matembezi *n* excursion

mateso *n* ordeal, torment

mathubuti *adj* foolproof

matibabu *n* therapy

matokeo *n* outcome

matule *n* vulgarity

matumaini *n* prospect

matumizi *n* expenditure

mauaji *n* murder

maudhi *n* displeasure

maudhui *n* substance

maumivu *n* ache, pain

maumivu ya jino *n* toothache

maungio *n* junction

mauzo *n* sale

mauzo ya jumla *n* wholesale

mavazi *n* clothes

mavi *n* crap

mawasiliano *n* contact

mazao *n* produce

maziga *n* casserole

mazingazi *n* mirage

mazingira *n* circumstance

mazishi *n* burial

maziwa *n* milk

mazoea *n* experience

mazungumzo *n* conversation

mba *n* dandruff

M

mbadhirifu *adj* extravagant

mbakaji *n* rapist

mbali *adv* far, away

mbali na *adv* aside from

mbali sana *adj* faraway

mbali zaidi *adv* farther, further

mbalimbali *adj* various

mbao *n* lumber, wood

mbawala *n* deer

mbaya *adj* awful, nasty

mbaya sana *adj* dire, ghastly

mbaya zaidi *adj* worse

mbayana *adj* apparent

mbebaji *n* bearer

mbegu *n* grain, seed

mbele *pre* ahead

mbele *adv* forward

mbele *n* front

mbele ya *adv* before

Mbelgiji *adj* Belgian

mbichi *adj* raw, fresh

mbili *adj* dual

mbilikimo *n* dwarf

mbinafsi *n* egoist

mbingu *n* heaven, sky

mbinguni *n* paradise

mbinu *n* tactics

mbinuufundi *n* technicality

mbishi *adj* stubborn

mbizi *n* plunge

mboga *n* vegetable

mbolea *n* manure

mboni *n* lense

mbu *n* mosquito

mbubujiko *n* outpouring

mbuga *n* prairie, park

mbunge *n* senator

mbuni *n* ostrich

mbunifu *adj* creative

mbuzi *n* goat

mbwa *n* greyhound

mbwa mwitu *n* wolf

mbweha *n* fox

mchana *n* afternoon

mchanga *n* sand

mchanga didimizi *n* quicksand

mchangamfu *adj* cheerful

mchanganyaji *n* mixer

mchanganyiko *n* blend

mchango *n* contribution

mchapishaji *n* publisher

mchawi *n* wizard, witch

mche *n* prism

mchele *n* rice

mchemraba *n* cube

mchepuo *n* diversion

mcheshi *adj* extroverted

mchezaji *n* actor, actress

mchezo *n* game, play

mchimba mgodi *n* miner

mchiriziko *v* trickle

mchirizo *n* curve

mchocheo *n* impulse

mchokozi *n* agitator

mchongezi *n* informer

mchoraji ramani *n* draftsman

mchoro *v* sketch

mchoro *n* sketch, layout

mchuaji *n* masseur

mchuano *n* competition

mchukuano *n* compatibility

mchukuzi *n* porter

mchumba *n* fiancé

mchungaji *n* chaplain

mchunguzi *n* explorer

mchuzi *n* gravy, sauce

mchwa *n* termite

Mdachi *adj* Dutch

mdadisi *adj* nosy

mdai *n* plaintiff

mdaiwa *n* debtor

mdalasini *n* cinnamon

mdanganyifu *adj* dishonest

mdhalimu *n* despot

mdhamini *n* guarantor

mdogo *adj* young

mdomo *n* lip, mouth

mdomo wa ndege *n* beak

mduara *n* circle

mdudu *n* bug

mdudu mharibifu *n* pest

mdundo *n* bounce

mea *v* germinate

mega *v* bite

mega kidogo *v* nibble

Mei *n* May

meja *n* major

mekanika *n* mechanic

meko *n* chimney

meli *n* ship

melodia *n* tune

mende *n* cockroach

meng'enya *v* crumble

meno *n* teeth

meno ya bandia *n* dentures

menya *v* peel

meta meta *v* glitter

metameta *v* sparkle

methali *n* proverb

meya *n* mayor

meza *v* gobble

meza kwa pupa *v* gulp down

M

mezwa *v* engulf
mfadhaiko *n* excitement
mfadhili *n* sponsor
mfalme *n* king, monarch
mfalme mkuu *n* emperor
mfano *n* example
mfano wa *n* semblance
mfanya magendo *n* smuggler
mfanyabiashara *n* trader
mfanyakazi *n* worker
mfarakano *n* schism
mfarishi *n* quilt
mfasiri *n* translator
mfereji *n* canal
mfereji daraja *n* aqueduct
mfidhuli *adj* arrogant
mfinyo *n* pinch, nip
mfu *adj* dead
mfua makufuli *n* locksmith
mfuaji *n* smith
mfuasi *n* follower
mfuata sheria *adj* law-abiding
mfuatano *n* sequence
mfuko *n* bag, sack
mfululizo *adj* consecutive
mfumbi *n* gutter
mfumo *n* organism
mfumuko *n* inflation

mfungwa *v* convict
mfungwa *n* prisoner
mfuniko *n* cover, lid
mfuo *n* groove
mfupa *n* bone
mfupa wa bega *n* collarbone
mfuto *n* annulment
mfyatuko *n* discharge
mgahawa *n* cafeteria
mgandamizo *adj* crushing
mgando *n* coagulation
mganga *n* doctor
mganga wa meno *n* dentist
mgao *n* distribution
mgawaji *n* supplier
mgawanyiko *n* parting
mgawanyo *n* allotment
mgawo *n* equation
mgeni *n* alien, stranger
mgeuko *n* transformation
mgeuzo *n* twist
Mgiriki *adj* Greek
mgodi *n* mine, quarry
mgombea *n* contender
mgomo *n* strike, walkout
mgomvi *adj* aggressive
mgongano *n* collision
mgongo *n* back, ridge

mgonjwa *adj* sick

mgonjwa *adj* ill

mgumu *adj* obstinate

mgunda *n* field

mgurumo *n* rumble

mguu *n* foot, leg

mhadhara *n* lecture

mhaini *n* deserter

mhalifu *n* felon, villain

mhamaji *n* emigrant

mhamiaji *n* immigrant

mhandisi *n* engineer

mhasibu *n* accountant

mhenga *n* ancestor

mhesabu kura *n* teller

mhimili *n* axis, pillar

mhubiri *n* preacher

mhudumu *n* attendant

mhudumu mkuu *n* butler

mhuni *n* hooligan

mhunzi *n* smith

mhuri wa posta *n* postmark

mia *adj* hundred

miadi *n* appointment

miaka kumi *n* decade

miaka mia *n* centenary

michezo *n* sport

miguu *n* feet

mila *n* custom

milele *n* eternity

milele *adv* forever

milenia *n* millennium

miligramu *n* milligram

miliki *v* own, possess

milikiwa na *v* belong

milimeta *n* millimeter

milionea *adj* millionaire

milioni *n* million

mimi *pro* I, myself

mimina *v* pour

mini *n* miniskirt

mintarafu *pre* regarding

mioshi *n* fumes

mipangilio *n* arrangement

mirithawa *adj* plentiful

misa *n* mass

mistari *n* stripe

mita *n* meter

miwani *n* eyeglasses

miwani ya jua *n* sunglasses

mizani *n* balance

mizigo *n* baggage

mjamaa *adj* socialist

mjamzito *adj* pregnant

mjane *n* widow

mjanja *adj* wily, shrewd

M

Mjapani *adj* Japanese

mjasirimali *n* entrepreneur

mjeledi *n* whip

mjenzi *n* builder

Mjerumani *adj* German

mjeuri *adj* arrogant

mji *n* town

mji mkubwa *n* metropolis

mjinga *adj* fool, stupid

mjini *n* downtown

mjomba *n* uncle

mjukuu *n* grandchild

mjumbe *n* envoy

mjusi *n* lizard

mjuzi *adj* expert

mkaa *n* coal

mkaa uchi *n* nudist

mkaaji *n* occupant

mkabala *n* opposite

mkaguzi *n* inspector

mkaidi *adj* opinionated

mkakati *n* strategy

mkali *adj* brusque

mkalimani *n* interpreter

mkamato *n* grip

mkamba *n* bronchitis

mkamwana *n* daughter-in-law

mkana Mungu *n* atheist

mkanda *n* belt

mkao *n* attitude

mkarara *n* chorus

mkarimu *adj* benevolent

mkasi *n* scissors

mkataba *n* treaty, charter

mkataji *n* chopper, cutter

mkate *n* bread

mkatili *adj* brute

mkato *n* cut

mkazi *n* inhabitant

mke *n* spouse, wife

mke wa lodi *n* countess

mke wa mfalme *n* empress

mkebe *n* can, canister

mkemia *n* pharmacist

mkereketwa *adj* extremist

mkesha *n* eve, vigil

mkia *n* tail

mkimbiaji *n* runner

mkimbizi *n* fugitive

mkoa *n* region, county

mkoba *n* briefcase

mkojo *n* urine

mkokoteni *n* cart

mkokotoo *n* calculation

mkoma *n* leper

mkono *n* arm, hand

mkono tele *n* handful

mkopo *n* loan

mkorofi *adj* bossy

mkorogo *n* dope

mkosefu *n* culprit, sinner

mkristo *adj* christian

mkubwa *n* elder

mkufu *n* necklace

mkufunzi *v* intern

mkuki *n* spear

mkulima *n* farmer

mkunga *n* midwife

mkuo *n* ingot

mkupuo *n* installment

mkurugenzi *n* director

mkurupuko *n* stampede

mkusanya *n* collector

mkusanyiko *n* assembly

mkutano *n* meeting

mkutubi *n* librarian

mkuu *n* chief, master

mkuu *adj* principal

mkwaruzo *n* graze, scratch

mkwe *n* son-in-law

mkweli *adj* truthful

mla njama *n* conspirator

mla rushwa *adj* corrupt

mla watu *n* cannibal

mlafi *n* glutton

mlafi *adj* greedy

mlalahoi *n* underdog

mlango *n* door, entrance

mlangobahari *n* channel

mlangoni *n* doorway

mlanguzi *n* middleman

mlegeo *n* backlash

mlemavu *adj* disabled

mlezi *n* patron

mlima *n* mountain

mlingano *n* uniformity

mlingano pacha *n* symmetry

mlingoti *n* mast

mlingoti wa taa *n* lamppost

mlinzi *n* guard

mlio *n* cry, wail

mlio mkali *n* howl

mlio wa bunduki *n* gunfire

mlio wa simu *n* dial tone

mlipuko *n* detonation

mlipwa *n* payee

mlo *n* meal

mlo wa jioni *n* dinner, supper

mlo wa mchana *n* lunch

mlokole *adj* fanatic

mlungula *n* blackmail

mluzi *n* whistle

M

Mmarekani *adj* American
mmea *n* herb, plant
mmilikaji *n* owner
mmisionari *n* missionary
mmomonyoko *n* disintegration
mnada *n* auction
mnafiki *adj* hypocrite
mnajimu *n* astrologer
mnanaa *n* mint
mnara *n* tower
mnara mdogo *n* turret
mnara wa taa *n* lighthouse
mnene *adj* overweight
mng'ang'anio *n* traction
mng'ao *n* glare, gleam
mngurumo *n* thunder
mno *adj* extreme
mnofu wa nyama *n* steak
mnong'ono *n* murmur
Mnorway *adj* Norwegian
mnunuzi *n* consumer
mnururisho *n* radiation
mnyama *n* animal
mnyiri *n* tentacle
mnyonge *adj* weak
mnyonya damu *n* vampire
mnyoo *n* worm
mnyororo *n* chain, leash

mnyumbuliko *n* declension
mnywaji *n* drinker
moja *adj* one
moja *n* single
moja kwa moja *adj* outright
moja tu *adj* single
molekuli *n* molecule
momonyoka *v* disintegrate
mota *n* motor
motisha *n* incentive
moto *v* blaze, fire
moto sana *adj* red-hot
moto wa kambi *n* bonfire
moyo *n* heart
mozaiki *n* mosaic
mpa silaha *v* arm
mpagani *n* heathen
mpagao *n* hysteria
mpaka *n* border, frontier
mpaka *adv* till, until
mpangaji *n* tenant
mpangilio *n* chronology
mpangishaji *n* lessor
mpango *n* plan, scheme
mpasuko *n* fracture, tear
mpasuo *n* slash, split
mpelelezi *n* detective
mpendwa *adj* beloved

mpenzi *adj* darling, dear
mpiga bunduki *n* gunman
mpiga fidla *n* violinist
mpiga kinanda *n* organist
mpiga mbizi *n* diver
mpiga piano *n* pianist
mpiga picha *n* photographer
mpiga rangi *n* painter
mpiganaji *n* combatant
mpigania haki *n* crusader
mpigo *n* blow
mpini *n* handle
mpinzani *n* opponent
mpira *n* ball
mpira wa miguu *n* football
mpira wa wavu *n* volleyball
mpishi *n* chef, cook
mpita njia *n* passer-by
mpito *n* transition
mpole *adj* polite
mpopi *n* poppy
mpotevu *adj* stray
mpotovu *adj* pervert
mpumbavu *n* idiot
mpumziko *n* repose
mpwa *n* nephew, niece
mpweke *adv* lonely
mpweke *n* recluse

mpwito *n* throb
mpya *adj* fresh, new
mpya kabisa *adj* brand-new
mraba *n* square
mradi *n* venture, project
mrasimu *n* bureaucrat
mratibu *n* coordinator
Mreno *adj* Portuguese
mrithi *n* heir
mrithi wa kike *n* heiress
mrudio *n* frequency
mrukaji *n* flier
mruko *n* jump, leap
Mrusi *adj* Russian
msaada *n* aid, help
msabazaji barua *n* postman
msafara *n* convoy
msafiri *n* traveler
msafishaji *n* cleaner
msaidizi *n* accomplice
msako *n* chase, search
msako wa mtu *n* manhunt
msala *n* lavatory
msalaba *n* cross
msalani *n* rest room
msaliaji *n* survivor
msaliti *n* traitor
msamaha *n* absolution

M

msambaza barua *n* mailman
msamiati *n* vocabulary
msanifu majengo *n* architect
msanii *n* artist
msasa *n* sandpaper
mseja *adj* unmarried
mshabiki *n* fan
mshabulizi *n* raider
mshahara *n* wage, salary
mshairi *n* poet
mshale *n* arrow
mshambulizi *n* assailant
mshangao *n* surprise
mshari *n* aggressor
mshauri *n* adviser
mshenzi *n* barbarian
mshikamano *n* cohesion
mshindani *n* contestant
mshindi *n* victor, winner
mshindilio *n* compression
mshindo *n* climax
mshindwa *n* loser
mshipa *n* artery, vein
mshiriki *n* collaborator
mshoni *n* tailor
mshono *n* stitch
mshtakiwa *n* defendant
mshtuko *n* jolt, shock

mshumaa *n* candle
msichana *n* girl, gal
msikilizaji *n* listener
msikiti *n* mosque
msikivu *adj* receptive
msimamizi *n* foreman
msimamo *n* consistency
msimbo wa posta *n* zip code
msimu *n* season
msindano *n* pine
msindikizaji *n* escort
msingi *n* foundation
msingiziwa *n* scapegoat
msiri *n* confidant
msisitizo *n* emphasis, stress
msitu *n* forest, jungle
msokoto *n* scroll, tangle
msomaji *n* reader
msomi *n* scholar
msomo *n* slogan
msongamano *n* congestion
Mspanish *n* Spaniard
mstari *n* line, queue
mstari wa mbele *n* forefront
mstatili *adj* oblong
mstatili *n* rectangle
msuko *n* braid
msukosuko *n* ordeal

msuli *n* muscle
msuluhishi *n* arbiter
msumari *n* nail, tack
msumeno *n* chainsaw
msusi *n* hairdresser
mswadajaribio *n* draft
Mswisi *adj* Swiss
mtabiri *n* herald
mtakatifu *n* saint
mtalaka *n* divorcee
mtalii *n* tourist
mtambo *n* mechanism
mtambuzaji *n* welder
mtanda *n* loom
mtandao *n* network, web
mtande *n* loom
mtangazaji *n* announcer
mtangulizi *n* predecessor
mtapeli *n* swindler
mtarajiwa *adj* would-be
mtaro *n* ditch, furrow
mtawa *n* abbot, friar, nun
mtawala *n* governor, ruler
mtazamaji *n* spectator
mtazamo *n* viewpoint, look
mtego *n* snare, trap
mtego wa kifo *n* death trap
mtego wa shimo *n* pitfall

mteja *n* customer
mteka nyara *n* kidnapper
mtekaji *n* conqueror
mteketeo *n* apocalypse
mtema *n* chopper
mtemi *n* chief
mtengenezaji *n* maker
mteremko *n* descent
mteremko *adv* downhill
mteteaji *n* defender
mtetemeko *n* shiver, tremor
mti *n* lumber, tree
mtihani *n* examination
mtiifu *adj* obedient
mtikisiko *n* vibration, jolt
mtindo *n* fashion, style
mtiririko *n* flow
mto *n* pillow, cushion
mto mdogo *n* stream
mto wa barafu *n* glacier
mtoa habari *n* informant
mtoaji *n* donor
mtoto *n* baby, child
mtoto mchanga *n* newborn
mtoto wa (simba) *n* cub
mtoto wa jicho *n* cataract
mtu *pro* someone
mtu *n* person

M

mtu anaejitolea *n* volunteer

mtu anayetubu *n* penitent

mtu mashuhuri *n* celebrity

mtu mzima *n* adult

mtu wa kawaida *n* layman

Mtu wa Mexico *adj* Mexican

mtu wa nje *n* outsider

mtuhumiwa *n* suspect

Mtukufu *n* Highness

mtukutu *adj* mischievous

mtulivu *n* calm

mtumaji *n* sender

mtume *n* apostle

mtumiaji *n* consumer

mtumishi *n* servant

mtumwa *n* slave

mtundu *adj* naughty

mtunga sheria *n* lawmaker

mtunza bustani *n* gardener

mtunza nyumba *n* housekeeper

mtunzaji *n* guardian

mtunzi *n* composer

mtupo *n* trajectory

Mturuki *adj* Turk

mtutumo *n* rumble

muafaka *n* consensus

muda *n* time, moment

muda mfupi *n* instant

muda si mrefu *adv* soon

mudi *v* sustain

mudu *v* cope, master

muhimu *adj* significant, vital

muhtasari *n* overview

muhula *n* term, session

muhuri *n* seal

muktadha *n* context

mume *n* husband, male

mundu *n* sickle

Mungu *n* God

mungu wa kike *n* goddess

murua *n* politeness

musiki *n* music

muuaji *n* murderer

muuguzi *n* nurse

muujiza *n* miracle

muumba *n* creator

muumini *n* believer

muundo *n* structure

muunga mkono *n* supporter

muungano *n* merger, union

muuza vitabu *n* bookseller

muuzaji *n* dealer, seller

mvamizi *n* intruder

mvinje *n* cypress

mvinyo *n* wine

mviringo *n* globe

mvivu *adj* lazy

mvua *n* rain, shower

mvua kubwa *n* downpour

mvua mawe *n* hail

mvua ya risasi *n* barrage

mvuke *n* moisture, steam

mvulana *n* boy

mvumo *n* buzz

mvutaji *n* smoker

mvutano *adj* deadlock

mvuto *n* strain, tension

mvuvi *n* fisherman

mwaga *v* shed, spill

mwagilia *v* irrigate

mwagilia maji *v* water

mwajiri *n* employer

mwajiriwa *n* employee

mwaka *n* year

mwaka mrefu *n* leap year

mwako *n* combustion

mwako wa radi *n* lightning

mwaliko *n* invitation

mwalimu *n* teacher, tutor

mwamba *n* reef

mwaminifu *adj* faithful, loyal

mwamuzi *n* referee

mwamvuli *n* chute

mwana falsafa *n* philosopher

mwana wa kiume *n* son

mwanaanga *n* astronaut

mwanachama *n* member

mwanafarasi *n* colt

mwanafunzi *n* learner, pupil

mwanaharamu *n* bastard

mwanahistoria *n* historian

mwanajeshi *n* conscript

mwanakijiji *n* villager

mwanamke *n* female

mwanamusiki *n* musician

mwanamwali *n* maiden

mwananchi *n* citizen

mwanariadha *n* athlete

mwanasayansi *n* scientist

mwanasesere *n* doll

mwanasiasa *n* politician

mwanaume *n* gentleman

mwandani *n* crony

mwandikiwa *n* addressee

mwandiko *n* manuscript

mwandishi *n* author, writer

mwanga *n* flare, glow

mwanga hafifu *n* glimmer

mwangalifu *adj* prudent

mwangalizi *n* custodian

mwangamizi *n* destroyer

mwanguko *n* fall

M

mwangwi *n* echo
mwanya *n* loophole
mwanzilishi *n* founder
mwanzo *n* beginning
mwanzo *adj* original
mwari *n* pelican
mwasherati *adj* promiscuous
mwashi *n* bricklayer
mwasi *n* anarchist, rebel
mwasisi *n* pioneer
mwathirika *n* victim
mwavuli *n* umbrella
mwayo *n* yawn
mwehu *adj* maniac
mweka hazina *n* treasurer
mweka rehani *n* pawnbroker
mwekezaji *n* investor
mwelekeo *n* indication, trend
mwema *adj* amiable
mwembamba *adj* slim
mwendeleo *n* reach
mwendo *n* movement
mwendopole *n* slow motion
mwenendo *n* demeanor
mwenyeji *n* host
mwenyekiti *n* chairman
mwenza *n* fellow, mate
mwenzi *n* partner, peer

mwerevu *adj* astute, smart
mwewe *n* hawk, kite
mwezi *n* month, moon
mwia *n* creditor
mwiba *n* thorn
mwibaji *n* singer
mwigo *n* dummy
mwili *n* body, flesh
mwinamo *n* decline
mwindaji *n* hunter
Mwingereza *adj* English
mwingilio *n* entry
mwingine *adj* other
mwinuko *n* altitude
mwisho *n* end, ending
mwisho *adj* last
mwisho *adv* lastly
mwisho wa wiki *n* weekend
mwishoni *adv* eventually
Mwislamu *adj* Muslim
Mwitaliano *adj* Italian
mwizi *n* burglar, thief
mwoga *n* coward
mwogeleaji *n* swimmer
mwoka *n* baker
mwokozi *n* savior
mwombaji *n* applicant
mwonekano *n* view

mwongo *adj* liar
mwongozo *n* guidance
mwonzi *n* beam, ray
mwosha vyombo *n* dishwasher
mwovu *adj* wicked
mwuaji *adj* bloodthirsty
mwujiza *n* mystery
Myahudi *n* Jew
myakinifu *adj* pragmatist
myasmini *n* jasmine
myeyungano *n* fusion
mzabibu *n* vine
mzaha *n* hoax
mzalendo *n* patriot
mzaliwa *adj* native
mzani *n* scale
mzawa *n* descendant
mzee *adj* elderly, old
mzembe *adj* negligent
mzigo *n* consignment
mzima *adj* sober
mzimamoto *n* fireman
mzimu *n* ghost
mzinga *n* hive
mzingile *n* labyrinth
mzingo *n* perimeter
mzio *n* allergy
mzio wa *adj* allergic

mzizi *n* root
mzoefu *adj* familiar
mzoga *n* carcass
mzozo *n* altercation
mzuka *n* apparition
Mzungu *adj* European
mzunguko *n* cycle, rotation
mzuri *adj* beautiful
mzururaji *n* wanderer

N

na *c* and
na *pre* with
na kuendelea *adv* onwards
na mawingu *adj* cloudy
na silaha *adj* armed
nabii *n* prophet
nadharia *n* theory
nadhifu *adj* tidy
nadi *v* auction
nadra *adv* barely
nafaka *n* cereal, corn
nafasi *n* slot, space

M
N

nafasi iliyowazi _n_ vacancy
nafasi tupu _adj_ blank
nafsi _n_ soul
nafuu _n_ respite
nafuu _adv_ rather
nahau _n_ idiom
najisi _v_ defile, rape
najisiwa _adj_ tainted
nakala _n_ copy, replica
nakala _v_ duplicate
nakala kivuli _n_ photocopy
nakili _v_ copy
nakshi _n_ décor
namba _n_ number
namna _n_ manner, style
namna ya kuishi _n_ lifestyle
nanasi _n_ pineapple
nane _adj_ eight
nanga _n_ anchor
nani _pro_ who, whom
nasua _v_ extricate
nathari _n_ prose
nati _n_ nut
nauli _n_ fare
nawiri _v_ bloom
nazi _n_ coconut
ncha _n_ point, tip
ncha ya kidole _n_ fingertip

nchi _n_ country
nchi ya asili _n_ homeland
ndala _n_ sandal
ndama _n_ calf
ndani _adv_ indoor
ndani _adj_ interior
ndani ya _pre_ within
ndani ya _pre_ inside
ndani ya mshipa _adj_ intravenous
ndani ya nchi _adv_ inland
ndani, rohoni _adv_ inwards
ndefu _adj_ tall, long
ndefu sana _adj_ lofty
ndege _n_ airplane, bird
ndege ya abiria _n_ airliner
ndevu nyingi _n_ beard
ndimu _n_ lime
ndio _adv_ yes
ndipo _c_ whereupon
ndizi _n_ banana
ndoa _n_ marriage
ndoana _n_ hook
ndogo _adj_ petite, small
ndogo zaidi _adj_ lesser
ndondi _n_ boxing
ndoo _n_ pail
ndoto _n_ dream
ndugu _n_ brother, comrade

ndui *n* smallpox
nduwari *n* swordfish
neema *n* grace
neemeka *v* thrive
nembo *n* seal, emblem
nena *n* groin
nena *v* remark
nenda *v* go
nenda kasi *v* speed
nenda kwa basi *v* bus
nenda mbele *v* pull ahead
nenda na kurudi *v* shuttle
nene *adj* thick, fat
nene sana *adj* corpulent
nenenene *adj* plump
nenepesha *v* fatten
neno *n* remark, word
neno kwa neno *adv* verbatim
nesi *n* nurse
ng'aa *v* gleam, shine
ng'aavu *adj* vivid
ngalawa *n* canoe
ngamia *n* camel
ng'amua *v* detect
ng'ang'ania *v* cling, stick to
ngano *n* wheat
ngano nyekundu *n* rye
ngao *n* fender, shield

ng'arisha *v* brighten
ng'ata *n* bite
ngawira *n* spoils
ngazi *n* ladder, stair
ngazi za umeme *n* escalator
nge *n* scorpion
ngeli *n* gender
ngiri *n* hernia
ng'oa *v* uproot
ngojea *v* await
ngoma *n* drum
ng'ombe *n* cattle, cow
ng'ombe maksai *n* oxen
ngome *n* garrison, fortress
ngozi *n* leather, skin
ngozi ya kichwa *n* scalp
ngumi *n* fist, punch
ngumu *adj* difficult, tough
nguo *n* garment, cloth
nguo za kulalia *n* pajamas
nguo za ndani *n* underwear
nguruma *v* roar, rumble
nguruwe *n* pig, pork
nguruwe pori *n* boar, hog
nguva *n* mermaid
nguvu *n* energy, power
nguvu kazi *n* manpower
nguvu ya wenzo *n* leverage

N

nguvu za kiume *n* virility
nguzo *n* pole, post, pillar
ni dhahiri *adv* obviously
ni wazi *adv* obviously
nia *n* intention, motive
nia nzuri *n* goodwill
nidhamu *n* discipline
nikeli *n* nickel
nikotini *n* nicotine
nimonia *n* pneumonia
ning'iniza *v* dangle, hang
nini *adj* what
nira *n* yoke
nishani *n* medal
nishani kubwa *n* medallion
nitrojeni *n* nitrogen
njaa *n* hunger
njama *n* conspiracy
njano *adj* yellow
nje *adj* exterior
nje *adv* outside, out, outdoors
nje ya mji *n* countryside
njegere *n* pea
njia *n* route, path, way, trail
njia isiyo toka *n* dead end
njia kati ya viti *n* aisle
njia pana *n* boulevard
njia panda *n* junction

njia ya *n* recipe
njia ya kuingilia *n* way in
njia ya kutokea *n* way out
njia ya reli *n* railroad
njiwa *n* dove, pigeon
njoo *v* come
njozi *n* fantasy
njozi za tamaa *v* daydream
nne *adj* four
noa *v* sharpen
nomino *n* noun
nondo *n* precedent
nong'ona *v* murmur
Norway *n* Norway
noti *n* note
Novemba *n* November
nozeli *n* nozzle
nta *n* wax
nta ya sikio *n* earwax
nufaika *v* avail, benefit
nufaisha *v* profit
nuika *v* concentrate
nuiza *v* wish
nuka *v* smell, stink
nukta *n* dot, point
nukta pacha *n* colon
nuna *v* grouch
nundu *n* bump**

nung'unika *v* whine

nungunungu *n* porcupine

nunua *v* purchase, buy

nuru *n* flash

nusa *v* sniff

nusu *n* half

nusu *adj* half

nusu kaputi *n* anesthesia

nusu kwa nusu *adv* fifty-fifty

nusura *adv* almost

nyakati *n* times

nyakua *v* grab, snatch

nyama *n* meat

nyama ya kuoka *n* roast

nyama ya ndama *n* veal

nyama ya pori *n* venison

nyama ya tunda *n* pulp

nyamaza *v* hush up, shut up

nyamazisha *v* silence

nyambua kitenzi *v* conjugate

nyanda *adj* broad

nyang'anya *v* seize, confiscate

nyang'au *adj* savage

nyangumi *n* whale

nyani *n* ape

nyanya *n* tomato

nyanyapaa *v* repulse

nyanyasa *v* abuse, molest

nyaraka *n* documentation

nyasi *n* hay, straw

nyati *n* bison, buffalo

nyatia *v* stalk

nyayo *n* trail, track

nyekundu *adj* red

nyembamba *adj* thin, slender

nyemelea *v* stalk

nyemelea *n* tiptoe

nyenje *n* cricket

nyenyekea *v* defer

nyenyekevu *adj* submissive

nyepesi *adj* fragile, light

nyesha *v* rain

nyeti *adj* delicate

nyeupe *adj* white

nyeusi *adj* black

nyeusi ti *adj* pitch-black

nyigu *n* wasp

nyima *v* deprive

nyima pumzi *v* asphyxiate

nyingi *adj* multiple

nyingi *n* plenty

nyingi kiasi *adj* sizable

nyingi sana *adj* prodigious

nyingine *adj* other

nyoa *v* shave

nyofu *adj* moral

N

nyoka *n* serpent, snake
nyonge *adj* feeble, frail, wretched
nyongeza *adj* additional
nyongeza *n* increase
nyongo *n* bile
nyonya *v* absorb, suck
nyonyoa *v* pluck
nyooka *adj* straight
nyoosha *v* flatten, smooth
nyota *n* star
nyoya *n* feather
nyuki *n* bee
nyuma *adv* back
nyuma *pre* behind
nyuma *n* rear
nyumba *n* house, condo
nyumba duni *n* slum
nyumba ya sanaa *n* gallery
nyumbu *n* mule
nyumbufu *adj* agile, elastic
nyundo *n* hammer
nyunya *v* drizzle
nyunyizia *v* sprinkle
nyusi *n* eyebrow
nyuzi *n* fiber
nywea *v* shrink
nywele *n* hair
nywelevu *adj* porous

nywila *n* password
nzi *n* fly
nzige *n* locust
nzima *adj* complete
nzito *adj* heavy
nzuri *adj* cute, pretty
nzuri kupita *adj* best
nzuri sana *adj* wonderful

O

oa *v* wed
oa tena *v* remarry
oa/olewa *adj* married
oasisi *n* oasis
Octoba *n* October
odorono *n* deodorant
ofisi *n* office, bureau
ofisi ya papa *n* papacy
ofisi ya tawi *n* branch office
oga *v* bathe
ogelea *v* swim
ogopa *adj* afraid
ogopa *v* chicken out

ogopesha *v* frighten
oka *v* bake, roast
okoa *v* bail out, rescue
okota *v* pick
oksijeni *n* oxygen
omba *v* beg, request
omba kwa *v* invoke
omba msamaha *v* apologize
ombaomba *n* beggar
ombea *v* intercede
ombi *n* petition
omboleza *v* lament
ona see, notice
ona aibu *v* blush
ona raha ya *v* savor
onanisha *v* harmonize
ondoa *v* clear, remove
ondoka *v* depart, leave
ondokana *v* rid of
ondolea haki *v* disqualify
ondosha *v* eliminate
onea *v* victimize
onea wivu *v* envy
onekana *v* manifest
onekana kama *v* seem
ongea *v* speak, talk
ongez *adv* plus
ongeza *v* add, increase, enlarge

ongezeka *v* escalate
ongezeko *n* buildup
ongoza *v* govern, lead
ongoza mkutano *v* chair
ongoza vibaya *v* mislead
oni *n* opinion
onja *v* taste
onya *v* admonish
onyesha *v* designate
onyesha *v* indicate, show
onyesha dalili *v* foreshadow
onyesha la awali *n* preview
onyesha mfano *v* exemplify
onyesha shauku *v* enthuse
onyesha uwiano *v* correlate
onyesho *n* spectacle
onyo *n* admonition
opera *n* opera
operesheni *n* operation
orodha *n* inventory
orodhesha *v* catalog, list
ororo *adj* smooth
ororo *n* smoothness
osha *v* wash, cleanse
ota *v* dream, grow
otea *v* guess
otesha *v* plant
oti *n* oatmeal

O

ovu *adj* malignant
ovyo *adj* sloppy
ovyo ovyo *adj* awkward
oza *v* decay, rot

P

pa kuotea moto *n* fireplace
pa kushukia *n* ramp
paa *n* antelope
paa angani *v* soar
paa samaki *v* scale
pacha *n* twin
padri *n* priest
pafu *n* lung
pagawa *v* possess
pai *n* pie, tart
painti *n* pint
paja *n* lap, thigh
paji *n* forehead
paji la uso *n* brow
paka *n* cat
paka *v* smear
paka rangi *v* color

paka vanishi *v* varnish
pakana *v* adjoin
pakana na *v* border on
pakua *v* unload
pale *adv* there
palilia *v* weed
paliwa *v* choke
pamba *v* adorn
pambana *v* struggle
pambano *n* duel, match
pambizo *n* margin
pambo *n* ornament
pamoja *adv* together
pamoja na *pre* along
pamoja na *adv* inclusive
pampu *n* pump
pana *adj* wide, broad
panda *v* ascend, go up
panda na shuka *v* fluctuate
pande kubwa *n* block
pandikiza *v* implant, sow
pandisha *v* hoist
pandisha daraja *v* upgrade
panga *v* organize, plan
panga ratiba *v* schedule
panga upya *v* reorganize
pango *n* cave, cavern
panji *n* dolphin

panua v widen, expand
panuka v branch out
panya n rat, mouse
panya buki n beaver
Papa n Pope
papasa v fondle
papatika v flutter
papo hapo adv instantly
parachuti n parachute
parokia n parish
paroko n parishioner
parura v claw
Pasaka n Easter
pasha moto v heat
pasipojulikana adv beyond
pasipoti n passport
pasua v rip apart, split
pasuka v rupture, burst
pata v acquire
pata kutu v rust
pata mimba v conceive
pata nafuu v recuperate
pata tena v regain
patana v bargain
patanisha v reconcile
patasi n chisel
patia v furnish, provide
patia nafasi v accommodate

patia vifaa n outfit
patikana adj available
pato n acquisition
pauni n pound
pazia n drape, curtain
pea n pair
pedeli n pedal
peke yake adj singlehanded
pekee adj alone, single
peku peku adj barefoot
pekua v ransack
peleleza v probe, spy
pembe n angle, side
pembe tano n pentagon
pembe ya ndovu n ivory
pembejeo n input
pembeni adj adjacent
pembeni adv apart, aside
pembetatu n triangle
penda adj fond
penda v love, like
pendekeza v recommend
pendekezo n proposal
pendelea v prefer
pendezesha v beautify
pendezwa v enchant
pendezwa mno v captivate
pendo adj affectionate

P

penduli *n* pendulum

penginepo *adv* elsewhere

penisilini *n* penicillin

penseli ya rangi *n* crayon

penya *v* penetrate

penya katika *v* permeate

penye miamba *adj* rocky

penye nafasi *adj* roomy

penyeza *v* infiltrate

pepesa *v* blink

pepesuka *v* stagger

peponi *n* paradise

pera *n* pear

peremende *n* candy

pesa *n* cash, money

pesa halali *adj* tender

petali *n* petal

pete *n* ring

petroli *n* gasoline

pezi *n* fin

pia *adv* also, too

piano *n* piano

picha *n* image, photo

pichi *n* peach

piga *v* assault, beat

piga chafya *v* sneeze

piga deki *v* mop

piga hatua ndefu *v* stride

piga honi *v* honk

piga kambi *v* camp

piga kelele *v* scream, yell

piga kengele *v* ring

piga kite *v* wail

piga kofi *v* slap, smack

piga kura *v* vote

piga lipu *v* plaster

piga magoti *v* genuflect

piga makasia *v* paddle

piga makofi *v* clap

piga mbizi *v* dive

piga mhuri *v* stamp

piga mluzi *v* whistle

piga msumeno *v* saw

piga mwayo *v* yawn

piga na bunduki *v* shoot down

piga na mawe *v* stone

piga na rungu *v* bludgeon

piga pasi *v* iron

piga picha *v* photograph

piga polishi *v* polish

piga rangi *v* paint

piga ribiti *v* rivet

piga rungu *v* club

piga simu *v* dial, phone

piga teke *v* lash out, kick

piga tupa *v* file

piga ukelele *v* shriek
piga uyole *v* cry out
pigana *v* battle
pigana mieleka *n* wrestling
pigania *v* champion
pigo *n* knock, smack
pigo la moyo *n* heartbeat
pika *v* brew, distill
pika kite *v* moan
pikapu *n* pickup
pikipiki *n* motorcycle
pili pili *n* pepper
pilikapilika *n* fuss
pilipili hoho *n* bell pepper
pima *v* measure
pima hatua *v* pace
pima muda *v* time
pima uzito *v* weigh
pimajoto *n* thermometer
pinda *v* curve, bend
pindo *n* fringe, hem
pindua *v* depose, oust
pinduka *v* capsize
pindukia *v* transcend
pinga *v* refute, rebut
pinga ngumi *v* punch
pingana *v* disagree
pingiti *n* torso

pingu *n* handcuffs
pini *n* pin, thumbtack
pipa *n* bin, trash can
pipa la karatasi *n* waste basket
pipi *n* candy, sweets
pishana *v* overlap
pita *v* lapse, pass
pitia *v* go over, review
pitisha *v* pass around
pitisha macho *v* glimpse
plagi *n* spark plug
plamu *n* plum
plamu kavu *n* prune
plani *n* blueprint
plastiki *n* plastic
platinamu *n* platinum
plutoniamu *n* plutonium
poa *v* mellow
pochi *n* handbag, purse
pochi ya pesa *n* wallet
pofua *v* blind
pokea *v* receive
pokezana *v* alternate
Poland *n* Poland
polepole *adv* slowly
polishi *n* polish
polisi *n* cop, police
pombe *n* liquor

P

pombe ya rum *n* rum
pomboo *n* dolphin
pomoni *n* brim
pona *v* heal, recover
ponda *v* mash, squash
pongeza *v* congratulate
pongezi *n* praise
ponyesha *v* cure
ponyoka *v* slip
pooza *v* paralyze
popo *n* bat
popote *c* wherever
pora *v* plunder
pori *n* jungle
poromoko *n* avalanche
posa *n* courtship
posho *n* allowance
posta *n* post office
posta ya mizigo *n* parcel post
posti *v* mail
posti-kadi *n* postcard
poswa *adj* engaged
potea *v* disappear
poteza *v* displace
potoa *adj* deprave
potosha *v* pervert, warp
povu *n* lather, foam
poza *v* cool, chill

profesa *n* professor
programu *n* program
propaganda *n* propaganda
protini *n* protein
pua *n* nose
pua na mdomo *n* muzzle
pukuchua *v* thresh
pukusa *v* shed
puliza *v* inflate, blow
pulizia *v* spray
puluki *adj* shoddy
pumbaza akili *v* hypnotize
pumu *n* asthma
pumua *v* breathe
pumzi *n* breath
pumzika *v* repose, rest
punda *n* donkey
punda milia *n* zebra
punde *adv* shortly
pungua *v* wane
pungua thamani *v* depreciate
pungufu *adj* deficient
punguga *v* minimize
punguza *v* reduce, trim
punguza *adj* moderate
punguza bei *v* discount
punguza nguvu *v* dilute
punguzo *n* discount

P

pupa *n* rash
puru *n* rectum
puto *n* balloon
puuza *v* override, ignore
puuzia *v* condone
pwani *n* beach, coast
pwani *adv* ashore
pweke *adj* introvert
pweza *n* octopus
pwita *v* pulsate, throb

R

rabbi *n* rabbi
rada *n* radar
radi *n* thunderbolt
rafadha *n* turbine
rafiki *n* buddy, friend
rafiki wa kike *n* girlfriend
rafiky *n* ally
rafu *n* hanger, shelf
raha *n* enjoyment
raha mustarehe *n* bliss
rahisi *adj* cheap, simple

rahisisha *v* facilitate
raia *adj* national
raia *n* citizen, subject
raisi *n* president
raketi *n* racket
ramani *n* map, chart
rambaza *v* surf
rambirambi *n* condolences
randa *v* loiter
randaranda *v* roam
rangi *n* color, paint
rangi ya asili *n* complexion
rangi ya udongo *adj* brown
rarua *v* maul
rasi *n* peninsula
rasilimali *n* assets
ratiba *n* schedule
ratibu *v* coordinate
ratili *n* pound
redio *n* radio
refu mno *adj* towering
refusha *v* lengthen
rehani *n* mortgage
rejea kwenye *v* refer to
rejesha kwao *v* repatriate
rejeshi *adj* reflexive
rejeta *n* radiator
rekebisha *v* adapt, adjust

P

R

reki *n* rake
reli *n* rail
reli za barafu *n* skate
remba *v* embellish
reptilia *n* reptile
ridhaa *n* compliance
ridhia *v* deign
ridhika *adj* content
ridhika *v* content
ridhisha *v* appease
rimu *n* rim
rinda *n* pleat
ringa *v* show off
risasi *n* ammunition
risiti *n* receipt
rithi *v* inherit
rithisha *v* bequeath
riwaya *n* novel
riziki *n* livelihood
robo *n* quarter
robota *n* bale
roho *n* spirit
rojo *n* puree
roketi *n* rocket
ropoka *v* babble
rosari *n* rosary
roshani *n* balcony
rubani *n* pilot

rubaruti *n* artichoke
rudi *v* return
rudi kawaida *v* normalize
rudi nyuma *v* retreat
rudia *v* repeat
rudisha *v* recall
rudishia *v* retaliate
rudishia kipigo *v* strike back
rudishia kupiga *v* hit back
rudufu *v* replicate
rufaa *n* appeal
ruhusa *n* allowance
ruhusu *v* allow, permit
ruka *v* leap, jump
rundika *v* pile, stack
rungu *n* club
runinga *n* television
rusha *v* toss, throw
rushia maji *v* splash
rushwa *n* kickback
rutuba *n* fertility
rutubisha *v* fertilize

R

S

saa *n* hour, time
saa ya ukutani *n* clock
saba *adj* seven
sababisha *v* cause, impact
sababu *n* reason, cause
sabini *adj* seventy
sadaka *n* alms, charity
sadikisha *v* convince
safari *n* journey, trip
safari ndefu *n* odyssey
safari ya kitalii *n* tour
safari ya ndege *n* flight
safi *adj* neat, tidy
safi kabisa *adj* immaculate
safihi *adj* impertinent
safina *n* ark
safiri *v* travel
safirisha *v* export
safisha *v* clean, purify
safisha kabisa *v* sterilize
safu *n* column
safu ya kizuizi *n* cordon
safura *n* anemia
saga *v* mince, grind

sagenti *n* sergeant
sahani *n* plate, disk
sahau *v* forget
sahihi *adj* precise
sahihisha *v* amend
saidia *v* aid, help
saikolojia *n* psychology
saini *v* sign
saini *n* signature
saini ndogo *n* initials
sajili *v* register
saka *v* track
sakafu *n* floor
sakitu *n* frost
sakramenti *n* sacrament
salaam *n* regards
salala *n* sirloin
salama *adj* safe
salamu *n* greetings
salfa *n* sulphur
salimia *v* greet
salimu amri *v* capitulate
salio *n* remnant
saliti *v* betray, sellout
samadi *n* dung
samaki *n* fish
sambamba *adv* abreast
sambamba *n* parallel

S

sambaza *v* scatter, spread
samehe *v* pardon, forgive
sampuli *n* sample
sana *adv* highly, very, widely
sanaa *n* art, humanities
sanaa bubu *v* mime
sanamu *n* effigy, statue
sanda *n* shroud
sanduku *n* suitcase
sanduku la posta *n* mailbox
sandwichi *n* sandwich
sanifu upya *v* recreate
sanjari *n* series
santuri *n* record
sarafu *n* coin, penny
sarakani *n* cancer
sarakasi *n* circus
sare *n* uniform
sarufi *n* grammar
saruji *n* cement
sasa *adv* now
sataranji *n* chess
satelaiti *n* satellite
sauti *n* sound, tone
sawa *adv* okay, right, smoothly
sawa *adj* right
sawa *adj* equal, same
sawa na *adj* equivalent

sawa sawa *adj* identical
sawadhisha *v* equate
sawadhisha *v* redress
sawasawa *adj* alike; even
sawasawa *adv* properly
sawazisha *v* balance
sawidi *v* draft
sawiri *v* depict, picture
sayansi *n* science
sayari *n* planet
sebule *n* lobby, lounge
sebuleni *n* living room
secunde *n* second
sehemu *n* fraction, portion
sehemu shiriki *n* component
sema *v* say, tell, utter
sema uongo *v* lie
sementi *n* cement
semesha *v* address
seminari *n* seminary
Semptemba *n* September
senata *n* senator
senati *n* senate
senene *n* cricket
sensa *n* census
sentensi *n* sentence
senti *n* cent, penny
sentimeta *n* centimeter

sepeto *n* spade

sera *n* policy

seremala *n* carpenter

serikali *n* government

sesere *n* toy

seti *n* set

shaba *n* copper

shaba nyekundu *n* bronze

shada *n* wreath

shadidi *adj* intensive

shahada *n* degree

shahawa *n* sperm

shahidi *n* eyewitness

shairi *n* lyrics, poem

shajara *n* almanac

shaka *n* quagmire

shakevale *n* buzzard

shakwa *n* gull

shakwe *n* seagull

shamba *n* farm

shamba kubwa *n* estate

shambulia *v* assault

shambulio *n* aggression

shambuliwa *v* beset

shangaa sana *v* confound

shangaza *v* astonish, baffle

shangazi *n* aunt

shangilia *v* cheer, applaud

shani *n* marvel, novelty

shanta *n* backpack

sharafa *n* sideburns

shari *adj* contentious

sharifu *v* regard

sharti *n* prerequisite

sharti la mwisho *n* ultimatum

shashi *n* gauze

shati *n* shirt

shauku *adj* ardent

shauku *n* enthusiasm

shauri *n* proposal

shauri vingine *v* dissuade

shauriana *v* confer

shavu *n* cheek

shawishi *v* entice, tempt

shayiri *n* barley

shela *n* veil

shemasi *n* deacon

shemeji *n* sister-in-law

shere *n* prank

sherehe *n* celebration

sherehekea *v* celebrate

sheria *n* decree, law

shetani *n* demon, devil

shida *n* hardship

shika *v* hold, catch

shika nafasi ya *v* supersede

S

shikana sana *v* clinch
shikilia *v* adhere
shikiliwa *v* obsess
shikwa *v* obsess
shimo *n* pothole, pit
shina *n* stalk, stem
shinda *v* vanquish
shinda tena *v* win back
shindana *v* compete
shindana mbio *v* race
shindikana *v* fall through
shindilia *v* compress
shindwa *v* fail, lose
shindwa kujali *v* neglect
shingo *n* neck
shinikiza *v* pressure
shinikizo *n* pressure
shira *n* syrup
shirika *n* corporation
shirika la ndege *n* airline
shiriki *v* participate
shirikiana *v* cooperate
shirikisho *n* affiliation
shitaki *v* indict, sue
shoka *n* ax
shona *v* stitch, sew
shtaki *v* prosecute
shtua *v* startle, shock

shua *v* launch
shubiri *n* span
shughuli *n* task, profession
shughulika na *v* tackle
shughulikia *v* process
shughulisha *v* preoccupy
shujaa *adj* courageous
shujaa *n* hero, knight
shuka *v* come down
shuka la juu *n* bedspread
shukrani *n* tribute
shuku *v* doubt, suspect
shukurani *n* gratitude
shukuru *v* thank
shule *n* school
shupavu *adj* intrepid
shuri *v* suggest
shurutisha *v* inflict
shurutisho *n* constraint
shusha *v* bring down
shusha cheo *v* demote
shusha pumzi *v* sigh
shusha thamani *v* devalue
shutuma *n* charge
shwari *adv* smoothly
si mtu *pro* no one
si popote *adv* nowhere
si rasmi *adv* unofficially

siafu *n* ant
siagi *n* butter
siasa *n* politics, regime
sidiria *n* bra
sifa *n* praise, flattery
sifia *v* exult, flatter
sifongo *n* sponge
sifu *v* commend, praise
sigareti *n* cigarette
sihi *v* entreat, implore
sihi sana *v* exhort
sijafu *n* cuff
siki *n* vinegar
sikia *v* hear
sikiliza *v* listen
sikiliza kwa siri *v* eavesdrop
sikio *n* ear
sikitika *v* regret
sikitika *adj* sorry
sikitikia *v* deplore, grieve
sikitiko *n* affliction
siku *n* day
siku hizi *adv* nowadays
siku moja *adv* someday
siku ya kazi *adj* weekday
silabi *n* syllable
silaha *n* weapon
silaha za vita *n* artillery

silika *n* instinct
silinda *n* cylinder
simama *adj* motionless
simama *v* base
simamia *v* supervise
simamisha *v* discontinue
simba *n* lion
simba jike *n* lioness
simika *v* inaugurate
simu *n* phone
sinagogi *n* synagogue
sindano *n* injection, shot
sindikiza *v* accompany
sinema *n* cinema, movie
singe *n* bayonet
singizia *v* insinuate
sinia *n* tray
sinyaa *v* wither, shrink
sinzia *v* doze, snooze
sio adilifu *adj* crude
sio halili *adj* illegal
sio kawaida *adj* abnormal
sio mtu *pro* nobody
sio mtu *adv* not
sio rasmi *adj* casual
sio ya kawaida *adj* bizarre
siri *n* secrecy
sisi *pro* we, us

S

sisi wenyewe *pro* ourselves
sisimka *v* shudder
sisimua *v* excite, thrill
sisitiza *v* assert, insist, underlie
sista *n* nun
sita *v* hesitate
sita *adj* six
sitaha *n* deck
sitasita *v* waver
sitiari *n* metaphor
sitini *adj* sixty
sitisha *v* cancel
siwa barafu *n* iceberg
skauti *n* scout
sketi *n* skirt
skrubu *n* screw
skuta *n* scooter
slesi *n* slice
soda *n* soda
sogea *v* budge
sogea mbele *v* move forward
sogelea *v* approach
sogeza *v* dislodge
soko *n* fair, market
sokota *v* intertwine
soksi *n* sock
sokwe *n* chimpanzee
soli *n* sole

soma *v* study, read
somea *v* major in
somo *n* lesson, course
somo kuu *n* major
sonara *n* jeweler
songa *v* crowd
songa mbele *v* advance
songamana *v* huddle
songasonga *v* mob
soseji *n* sausage
Spain *n* Spain
spika *n* speaker
spishi *n* species
staafu *v* retire
staajabisha *v* amaze
staajabu *adj* aghast
staajabu *v* wonder
staarabisha *v* civilize
stadi *adj* skillful
staha *n* modesty
stahili *v* deserve
stahilifu *adj* deserving
stahimili *v* endure, bear
stakabadhi *n* sale slip
starehe *n* leisure
stashahada *n* diploma
stawi *v* bloom
stempu *n* postage

suala *n* issue, matter
subira *n* patience
subiri *v* hang on, wait
subu *v* mold
sufu *n* wool
sufuri *n* zero
sufuria *n* pan, pot
sufuria *n*
sugu *n* wart
sugu *adj* chronic
sugua *v* rub, scour
sugua kwa brashi *v* brush
sugua sana *v* scrub
sujudu *v* adore
sukari *n* sugar
sukuma *v* push, shove
sukutua *v* gargle
suluba *n* torture
sulubu *n* crucifixion
sulubu *v* crucify, torture
suluhia *adj* adaptable
suluhisha *v* conciliate
suluhisho *n* resolution
suluhu *n* settlement
sumaku *n* magnet
sumbua *v* bother, hassle
sumbufu *adj* bothersome
sumbuka *v* agonize

sumbuliwa *v* put out
sumbuliwa na *v* suffer from
sumu *n* poison
sumu ya nyoka *n* venom
sungura *n* hare, rabbit
supu *n* broth, soup
sura *n* feature, looks
sura ya nchi *n* landscape
surua *n* measles
suruali *n* slacks, pants
susa *v* boycott
suti *n* suit
suuza *v* rinse
swali *n* inquiry
Sweden *n* Sweden
sweta *n* sweater
swichi *n* switch
Swideni *adj* Sweedish

S

T

taa *n* lamp, lighting
taa kubwa *n* floodlight
taabu *n* tribulation
taadabu *v* behave
taahira *adj* retarded
taalamisha *v* enlighten
taalimu *v* specialize
taaluma *n* vocation
taamali *v* meditate
taarifa *n* notification
taarifu *v* inform
taasisi *n* institution
tabaka *n* caste
tabaka ya chini *n* ground floor
tabaruku *v* dedicate
tabasamu *v* smile
tabasamu *n* smile
tabia *n* behavior
tabia *adj* characteristic
tabia mbaya *n* misconduct
tabiri *v* foretell
tafakari *v* ponder
taflisi *n* seizure
tafrija *n* feast

tafsiri *v* interpret
tafsiri visivyo *v* pervert
tafua *v* look through
tafua kimbilio *v* recourse
tafuna *v* munch, chew
tafuta *v* find, locate
tafuta ushauri *v* consult
tahadhari *n* caution
tahadharisha *v* alert
tahajia *n* spelling
tahayari *n* timidity
tahira *adj* moron
tai *n* necktie
tai mzoga *n* vulture
taifa *n* nation
taifa kubwa *n* superpower
taifisha *v* nationalize
tairi *v* circumcise
taja *v* mention
taja herufi *v* spell
taji *n* crown
tajiri *adj* wealthy, rich
tajirisha *v* enrich
taka *v* desire, want
takasa *v* purify, purge
takataka *n* rubbish, refuse
takatifu *adj* holy, sacred
takwimu *n* statistic

talaka *n* divorce

taliki *v* divorce

tamaa *n* ambition

tamaa kubwa *n* hangup

tamani *v* covet, lust

tamba *v* brag

tambara *n* rag

tambarare *adj* flat

tambua *v* realize, discern

tambua ugonjwa *v* diagnose

tambulisha *v* introduce

tambuza *v* weld

tamka *v* proclaim

tamka ghafla *v* exclaim

tamko *n* declaration

tamu *adj* delicious

tanbihi *n* footnote

tandu ya buibui *n* spiderweb

tanga *n* sail

tangatanga *v* stray

tangawizi *n* ginger

tangaza *v* announce

tangazo *n* broadcast

tangi *n* tank

tangi la maji *n* cistern

tangi samaki *n* aquarium

tango *n* cucumber

tangu *c* since

tangua *v* quash

tangulia *v* precede

tangulia *adj* front

tangulia kufanya *v* preempt

tanguliza *adj* front

tani *n* ton

tania *v* joke, tease

tano *adj* five

tanuri *n* oven

tanzu *adj* subsidiary

tao *n* arc, arch

tapakaa *adj* infested

tapanya *v* squander

tapatapa *v* writhe

tapeli *v* cheat, swindle

tapeli *n* cheater

tapika *v* vomit

tapo *n* nut

tarajia *v* anticipate

tarajio *n* expectancy

tarakimu *n* digit, number

taratibu *adj* gradual

taraza *n* embroidery

tarehe *n* date

tarikhi *n* chronicle

tarishi *n* courier

tarizi *v* embroider

tarumbeta *n* trumpet

tasa *adj* barren, childless
tasbihi *n* rosary
tashtiti *n* satire
tasnifu *n* thesis
taswira *n* portrait
tatanisha *adj* ambiguous
tatanisha *v* complicate
tathmini *v* assess
tathmini *n* assessment
tatiza *v* confuse
tatizo *n* problem
tatu *adj* three
tatua *v* solve, sort out
taulo *n* towel
tauni *n* plague
tausi *n* peacock
tawa *adj* virtuous
tawala *v* dominate, reign
tawala huria *n* anarchy
tawala tawala *v* boss around
tawaliwa *adj* addicted
tawanya *v* dispel
tawanyisha *v* space out
tawaza *v* bestow
tawi *n* bough, branch
taya *n* jaw
tayari *adv* already
tayari *adj* ready

tayarisha *v* compile
tazama *v* gaze, look
tazamio *n* expectancy
tega *v* snare
tegemea *v* depend, rely on
tegemeo *n* expectation
tegua *v* defuse
teguka *v* sprain
teka *v* hijack, capture
teka nyara *v* abduct, kidnap
teke *n* boot
tekeleza *v* ravage, enforce
teknologia *n* technology
teksi *n* cab
tele *adj* ample
telegramu *n* telegram
telekeza *v* abandon
teleza *v* glide, slip
tema *v* spit
tembea *v* pace, walk
tembea kama askari *v* march
tembea tembea *v* stroll
tembelea *v* visit, drop in
tembo *n* elephant
tena *adv* again
tenda *v* perform
tenda dhambi *v* sin
tendea *v* treat

tendo *n* action
tenga *v* cut off, isolate
tengamaji *n* watershed
tenganisha *v* separate
tengeneza *v* fabricate
tengeneza tena *v* remake
tengenezwa na *v* comprise
tengua *v* repeal
tenisi *n* tennis
teremka *v* get off
tesa *v* torment
teseka *v* agonize, suffer
teta *v* gossip
tete *n* reed
tetea *v* advocate
tetekuwanga *n* chicken pox
tetemeka *v* shiver, quiver
tetesi *n* hearsay, rumor
teua *v* appoint
tezi *n* gland, prostate
thabiti *adj* staunch
thamani *n* value, cherish
thelathini *adj* thirty
theluji *n* snow
themanini *adj* eighty
theologia *n* theology
thibitisha *v* affirm, certify
thubutu *v* dare, venture

thurea *n* chandelier
tia alama *v* earmark
tia bumbuwazi *v* daze
tia dau *v* stake
tia doa *v* blemish, stain
tia hamasa *v* motivate
tia hofu *v* dismay
tia kasumba *v* brainwash
tia kilema *v* maim
tia maiti dawa *v* embalm
tia moyo *v* encourage
tia nanga *v* moor
tia rangi *v* dye
tia saini *v* sign
tia scrubu *v* screw
tia sumu *v* poison
tia ukungu *v* blur
tia uzi *v* thread
tia wasiwasi *adj* distressing
tiara *n* kite
tiba *n* medication
tibu *v* redress
tibua zaidi *v* worsen
tii *v* abide by, heed
tiifu *adj* pious
tikisa *v* wag, jolt
tikisa sana *v* convulse
tikisatikisa *v* wiggle

tikisika *v* vibrate

tikiti *n* watermelon

tikiti maji *n* melon

tilia *v* darn

tilia shaka *v* mistrust, distrust

timamu *adj* lucid, sane

timiza *v* fulfill

timu *n* team

tindikali *n* acid

tingisha *v* jerk, shake

tini *n* fig

tipwatipwa *adj* obese

tiririka *v* drip, flow

tisa *adj* nine

tisha *v* terrify, scare

tishia *v* threaten

tishia kikatili *v* terrorize

tishio *n* threat

tisini *adj* ninety

titia *v* bog down

toa *v* emit, yield

toa damu *v* bleed

toa hatiani *v* acquit

toa hoja *v* reason

toa hongo *v* graft

toa huduma *v* service

toa kauli *v* profess

toa leseni *v* license

toa maji *v* drain

toa mimba *n* abortion

toa msaada *v* donate

toa muhtasari *v* sum up

toa taarifa *v* notify

toa tahadhari *v* warn

toa upepo *v* deflate

toa upya *v* reproduce

toa ushaidi *v* testify

toa ushauri *v* counsel

toa wazi *v* divulge

toa wazo *v* comment

toba *n* penance

toboa *v* drill, pierce

tochi *n* torch

tofaa *n* apple

tofali *n* block, brick

tofauti *adj* assorted

tofauti *n* variety

tofautiana *v* differ, vary

tofautisha *v* contrast

tohara *n* purgatory

toka *v* go away

toka *c* since

toka damu *n* bleeding

toka jasho *v* perspire

toka nje *v* go out

tokana na *v* derive

tokea v occur, happen

tokea hapo adv since then

tokea tena v recur

tokeo n ocurrence

tokep n sequel

tokeza n bulge

tokezea v turn up

tokezea tena v reappear

toleo n version, edition

tombo n quail

tone n drop, drip

tonge la barafu n ice cube

tongoza v seduce

tope n mud

tora n regularity

toroka v escape, flee

toroli n wheelbarrow

tosheleza v quench

tovuti n web site

toweka v vanish

toza faini v fine

toza kwa lazima v extort

trauti n trout

trekta n tractor

trela n trailer

treni n train

tropiki n tropic

tu adv solely, only

tua v land, settle

tuama v stagnate

tubu v confess, repent

tufe n sphere

tuhuma n accusation

tuhumu v accuse

tuili adj belated

tukana v affront, insult

tukio n incident, event

tukuza v glorify, exalt

tukwa n tonsil

tulia v settle down

tulivu adj calm, serene, composed

tuliza v placate, mitigate

tuma v dispatch, send

tumaini n hope

tumbaku n tobacco

tumbili n monkey

tumbo n stomach, belly

tumbukiza v plunge

tume n commission

tumia v utilize, use, exert, consume

tumia busara v rationalize

tumia mashine v mechanize

tumia nguvu za v tap into

tumia tena v recycle

tumikia v minister, serve

tuna v emboss

T

tunda *n* fruit
tundika *v* hang, put up
tundu *n* hole
tundu la hewa *n* vent
tundu la pua *n* nostril
tunga *v* concoct
tunga papo hapo *v* improvise
tunga sheria *v* legislate
tunga usaha *v* fester
tungua *v* shoot
tunza *v* cherish, care for
tunzo *n* prize
tupa *v* dump, cast
tupu *adj* empty, void
turubai *n* canvas
turuhani *n* bonus
tusi *n* affront, insult
tuta *n* spur
tutuma *v* rumble
tuza *v* award
tuzo *n* reward, award
twa kwa nguvu *v* conquer
twaa *v* take over
twanga *v* pound
tweka *v* sail
tweta *v* gasp
twiga *n* giraffe

U

ua *v* assassinate
ua kwa umeme *v* electrocute
uachiaji huru *n* liberation
uadilifu *n* ethics, virtue
uadui *n* animosity
uaguzi *n* oracle
uaminifu *n* integrity, loyalty
uamuzi *n* decision
uanamaji *n* navy
uandikishaji *n* enrollment
uangalifu *adj* careful
uangalifu *n* prudence
uangalizi *n* care, custody
uangamizi *n* destruction
uanzishaji *n* activation
uanzishaji upya *n* renewal
uashi *n* mutiny
uasi *n* disloyalty
ubaba *n* fatherhood
ubadhirifu *n* extravagance
ubadili *n* avarice
ubadilishaji *n* replacement
ubaguzi *n* discrimination
ubalozi *n* embassy

ubamba *n* slab

ubani *n* incense

ubao *n* blackboard

ubao mgumu *n* hardwood

ubao wa kurukia *n* springboard

ubapa *n* blade

ubaridi *n* coldness

ubashiri *n* prophecy

ubatizo *n* baptism

ubavu *n* flank, rib

ubavuni *pre* alongside

ubaya *n* malice

ubeberu *n* imperialism

Ubelgiji *n* Belgium

ubepari *n* capitalism

ubeti *n* verse

ubikira *n* chastity

ubinafsi *n* selfishness

ubishani *n* dispute

ubishi *n* obstinacy

uboho *n* marrow

ubongo *n* brain

ubora *n* quality

ubunifu *n* creativity

ucha Mungu *n* piety

uchachu *n* ferment

uchafu *n* filth

uchafuzi *n* pollution

uchaguzi *n* choice, option

uchaji *n* reverence

uchakavu *n* deterioration

uchale *n* slash

uchambuzi *n* analysis

uchanga *n* immaturity

uchawi *n* witchcraft

uchengele *n* bowels

uchi *adj* naked

uchi *n* nudity

uchochezi *n* insinuation

uchokezi *n* boredom

uchovu *n* exhaustion

uchoyo *n* meanness

uchu *n* passion

uchukuaji *n* intake

uchungu *n* bitterness

uchunguzi *n* inquest

udadisi *n* inquisition

udanganyifu *n* fraud

udevu *n* antenna

udhaifu *n* limitation

udhalilishaji *n* mortification

udhalimu *n* tyranny

udhanifu *n* implication

udhi *v* irritate, bug

udhia *n* burden

udhibiti *n* censorship

U

udobi *n* laundry

udogo *n* miniature

udongo *n* dirt, soil

udume *n* manliness

uduni *n* degradation

uelekeo *n* direction

uelewano *n* harmony

uelimishaji *n* pedagogy

ufa *n* crack, rift

ufa mdogo *n* crevice

ufafanuzi *n* clarification

ufagio *n* broom

ufahamu *n* awareness

ufahari *n* splendor

ufalme *n* kingdom

ufananaji *n* similarity

Ufaransa *n* France

ufasaha *n* eloquence

ufasiki *n* immorality

ufidhuli *n* rudeness

Ufini *n* Finland

ufisadi *n* corruption

ufito *n* rod

ufizi *n* gum

ufufuo *n* resurrection

ufugaji wa ndege *n* poultry

ufuko *n* coast

ufukufuku *n* provocation

ufukwe *n* seashore

ufukwe *adj* seaside

ufukweni *adv* ashore

ufukweni *n* shore

ufumbuzi *n* solution

ufundi *n* skill

ufundishaji *n* pedagogy

ufungaji *n* closure

ufunguo *n* key

ufunuo *n* revelation

ufupi *n* brevity

ugaidi *n* terrorism

ugandamizaji *n* oppression

ugeugeu *n* instability

ughushi *v* counterfeit

Ugiriki *n* Greece

ugo *n* fence

ugomvi *n* conflict, strife

ugonjwa *n* sickness, illness

ugonvi *n* scuffle

ugua *adj* ailing

ugua *v* sicken

ugumu *n* bottleneck

uguza *v* care for

uhaba *n* shortage

uhai *n* animation

uhaini *n* treason

uhakika *n* certainty; precision

U

uhakika *adj* certain

uhalali *n* validity, legality

uhalalishaji *n* warrant

uhalifu *n* crime, felony

uhalifu wa kitoto *n* delinquency

uhalisi *n* authenticity

uhami *n* insulation

uhamiaji *n* immigration

uhamisho *n* transfer

uharamia *n* piracy

uharibifu *n* damage

uharibifu *adj* wasteful

uhasi *n* insurgency

uhasibu *n* bookkeeping

Uholanzi *n* Holland

uhuru *n* freedom

uhusiano *n* rapport, liaison

uimara *n* firmness

uimara *adj* constant

uimbaji *n* chant

Uingereza *n* Britain

uingiaji *n* influx

uingiliaji *n* intrusion

ujamaa *n* fellowship

ujana *n* adolescence

ujanja *n* trick, ruse

ujanja *adj* devious

Ujapani *n* Japan

ujasiri *n* bravery

ujasusi *n* espionage

ujauzito *n* pregnancy

Ujerumani *n* Germany

ujia *n* lane, path

ujinga *n* ignorance

ujinsia *n* sexuality

ujira *n* wage

ujirani *n* neighborhood

ujumbe *n* errand, mission

ujumi *adj* aesthetic

ujuzi *n* knowledge

ukaaji *n* occupation

ukadiri *n* mediocrity

ukaguzi *n* check, survey

ukaidi *n* defiance

ukakamavu *n* fitness

ukale *adj* conservative

ukali *n* ferocity

ukame *n* drought

ukamilifu *n* perfection

ukanda *n* strap

ukanushaji *n* denial

ukapera *n* celibacy

ukarabati *n* reparation

ukaribu *n* proximity

ukarimu *n* kindness

ukataaji *n* refusal

U

ukatavu n abandonment
ukatili n atrocity, cruelty
ukatizaji n interruption
Ukatoliki n Catholicism
ukawaida n mediocrity
ukelele n scream, shriek
ukengefu n aberration
ukimbizi n defection
ukimya n silence, hush
ukinaifu n monotony
ukingo n verge, edge; profile
ukingoni n brink
ukirithimba n monopoly
ukiwa n abandonment
ukoga n tartar
ukoloni n colonization
ukoma n leprosy
ukomavu n maturity
ukombozi n redemption
ukomunisti n communism
ukoo n ancestry, clan
ukosefu n lack
ukosefu wa haki n unfairness
ukosekanaji n absence
ukosi n collar
ukosoaji n criticism
Ukristo n Christianity
ukuaji n growth

ukubwa n magnitude, size
ukulima n farming
ukumbi n lobby, hall
ukumbusho n anniversary
ukungu n fog, haze, mist
ukunjufu n warmth
ukurasa n page
ukurutu n rash
ukuta n wall
ukuzaji n enlargement
ukweli n honesty, truth
ukweli wa n realism
ukwepaji n evasion
ulafi n greed
ulaghai n deceit
ulaini n softness
ulainishaji n lubrication
ulaji n consumption
ulanzi n bamboo
Ulaya n Europe
ulazima n necessity
ulevi n drunkenness
ulezi n patronage
ulili n shrine
ulimi n tongue
ulimi wa moto n flame
ulimwengu n universe
ulinganifu n coincidence

ulipizi *n* retaliation
uliza *v* ask, question
uliza *adj* prompt
uma *n* fork
umaarufu *n* greatness
umaji *n* fluid
umakini *n* conciousness
umama *n* motherhood
umande *n* dew
umaskini *n* poverty
umati *n* crowd, throng
umba *v* create
umbali *n* distance
umbea *n* gossip
umbile *n* looks
umbo *n* shape, form
umbua *v* denigrate
umeme *n* electricity
umeng'enyaji *n* digestion
umilikaji *n* ownership
umiliki *n* possession
umio *n* esophagus
umiza *v* harm, hurt
umma *adj* grassroots
umoja *n* unity, league
umri *n* age
umuhimu *n* importance
umwagiliaji *n* irrigation

unafiki *n* hypocrisy
unafuu *n* relief
unajimu *n* astrology
unda *v* constitute
undani *n* intimacy
undugu *n* brotherhood
unene *n* thickness
unga *n* cocaine, heroin
unga mkono *n* boost, support
ungana *v* ally, unite
unganisha *v* connect, link
ung'aro *n* brightness
unguza *v* burn, scorch
ungwana *n* gentleness
ununuzi *n* purchase
unyama *n* bestiality
unyang'anyi *n* confiscation
unyanyasaji *n* harassment
unyeleo *n* pore
unyenyekevu *n* meekness
unyenyezi *adj* hazy
unyevu *n* humidity
unyonge *n* weakness
unyong'onyevu *n* depression
unywaji kidogo *n* sip
uoevukaji *n* condensation
uoga *n* fear, fright
uondoaji *n* disposal

U

uonevu *n* injustice
uongo *n* illusion, lie
uongozi *n* leadership
uoto *n* vegetation
uovu *n* wickedness
uoza *n* rot
uozo wa mwili *n* gangrene
upadri *n* priesthood
upamba *n* sickle
upana *n* breadth, width
upande *n* facet, side
upande mmoja *adj* unilateral
upanuzi *n* expansion
upapi *n* strip
upasuaji *n* incision
upatikanaji *n* availability
upekee *n* oddity
upelelezi *n* espionage
upendeleo *n* bias, interest
upendeleo *adj* partial
upendo *n* affection, love
upenyezi *n* insinuation
upenyo *n* gap
upeo *n* scope, reach
upeo wa furaha *n* ecstasy
upeo wa kuona *n* visibility
upeo wa macho *n* horizon
upepo *n* wind

upepo mwanana *n* breeze
upesi *adj* hasty
upigaji kura *n* voting
upigaji picha *n* photography
upinde *n* bow
upinde wa mvua *n* rainbow
upinzani *n* resistance
upofu *n* blindness
upokezi *n* receipt
upole *n* compassion
upole *adj* indulgent
uporaji *n* mugging
upotovu *n* depravity
upungufu *n* deficiency
upuuzi *n* nonsense
upweke *n* loneliness
upya *adv* afresh, anew
upya *n* freshness
urafiki *n* friendship
urahisi *n* ease
uraia *n* nationality
uraisi *n* presidency
urasimu *n* bureaucracy
uratibu *n* coordination
urefu *n* height, length
Ureno *n* Portugal
urithi *n* heritage, legacy
urujuani *n* violet

U

urukaji *n* jump
Urusi *n* Russia
usafi *n* cleanliness
usafihi *n* impertinence
usaha *n* pus
usahihi *n* accuracy
usaidizi *n* assistance
usaili *n* interview
usajili *n* registration
usalama *n* safety
usaliti *n* betrayal
usambazaji *n* dispersal
usambazaji joto *n* heating
usanii *n* artwork
usawa *n* equality
usemi *n* axiom, saying
useremala *n* carpentry
ushaidi *n* testimony
ushaidi dhahiri *n* smoking gun
ushairi *n* poetry
usharika *n* congregation
ushaufu *n* pretension
ushauri *n* advice, counsel
ushawishi *n* temptation
ushenzi *n* barbarism
ushikiliaji wa nguvu *n* holdup
ushindano *n* rivalry
ushindi *n* victory

ushirika *v* affiliate
ushirika *n* fellowship
ushirikiano *n* association
ushirikina *n* superstition
ushoroba *n* corridor
ushujaa *n* heroism
ushupavu *n* boldness
ushuru *n* tax, toll
usia *n* testament
usikivu *n* attention
usiku *n* night
usiku huu *adv* tonight
usimamizi *n* supervision
usingizi *n* doze
uso *n* face, surface
uso kwa uso *adv* head-on
ustaarabu *n* civilization
ustadi *n* skill
ustawi *n* welfare
usukani *n* helm, rudder
usuluhishi *n* arbitration
usumaku *n* magnetism
usumbufu *n* nuisance
ususu *n* hallway
Uswisi *n* Switzerland
uta *v* eliminate
utaalamu *n* proficiency
utabiri *n* prediction

U

utafiti _n_ research
utajiri _n_ wealth
utakatifu _n_ holiness
utalii _n_ tourism
utamaduni _n_ culture
utambi _n_ membrane
utambulisho _n_ identity
utamu _n_ sweetness
utangazaji _n_ publicity
utangulizi _n_ introduction
utanguzi _n_ reversal
utani _n_ farce, mockery
utapeli _adj_ devious
utapeli _n_ swindle, scam
utapiamlo _n_ malnutrition
utaratibu _n_ routine, process
utari _n_ harp
utata _n_ complexity
utawa _n_ devotion
utawala _n_ reign
utawala juu ya _n_ lordship
ute wa yai _n_ egg white
utekaji _n_ conquest
utendaji _n_ performance
utendaji bora _n_ efficiency
utenzi _n_ industry
utepe _n_ ribbon
utepetevu _n_ apathy

utetezi _n_ intercession
uteuzi _n_ assignment
uthabiti _adj_ constant
uthabiti _n_ stability
uthibitisho _n_ evidence
uti wa mgongo _n_ backbone
utii _n_ allegiance
utiifu _n_ obedience
utiifu wa desturi _n_ conformity
utiko _n_ ridge
utimizaji _n_ fulfillment
utoaji _n_ provision
utokaji _n_ exodus
utomvu _n_ sap
utoto _n_ boyhood
utotoni _n_ childhood
utovu _n_ lack
utovu wa adabu _n_ indecency
utozaji _n_ imposition
utukufu _n_ glory, splendor
utukufu _adj_ sublime
utukutu _n_ mischief
utulivu _n_ composure
utumbo _n_ bowels
utumbo mpana _n_ colon
utume _n_ prophecy
utumiaji _n_ exploitation
utumwa _n_ slavery

utundu *n* mischief

utunzaji *n* care, custody

utunzi *n* composition

utupu *n* emptiness

utupu *adj* nude

Uturuki *n* Turkey

utusitusi *n* gloom

utuzaji *n* maintenance

uumbaji *n* creation

uunganishaji *n* synthesis

uungu *n* deity

uungwana *n* nobility

uuzaji *n* sale

uvamizi *n* invasion

uvimbe *n* cyst, swelling

uvivu *n* laziness

uvujaji *n* leakage

uvumbi *n* remains

uvumbuzi *n* discovery

uvumi *n* rumor

uvumilivu *n* restraint

uwakala *n* agency

uwanachama *n* membership

uwanda *n* plain, space

uwanda wa juu *n* plateau

uwanja *n* yard

uwanja wa nyasi *n* lawn

uwazi *n* candor

uwazo *n* imagination

uwekaji wa sumu *n* poisoning

uwekevu *n* economy

uwekezaji *n* investment

uweza wa ajabu *n* prodigy

uwezekano *n* possibility

uwezo *n* ability

uwezo wa kuona *n* sight

uwiano *n* proportion

uwizi *n* robbery

uwongo *n* fallacy

uyoga *n* fungus

uza *v* sell

uzalishaji *n* production

uzazi *n* maternity

uzee *n* old age

uzembe *adj* careless

uzembe *n* negligence

uzi *n* string, thread

uzima *n* vitality

uzinzi *n* infidelity

uzio *n* blockade

uzio wa ngazi *n* handrail

uzito *n* gravity, weight

uziwi *n* deafness

uzoefu *n* acquaintance

uzuiaji *n* repression

uzuizi *n* prohibition

U

uzuni *n* melancholy
uzuri *n* beauty
uzushi *n* calumny
uzuzu *n* clumsiness

V

va uso *v* blush
vaa *v* dress, wear
vamia *v* assail, attack
vanishi *n* varnish
vazi *n* clothing
vema *adv* right
vetebra *n* vertebra
viatu *n* footwear
vibaya *adv* badly, badly
viburudisho *n* refreshment
vice *n* vice
vichekesho *n* humor
vifaa *n* equipment
vifaa vya ofisi *n* stationery
vifaa vya ujenzi *n* hardware
vifungo *n* parenthesis
vifusi *n* rubble

vigae *n* tile
vigezo *n* terms
vijazio *n* stuffing
vikomo *n* extremities
vilia *n* cutlery
vilivyomo ndani *n* contents
vimba *n* bulge, swell
vinginevyo *adv* otherwise
vinjari *v* cruise
vinya *v* tremble
vipande *adv* asunder
vipengele *n* parameters
vipi *adv* how
vipimo *n* measurement
viringisha *v* roll, twist
virusi *n* virus
vita *n* war
vita vidogo *n* skirmish
vita vitakatifu *n* crusade
vitamini *n* vitamin
vitendo *n* exploit
vitisho *n* terror
vitu *n* goods, stuff
vitu laini *n* padding
viungo *n* seasoning
viwili *n* couple
vizazi *n* loin
vizuri *adv* clearly

U
V

vocha *n* voucher
volkeno *n* volcano
volteji *n* voltage
vua *v* undress
vugu vugu *adj* lukewarm
vuguvugu *adj* tepid
vuja *v* leak
vuka *v* span
vuka mpaka *v* overstep
vukiza *v* evaporate
vuma *v* howl, growl
vumaika *v* toil
vumbi *n* dust
vumbua *v* discover
vumilia *v* tolerate
vumisha *v* sound out
vuna *v* harvest
vunja *v* sever, break
vunja ili kuingia *v* break in
vunja kufungua *v* break open
vunja moyo *v* dishearten
vunja vunja *v* wreck
vunjavunja *v* splinter
vunjika *v* dissolve
vuruga *v* upset, disrupt
vurugu *n* chaos, tumult
vurumai *n* uproar
vuta *v* tow, haul

vuta kwingine *v* distract
vuta maji *v* flush
vuta masika *v* row
vuta ndani *v* ingest
vutia *n* allure, attract
vutia sana *v* fascinate
vutiwa *v* gravitate
vyakula *n* foodstuff
vyote *pro* everything

W

wachache *n* minority
wachezaji *n* player
wafanyakazi *n* personnel
wahi *v* catch up
wajibika *adj* accountable
wajibu *n* obligation
waka *adj* ablaze, alight
wakala *n* middleman
wakati *c* as, while
wakati *pre* during
wakati *n* period
wakati huo *adv* meantime

wakati upasao *adj* punctual

wake *n* wives

wakfu *n* dedication

wakia *n* ounce

wakifia *v* evaluate

wakili *n* attorney

wakilisha *v* represent

wakwe *n* in-laws

wala *adj* neither

wali *n* rice

walio tengana *adj* estranged

wambiso *n* attachment

wanaume *n* men

wanawake *n* women

wanga *n* starch

wangia *v* haunt

wangwa *n* lagoon

wanyama pori *n* wildlife

wao *pro* they

wao kwa wao *adj* each other

wapi *adv* where

waraka *n* document

waridi *adj* pink

waridi *n* rose, pink

warsha *n* workshop

washa *v* turn on, light

washwa *v* itch

wasi *n* misgivings

wasifu *n* biography

wasili *v* show up

wasiliana *v* communicate

wasiliana na *v* contact

wasilisha *v* convey, deliver

wasio tengana *adj* inseparable

wasiwasi *n* anxiety

wastani *adj* medium

wastani *n* moderation

wateja *n* clientele

wati *n* watt

watoto *n* children

watu *n* folks, people

wavu *n* net

wavu wa wire *n* mesh

wawili *n* couple

waya *n* wire

waza *v* suppose

wazazi *n* parents

wazi *adj* ajar

wazia *v* envisage

wazimu *n* insanity

wazimu *adj* crazy

waziri *n* minister

waziwazi *adv* plainly

wazo *n* idea, concept

wazo bunifu *n* inspiration

wazo la ghafla *n* whim

W

weka v rank
weka v install, set
weka akiba v save
weka alama v mark
weka fremu v frame
weka grisi v grease
weka huru v emancipate
weka jela v imprison
weka katikati v center
weka kiraka v patch
weka kizuizini v detain
weka ndani v contain
weka pamoja na v include
weka pembeni v put aside
weka rehani v pawn
weka sawa v beef up
weka tarehe v date
weka umeme v electrify
weka uzi v thread
weka wazi v expose
wekevu adj economical
wekeza v invest
wema n goodness
wembe n razor, blade
wengi adj many
wengi wao adj most
wenyewe pro themselves
wenzo n lever

werevu n ingenuity
weupe n fairness
weusi n blackness
wewe pro you
weza v manage, cope
weza kufanya v can
wezekana adv likely
wezesha v enable
wifi n sister-in-law
wigi n wig
wika v crow
wiki n week
wilaya n district
wima adj rampant
wimbi n wave, surge
wimbi kubwa n tidal wave
wimbi la joto n heatwave
wimbo n hymn, song
wimbo wa taifa n anthem
winchi n crane
winda v hunt
windo n prey
wingi n majority, bulk
wingu n cloud
wino n ink
witiri adj odd
wito n motto
wivu n jealousy

W

wizara *n* ministry
wizi *n* burglary
wizi kwa silaha *n* heist
wodi *n* ward
woga *n* cowardice
wote wawili *adj* both

Y

ya   *pre* for, of
yaani *adv* namely
yabisi kavu *n* arthritis
yai *n* egg
yake *pro* hers, his
yako *adj* your, yours
yakuti *n* saphire
yaliyo tuama *adj* stagnant
yamkini *adj* possible
yangu *pro* mine
yangu *adj* own, my
yatima *n* orphan
yaya *n* nanny
yayusha *v* melt
yetu *adj* our

yeye *pro* he, she
yeye *adj* her
yeye mwenyewe *pro* herself
yeyote *pro* anybody
yeyuka *v* thaw
yeyusha barafu *v* defrost
yote *adj* all, entire
yowe *n* scream
yoyote *adj* any, either
yumba *adj* ambivalent
yumba *v* waver
yumbayumba *v* wobble
yupi *pro* whom

Z

zaa *v* procreate
zabibu *n* grape, raisin
zabuni *n* bid, offer
zahanati *n* clinic
zaidi *adv* else, more
zaidi *c* even more
zaidi ya *pre* besides
zaidi ya hapo *adv* moreover

W
Y
Z

zaituni *n* olive

zaliana *v* procreate

zama *v* drown, sink

zama ndani *v* sink in

zamani *adj* ancient

zamani *adv* formerly

zamani za kale *n* antiquity

zambarau *adj* purple

zamisha *v* submerge

zamu *n* shift

zana za vita *n* munitions

zao *n* crop, harvest

zari *n* czar

zatiti *v* consolidate

zawadi *n* award, prize

zawadia *v* reward

zebaki *n* mercury

zege *n* concrete

zetu *pro* ours

zezeta *adj* backward

ziada *n* excess, surplus

ziara *n* visit, outing

ziba *v* plug, clog

zidi *v* outdo, surpass

zidi kwa haiba *v* overshadow

zidi mbio *v* outrun

zidi nguvu *v* overwhelm

zidi umaridadi *v* outshine

zidi uzito *v* outweigh

zidi wingi *v* outnumber

zidisha *v* exceed, overdo

zidisha chumvi *v* overstate

zidisha nguvu *v* intensify

zidisha mara mbili *v* double

zidiwa na *adj* swamped

zima *v* quell, suppress

zima simu *v* hang up

zimia *v* faint, pass out

zimua *v* water down

zinazo stahili *n* dues

zindua *n* disillusion

zinga *adj* gigantic

zingatia *v* note

zingia *v* blockade

zingio *n* blockade

zingira *v* blockade, siege

zinifu *adj* lewd

zinki *n* zinc

zipu *n* zipper

zirai *v* collapse

ziua *v* meditate

ziwa *n* lake

zizi *n* barn, stable

zoea *adj* used to

zoea *v* accustom

zoea mazingira *v* acclimatize

Z

zoezi *n* rehearsal

zoloto *n* larynx

zomea *v* hiss

zubaa zubaa *v* linger

zubaisha *v* stun

zuia *v* curb, hinder

zuia kusema *v* muzzle

zuia njia *v* seal off

zuia njiani *v* intercept

zuka *v* break out

zuka tena *v* resurface

zulia *n* carpet

zulufu *adj* senile

zumaradi *n* emerald

zumari *n* clarinet

zumgumza *v* chat

zunguka *v* circle, revolve

zungusha *v* rotate, spin

zungushia *v* revolve

zungusho *n* fencing

zuologia *n* zoology

zurura *v* wander, roam

Z

Word to Word Bilingual Dictionary Series

Arabic
ISBN 0-933146-41-8

Bengali
ISBN 0-933146-30-2

Cambodian
ISBN 0-933146-40-X

Chinese
ISBN 0-933146-22-1

Farsi
ISBN 0-933146-33-7

French
ISBN 0-933146-36-1

German
ISBN 0-933146-93-0

Gujarati
ISBN 0-933146-98-1

Haitian-Creole
ISBN 0-933146-23-X

Hindi
ISBN 0-933146-31-0

Japanese
ISBN 0-933146-42-6

Korean
ISBN 0-933146-97-3

Pashto
ISBN 0-933146-34-5

Polish
ISBN 0-933146-64-7

Portuguese
ISBN 0-933146-94-9

Punjabi
ISBN 0-933146-32-9

Romanian
ISBN 0-933146-91-4

Russian
ISBN 0-933146-92-2

Spanish
ISBN 0-933146-99-X

Swahili
ISBN 0-933146-55-8

Tagalog
ISBN 0-933146-37-X

Thai
ISBN 0-933146-35-3

Turkish
ISBN 0-933146-95-7

Vietnamese
ISBN 0-933146-96-5

Ukrainian
ISBN 0-933146-25-6

Urdu
ISBN 0-933146-39-6

Order Information

To order our Word to Word Bilingual Dictionaries or any other products from Bilingual Dictionaries, Inc., please contact us at (951) 461-6893 or visit us at **www.BilingualDictionaries.com**. Visit our website to download our current Catalog/Order Form, view our products, and find information regarding Bilingual Dictionaries, Inc.

 **Bilingual Dictionaries, Inc.**

PO Box 1154 • Murrieta, CA 92562 • Tel: (951) 461-6893 • Fax: (951) 461-3092
www.BilingualDictionaries.com